BLUE RIBBON

COUNTRY

# CANNING

STATE FAIR AWARD–WINNING TRADITIONAL
& MODERN FAVORITE RECIPES

In Compliance with the USDA Complete
Guide to Home Canning

DIANE ROUPE

*photographs by* ERIN SCOTT

EGG&DART®

*To Dee and Gary Staples,*
*my sister-in-law and brother*

ℳ

# CONTENTS

RECIPE INDEX . . . . . . . . . . . . . . . . . . . . . . .8

## FUNDAMENTALS OF CANNING

INTRODUCTION
The Rewards of Canning. . . . . . . . . . 12

CANNING SAFETY . . . . . . . . . . . . . . . . . . .14

PREPARATIONS FOR CANNING
Selection of Foods for Canning. . . . . . 15
Canning Equipment. . . . . . . . . . . . . . 15
Recipe Guidelines and
Special Information . . . . . . . . . . . 17
Time Allocation . . . . . . . . . . . . . . . . 18

CANNING PROCEDURES
Jars and Lids . . . . . . . . . . . . . . . . . .19
Filling the Jars. . . . . . . . . . . . . . . . . 21
Processing Fundamentals . . . . . . . . . 23
Unsafe Canning Methods. . . . . . . . . . .26
The Boiling Point of Water
by Altitude. . . . . . . . . . . . . . . . . .28
Boiling-Water Bath Canning. . . . . . . .28
Pressure Canning . . . . . . . . . . . . . . . 31

STORING AND HANDLING
CANNED FOODS . . . . . . . . . . . . . . . . .34

SPECIAL TECHNIQUES
Blanching. . . . . . . . . . . . . . . . . . . . .36
Chopping Nuts . . . . . . . . . . . . . . . . .36
Grating Citrus Rind . . . . . . . . . . . . . .37
Grinding Most Foods Other than
Nuts and Coffee Beans. . . . . . . . . .37
Making a Cheesecloth Bag for
Herbs or Spices . . . . . . . . . . . . .38

Peeling Pearl Onions . . . . . . . . . . . . .38
Preparing Mangos. . . . . . . . . . . . . . .38
Seeding and Coring Tomatoes. . . . . . .39
Using Fresh Ginger. . . . . . . . . . . . . . .39

GLOSSARY . . . . . . . . . . . . . . . . . . . . . . 40

## CANNING RECIPES
(Complete Recipe Index on page 8)

Fruits and Spiced Fruits
without Vinegar . . . . . . . . . . . . . . .45
Vegetables. . . . . . . . . . . . . . . . . . . . .81
Meats and Fish . . . . . . . . . . . . . . . 101
Pickles. . . . . . . . . . . . . . . . . . . . . . .109
Fermented Foods . . . . . . . . . . . . . . 133
Relishes and Salsas . . . . . . . . . . . . . 141
Savory and Sweet Sauces . . . . . . . . . 165
Jams . . . . . . . . . . . . . . . . . . . . . . . 173
Jellies . . . . . . . . . . . . . . . . . . . . . . 195
Preserves . . . . . . . . . . . . . . . . . . . 215
Conserves. . . . . . . . . . . . . . . . . . . . 221
Marmalades. . . . . . . . . . . . . . . . . . 231
Butters . . . . . . . . . . . . . . . . . . . . . 237

SOURCES CONSULTED . . . . . . . . . . . . . . .245

ACKNOWLEDGMENTS . . . . . . . . . . . . . . .247

INDEX . . . . . . . . . . . . . . . . . . . . . . . .248

METRIC CONVERSION TABLES . . . . . . . . . 252

VOLUME AND WEIGHT MEASURES . . . . . . . 253

ABOUT THE AUTHOR. . . . . . . . . . . . . . . . 255

# RECIPE INDEX

🎗 Designates a recipe for which the author won a blue ribbon (first place) at the Iowa State Fair.

🎗 Designates a recipe for which the author won a red ribbon (second place) at the Iowa State Fair.

## FRUITS AND SPICED FRUITS WITHOUT VINEGAR

🎗 Apples . . . . . . . . . . . . . . . . . . . . . . 46
Applesauce . . . . . . . . . . . . . . . . . . .47
🎗 Apricots . . . . . . . . . . . . . . . . . . . . . .50
🎗 Blueberries. . . . . . . . . . . . . . . . . . . 53
🎗 White Cherries . . . . . . . . . . . . . . . .54
Fruit Cocktail . . . . . . . . . . . . . . . . . 55
Gooseberries . . . . . . . . . . . . . . . . . .58
Grapes . . . . . . . . . . . . . . . . . . . . . . .60
🎗 Kiwis . . . . . . . . . . . . . . . . . . . . . . . .61
🎗 Mixed Fruit. . . . . . . . . . . . . . . . . . .62
🎗 Peaches . . . . . . . . . . . . . . . . . . . . . 64
🎗 Pears Amaretto . . . . . . . . . . . . . . . .65
🎗 Pears (Plain) . . . . . . . . . . . . . . . . . .66
🎗 Plums in Port Wine. . . . . . . . . . . . .67
Plums (Plain) . . . . . . . . . . . . . . . . .68
🎗 Raspberries (Red or Black) . . . . . . . .68
Rhubarb. . . . . . . . . . . . . . . . . . . . . .70
🎗 Strawberries . . . . . . . . . . . . . . . . . .72
🎗 Spiced Apple Rings . . . . . . . . . . . . . 75
🎗 Peppermint Pears . . . . . . . . . . . . . . 78

## VEGETABLES

🎗 Asparagus Spears. . . . . . . . . . . . . . .82
Cut Asparagus . . . . . . . . . . . . . . . .84
🎗 Green and Wax Beans . . . . . . . . . . .84
Carrots . . . . . . . . . . . . . . . . . . . . . .87
Whole-Kernel Corn . . . . . . . . . . . . .89
🎗 Corn with Red Peppers and Basil . . . .90
Cream-Style Corn. . . . . . . . . . . . . . .92
🎗 Tomatoes . . . . . . . . . . . . . . . . . . . .95
🎗 Tomato Juice . . . . . . . . . . . . . . . . .97

## MEATS AND FISH

Cubes, Strips, or Chunks of Boneless Meat . . . . . . . . . . . . . . .102
🎗 Brandied Mincemeat . . . . . . . . . . . .105
Salmon in Pint Jars . . . . . . . . . . . . .106

## PICKLES

Bread and Butter Pickles . . . . . . . . .110
Easy Refrigerator Sweet Dill Pickles. . . . . . . . . . . . . . . . . . 111
🎗 Dilly Beans. . . . . . . . . . . . . . . . . . . 112
Pickled Beets . . . . . . . . . . . . . . . . . 115
🎗 Pickled Mixed Vegetables. . . . . . . . . 119
Marinated Mushrooms . . . . . . . . . .120
Pickled Okra . . . . . . . . . . . . . . . . . 122
🎗 Melon Ball Pickles. . . . . . . . . . . . . 123
🎗 Spiced Peaches. . . . . . . . . . . . . . . . 125
🎗 Spiced Seckel Pears . . . . . . . . . . . . . 127
🎗 Watermelon Rind Pickles. . . . . . . . . 129

## FERMENTED FOODS

Fermented Dill Pickles . . . . . . . . . . .134
Fermented Kosher Dill Pickles . . . . .136
🎗 Sauerkraut. . . . . . . . . . . . . . . . . . . .136

## RELISHES AND SALSAS

- Bell Pepper Relish . . . . . . . . . . . . . .142
- Chili Sauce. . . . . . . . . . . . . . . 143
- Corn Relish . . . . . . . . . . . . . . .146
- Jicama Relish. . . . . . . . . . . . . . .148
- Peach Chutney . . . . . . . . . . . 150
- Piccalilli . . . . . . . . . . . . . . . . . 152
- Zucchini Relish. . . . . . . . . . . . . 154
- Mango Salsa. . . . . . . . . . . . . . . 156
- Peach-Apple Salsa. . . . . . . . . . . . 159
- Tomato-Chile Salsa . . . . . . . . . . . 161

## SAVORY AND SWEET SAUCES

- Tomato Catsup . . . . . . . . . . . . . .166
- Spaghetti Sauce . . . . . . . . . . . . . .168
- Cherry Sauce. . . . . . . . . . . . . . . .170
- Cherry Sauce with Kirschwasser . . . 171
- Tutti-Frutti Ice Cream Topping . . . . 171

## JAMS

- Apricot Jam . . . . . . . . . . . . . . . . 175
- Blueberry Jam. . . . . . . . . . . . . . .177
- Cherry Jam . . . . . . . . . . . . . . . . 178
- Gooseberry Jam. . . . . . . . . . . . . .180
- Grape Jam . . . . . . . . . . . . . . . . .182
- Peach Jam. . . . . . . . . . . . . . . . . 183
- Pineapple Jam . . . . . . . . . . . . . . 185
- Red Plum Jam . . . . . . . . . . . . . . 186
- Red Raspberry Jam . . . . . . . . . . . 188
- Seedless Wild Black Raspberry Jam. . . . . . . . . . . . .189
- Strawberry Jam. . . . . . . . . . . . . .190
- Tutti-Frutti Jam . . . . . . . . . . . . . 192

## JELLIES

- Apple Jelly . . . . . . . . . . . . . . . . .196
- Blackberry Jelly. . . . . . . . . . . . . .198
- Cherry Jelly . . . . . . . . . . . . . . . .200
- Grape Jelly . . . . . . . . . . . . . . . . 203
- Red Raspberry Jelly . . . . . . . . . . . 204
- Strawberry Jelly . . . . . . . . . . . . .206
- Wild Black Raspberry Jelly . . . . . . .207
- Basil Jelly . . . . . . . . . . . . . . . . .209
- Mint Jelly . . . . . . . . . . . . . . . . . 210
- Blush Wine Jelly . . . . . . . . . . . . . 212

## PRESERVES

- Cherry Preserves. . . . . . . . . . . . . 216
- Strawberry Preserves . . . . . . . . . . 218

## CONSERVES

- Apricot-Almond Conserve. . . . . . . . 223
- Gooseberry Conserve . . . . . . . . . . 225
- Grape Conserve. . . . . . . . . . . . . .226
- Rhubarb-Strawberry Conserve . . . .228

## MARMALADES

- Kumquat Marmalade. . . . . . . . . . . 232
- Orange Marmalade. . . . . . . . . . . .234

## BUTTERS

- Apple Butter. . . . . . . . . . . . . . . . 238
- Apricot Butter . . . . . . . . . . . . . . 239
- Pear Butter. . . . . . . . . . . . . . . . .240
- Wild Plum Butter . . . . . . . . . . . . . 243

Asparagus, Apricot Jam, and Blueberry Jam

# FUNDAMENTALS OF CANNING

# INTRODUCTION

## THE REWARDS OF CANNING

"Putting by" the bounty of their gargan-
tuan gardens and fruit groves for the long
winter months ahead was a summer and
early fall priority for prairie frontier
farmwives. Once a vital facet of subsistence,
home canning—though never a lost art—
is front and center in current food fashion
among dedicated home cooks whose
mothers and grandmothers passed along
this kitchen art, haute cuisine devotees,
and a myriad of others who have discov-
ered the pleasure and benefits of canning
for the first time.

Not only does canning result in superior
food and year-round enjoyment of seasonal
garden yield, but passionate canners
describe the endeavor as "surefire eupho-
ria!" Gloating over jars of gorgeous Strawberry Jam cooling on the kitchen counter
and the exhilaration of lifting quart jars of
glowing Pears Amaretto out of a boiling-
water canner elicit some of the all-time
highs in culinary adventure.

Home-canned foods are sensational tasting,
strikingly beautiful, and uniquely superior.
It is virtually impossible to duplicate in
commercially canned foods—regardless of
how fancy they are purported to be—the
supreme flavor and quality of home-canned
products. Volume canning simply does
not permit the TLC possible with home
canning, which starts with the fastidious
hand selection of products ripened to the
optimum point before processing. Foods

often go from the garden to the jar in the
same day.

Additives, such as chemical preservatives
and artificial flavorings, are anathema to
home canners. There is no need for artificial coloring, either. Mother Nature's
own spectacular colors are vividly cap-
tured and retained in jars carefully stored
in a dark, cool, dry, special storage place
until called into service in the kitchen. (Of
course, bright red and green coloring is
traditionally added to a very few canned
items, such as Spiced Apple Rings and
Peppermint Pears.

Besides the sheer natural beauty of home-
canned food products, jars can be master-
pieces of food arrangement—a true art
form for those so inclined. From uniform
peach halves overlapped symmetrically, to
green beans each precisely measured and
standing vertically in the jar (sometimes
alternating with wax beans), the sky's
the limit when it comes to imaginative
presentations worthy of exhibition.

While most of the time-honored canned
items, such as Bread and Butter Pickles and
Chili Sauce, are as popular with canners
today as they were in the 1860s, the canning
of "designer" products, such as Jicama
Relish, Marinated Mushrooms, and
Kumquat Marmalade, is "in."

One of the greatest pluses about canning is
the longevity of the end result—a triumph
over the perennial bane of good cooks
who see days of planning, marketing, and

preparation perish before their eyes in one short hour at the Thanksgiving table. Canning allows repeat, star performances over months, with not one iota of additional effort.

There are other benefits. No gift is more fashionable or appreciated by a host or hostess greeting you at the door than a jar of Raspberry Jam, Melon Ball Pickles, or some other delicacy you have painstakingly canned yourself. And with a cache of canned delectables, the holiday gift-giving dilemma is a thing of the past. Anyone would love to receive a beautiful jar of home-canned Plums in Port Wine or Bell Pepper Relish, hand labeled and made "gifty" with a white doily draped over the lid and tied with a satin ribbon.

While the joy of giving away these gems in jars is enormously rewarding, the gratification derived from serving home-canned foods to your family can only be described as soul satisfying. Canning can be a binding family ritual passed down through the generations. Canning one or two traditional family favorites can help busy, working parents fulfill their role as links in the perpetuation of long-standing, family food customs. Canning also can be a grand family project.

If you raise your own vegetables and fruits, the bliss is doubled. You're in for a real thrill when tomatoes used in the preparation of Swiss Steak you serve to friends in January were started indoors from seeds in April and canned straight from your garden in July. Add to the praise from around the table the feeling of pioneer self-sufficiency

gained from helping nature carry out its plan of seed to nourishment, and you have a memory not to be forgotten.

Canning commands dedication, time, and creativity, and it takes study, patience, and practice. But if you're looking for something challenging, worthwhile, and really fun to add to your repertoire of life experiences and accomplishments, canning may be just your ticket.

# CANNING SAFETY

Food safety is of utmost importance in home canning. When canning any food product, it is *critically important* to follow recipes, procedures, and instructions that adhere to the most current guidelines for safe canning adopted by the United States Department of Agriculture. *The recipes, procedures, and instructions in* Blue Ribbon Country Canning *conform to the latest USDA guidelines for safe canning as of the publication of this book.*[1]

The deadly *Clostridium botulinum* bacteria can survive and grow in jars of food that do not conform to safe recipes, procedures, and processing, and/or have not been properly stored. While this fact underscores the importance of judicious handling, the potential threat of food poisoning and botulism need not be a reason to avoid the considerable pleasure and benefits derived from home canning. Responsible, safe canning is reliably achieved by following the USDA guidelines and recipes that conform to them.

Proper storage and handling of canned foods is an important factor in maintaining canning safety. See Storing and Handling Canned Foods (page 34) for information on the subject, including Opening Jars of Canned Foods and Disposition of Suspect Jars of Canned Foods.

## ADDITIONAL CANNING SAFETY INFORMATION

For additional information on the endorsed principles and techniques of safe canning, the USDA guidelines are available online or in hard copy as follows:

[1]*Complete Guide to Home Canning* Agriculture Information Bulletin No. 539, United States Department of Agriculture. National Institute of Food and Agriculture, August 2009

Available:

a. Online at http://nchfp.uga.edu/ publications/publications_usda.html

b. Hard copy from Purdue University Extension at http://www.extension.purdue.edu/ USDAcanning/orderform.pdf

Also, the local Extension Service office serving your county may be contacted for expert information on safe canning. Some Extension Service offices operate a hotline to help answer canning questions.

## FINAL WORD

The USDA guidelines and precautionary warnings should not discourage interest in the enjoyable pursuit of canning. If the recommended guidelines are followed, canning and the sublime pleasure of eating exquisite canned foods can be enjoyed with safety.

# PREPARATIONS FOR CANNING

## SELECTION OF FOODS FOR CANNING

Home-can only the highest-quality food products. Mediocre raw materials can only result in mediocre canned goods. Use very fresh, unblemished produce ripened to the optimum stage. Plan your canning calendar around the availability of fresh foods, preferably locally grown, at their peak of quality. Many good canners have their own well-tended gardens—the ideal source for fine, fresh produce. Also, befriend a knowledgeable food-market produce manager, who will help obtain products you want. The availability of superior food products dictates what foods you can and when you can them.

Many vegetables begin to lose their vitamins immediately after they are harvested. If harvested vegetables are not promptly cooked or preserved, close to one-half of their vitamins may be lost in only a few days.

Although one third to one half of vitamins A and C, thiamin, and riboflavin may be lost during the heating process in canning, the amounts of other vitamins in properly canned foods are only slightly lower than in fresh foods.

Given these facts, when top-quality vegetables are canned promptly after harvest, they can be more nutritious than fresh produce in supermarkets.

## CANNING EQUIPMENT

Before embarking on canning, it is necessary to acquire the proper equipment. The basic items required for canning most food products are enumerated on the Canning Equipment List, on the following pages. Of course, not all the listed items are needed for canning every kind of food.

Not shown on the list is specialized equipment, such as an apple "peeler" (parer) (see illustration, page 47) and a cherry pitter (see illustration, page 170), which are useful in the canning of specific food products.

Study the recipe you plan to use well in advance of canning to make certain the needed equipment is at hand. Good equipment is a must in order to can foods safely and proficiently.

CANNING EQUIPMENT LIST

- ⊙ 7-quart boiling-water canner
- ⊙ 12-quart dial-gauge or weighted-gauge pressure canner (for canning vegetables, meats, fish, chicken, and other low-acid foods requiring pressure canning)
- ⊙ 8-quart, heavy-bottomed, stainless steel kettle with cover (for canning most sweet spreads)
- ⊙ 12-quart, heavy-bottomed, stainless steel kettle with cover (for general canning)
- ⊙ 16-quart, heavy-bottomed, stainless steel kettle with cover (for canning large quantities and retaining prepared fruits in vinegar solution)
- ⊙ 3-quart stainless steel saucepan with cover (for heating jar lids [and bands])
- ⊙ Large, medium, and small stainless steel saucepans with covers
- ⊙ 5-gallon stoneware crock (for fermenting pickles and sauerkraut)
- ⊙ Crack-free, unchipped, half-pint, pint, and quart Mason-type canning jars. Widemouthed Mason-type canning jars are necessary when canning large-sized, solid foods
- ⊙ *New*, self-sealing jar lids (self-sealing lids may be used only once)
- ⊙ Clean, unrusted jar bands (bands may be reused if not rusted or bent)
- ⊙ Blancher
- ⊙ Food mill (see illustration, page 72)
- ⊙ Meat grinder (see illustration, page 38)
- ⊙ Large and small sieves
- ⊙ Colander

- ⊙ Jar lifter (for lifting jars in and out of the canner)
- ⊙ Magnetic lid wand (for lifting jar lids and bands out of hot water)
- ⊙ Widemouthed canning funnel (for filling jars)
- ⊙ Mixing bowls
- ⊙ 1-cup, 2-cup, and 4-cup glass measuring cups with pouring spouts
- ⊙ Set of fractional measuring cups
- ⊙ Set of measuring spoons
- ⊙ Large, stainless steel mixing spoon
- ⊙ Large, stainless steel, slotted mixing spoon
- ⊙ Medium wooden mixing spoon with long handle (for stirring and handling fragile foods)
- ⊙ 4 tableware, stainless steel tablespoons (for skimming jellied products)
- ⊙ 4 tableware, stainless steel teaspoons (for skimming jellied products)
- ⊙ Sharp, thin-bladed paring knife
- ⊙ Sharp, thin-bladed slicing knife (the size of a steak knife)
- ⊙ Plastic knife or narrow, rubber spatula (for removing air bubbles from packed jars)
- ⊙ Potato masher (for crushing fruits used in some jellied products)
- ⊙ Vegetable parer
- ⊙ Vegetable brush
- ⊙ Candy thermometer
- ⊙ Kitchen scale

- ⊙ Timer
- ⊙ *Untreated* cheesecloth
- ⊙ Cotton flannel (for straining) (purchase from a fabric store)
- ⊙ Medium wooden board (for cooling processed jars)
- ⊙ Large wooden board (for filling jars)
- ⊙ Clean tea towels
- ⊙ Small sponge (for wiping jar rims and threads)
- ⊙ Pot holders
- ⊙ Rubber gloves (to wear when stirring and handling hot foods and jars)
- ⊙ Blender (for preparing some products)
- ⊙ Food processor (not necessary, but convenient for preparing some products)

## RECIPE GUIDELINES AND SPECIAL INFORMATION

For safe canning, it is extremely important to use tested recipes that comply with the United States Department of Agriculture's *Complete Guide to Home Canning* (see Canning Safety, page 14). All ninety-five recipes in *Blue Ribbon Country Canning* conform to the most current USDA guidelines as of the publication of this cookbook.

### MEASURING OR WEIGHING INGREDIENTS

Measure or weigh ingredients accurately. Proportions of fresh foods to other ingredients not only affect flavor, but also may affect safety.

### JELLIED PRODUCTS

Jellies, jams, preserves, conserves, and marmalades require a correct balance of fruit, sugar, pectin, and acid to achieve the desired jellying and texture. Therefore, do not reduce the amount of sugar called for in recipes for these items, as a runny product will be the consequence. Too little sugar also may allow the growth of yeasts and molds. If a lower-sugar jellied product is desired, select a special recipe that meets this requirement (see Lower-Sugar Jellied Products, page 18).

In recipe procedures for jellied products made with added pectin, the term "rolling boil" means a full, rapid boil that cannot be stirred down (see Rolling Boil, page 40). To achieve a firm enough gel, it is important to bring mixtures with added pectin to a full rolling boil before commencing to count the specified boiling time—most often 1 minute. On the other hand, exceeding the specified time at which these mixtures remain at a rolling boil, even by a portion of a minute, may result in jellied products that are too stiff.

Be sure to check the expiration date on packages of fruit pectin. Unsatisfactory gelling may result from the use of old pectin.

Some recipes for jellied products found in sources other than *Blue Ribbon Country Canning* call for the addition of butter or margarine to help control foaming during cooking. This is not recommended because butter or margarine may affect the flavor of stored jellied products. Skimming the foam off jellied product mixtures is not difficult; however, the procedure should be done expeditiously when making most jellied products so that the skimmed mixture can be poured into the jars before it begins to gel.

Do not double recipes for jellied products as a soft gel may result. Make one batch at a time.

## LOWER-SUGAR JELLIED PRODUCTS

To make lower-sugar jellied products, special recipes must be used. Such recipes are not included in *Blue Ribbon Country Canning*.

Special boxes of modified pectin that include recipes for lower-sugar jams and jellies usually are available at supermarkets where canning items are displayed.

## PICKLES AND RELISHES

### Vinegar

For food safety as well as taste and texture, it is important not to change the proportions of vinegar, water, and food in recipes for pickles and relishes. The acidity level of these canned products is critical to their safety as well as their flavor. Use *commercial* bottled vinegar of 5 percent acidity (50-grain acetic acid). Either cider or white distilled vinegar may be used. Cider vinegar has good, mellow flavor, however, it may darken white or light-colored vegetables and fruits, such as cauliflower, onions, and pears. White vinegar is preferable for use in canning such foods. Do not use homemade vinegar or other vinegars of unknown acidity.

### Salt

Use only canning (or pickling) salt in most pickle and relish products. Canning (or pickling) salt is a pure granulated salt. Other salts, including some sea salts, contain anticaking or iodine additives that may cause cloudy brine (see page 40). Do not use flake salt because it varies in density.

Do not alter the type and amount of salt called for in recipes for fermented pickles and sauerkraut. The type and amount of salt called for in approved recipes for these products are vital to their safety as well as their texture and flavor. The brine in these fermented products draws moisture and natural sugar from the vegetables. Lactic acid, which prevents their spoilage, is then produced.

While fresh-pack pickles and relishes are safely acidified with vinegar in tested recipes, reducing or eliminating the salt in these products may impair the quality of their texture and flavor.

## TIME ALLOCATION

Canning demands major chunks of time. It cannot be hurried. Blanching, peeling, paring, chopping, grinding, straining, boiling, jar filling, and processing are among the tasks that can consume hours of uninterrupted time when canning large quantities of food safely. Canning is fun and one of the most rewarding culinary challenges when approached methodically and with a relaxed attitude. It is a food art jealous of time and patience.

# CANNING PROCEDURES

## JARS AND LIDS

Use only standard Mason-type jars made for home canning. They are available in half-pint, pint, 1½-pint, and quart sizes. Half-pint, pint, and quart jars are the most commonly used, and are the only three sizes of jars specified in *Blue Ribbon Country Canning*. Although half-gallon Mason-type canning jars are available, they are recommended only for canning very acid juices.

Food should be canned only in the size or sizes of jars prescribed in the recipe. The safe processing time for a particular food often differs with the size of the jar. Jars used for canning should be completely free of cracks and chips.

Canning jars come with either regular (about 2⅜ inches) or widemouthed (about 3 inches) openings. Certain foods, such as larger solid foods, are more readily packed in widemouthed jars. Widemouthed jars with straight sides also lend themselves well to many artistic arrangements of canned foods.

The use of mayonnaise-type jars for canning is not recommended. Mayonnaise-type jars are tempered less than Mason-type jars, making them more subject to breakage. Mayonnaise-type jars especially should not be used for canning foods processed in a pressure canner due to the breakage hazard. In addition, mayonnaise-type jars have a more narrow sealing surface, making them more prone to sealing failures. Mason-type

canning jars are not expensive. Given the time and effort involved in canning, it follows that only the best jars should be used.

Use standard two-piece, self-sealing metal lids, which consist of a flat, metal lid containing sealing compound around the outer edge, and a metal band that screws onto the jar. The flat, metal lids should be used only *once*, however, the metal bands may be used repeatedly provided they are rust free and not bent. Metal lids may be purchased separately to pair with useable metal bands on hand. Although unused metal lids may be useable up to 5 years from their date of manufacture, it is a good practice to purchase only the quantity of metal lids needed for a single year's canning.

The old-style, porcelain-lined, zinc lids used with rubber rings, as well as jars with wire bails and glass caps used with rubber rings are not recommended for safe canning.

### PREPARING AND STERILIZING JARS

As a first step, new or used canning jars should be washed in hot detergent water and rinsed thoroughly. Jars may be washed in a dishwasher.

While it is unnecessary to presterilize jars used to can foods processed 10 minutes or more in a boiling-water canner at altitudes of 0 to 1,000 feet above sea level (add 1 additional minute for each 1,000 feet of elevation above 1,000 feet), or jars used to can foods processed in a pressure canner, I make the practice of doing so and call for the procedure in all the canning recipes in *Blue Ribbon Country Canning*. Jars used to can foods processed less than 10 minutes in a boiling-water canner at altitudes of 0 to 1,000 feet (add 1 additional minute for each 1,000 feet of elevation above 1,000 feet) *must* be presterilized. (See The Boiling Point of Water by Altitude, page 28, for information on how to find out the altitude of your canning location.) Also, jars used to can cucumber pickles processed by low-temperature pasteurization (see page 24) *must* be presterilized.

To presterilize canning jars, place them, right side up, in the rack in a boiling-water canner. Fill the canner with hot (not boiling) water to cover the jars 1 inch. Cover the canner and place it over high heat. Bring the water to a boil and boil the jars for 10 minutes in locations with altitudes of 1,000 feet or less above sea level. In locations with altitudes of 1,001 feet or more above sea level, add 1 minute boiling time for each additional 1,000 feet above sea level.

When the proper boiling time for sterilization has elapsed, turn off the heat under the canner and leave the sterilized jars immersed in the water. Reheat the water to near boiling and remove the jars from the canner immediately or shortly before filling them with food. Use a jar lifter to remove the jars from the canner. Wear rubber gloves to avoid burns from the steam and hot water. Pour the hot water in the jars back into the canner. Place the jars, upside down, on a clean tea towel covering a very large wooden board or other work surface on which you will fill the jars. Turn each jar upright immediately before filling it. The hot water in the canner may be used for processing filled jars in the canner by the boiling-water bath method (page 28).

PREPARING LIDS AND BANDS

Wash new metal lids and new or used metal bands in hot detergent water and rinse them thoroughly. Place the lids and bands, single layer, on two layers of paper towels situated away from food, and let them stand.

Carefully follow the manufacturer's instructions to prepare the lids and bands shortly before placing them on jars filled with food. Generally, place both the lids and bands in a 3-quart saucepan and cover them with hot water. Cover the saucepan and bring the water to a *simmer* (page 41), not a boil. Simmer the lids and bands for 10 minutes in locations with altitudes of 1,000 feet or less above sea level. In locations with altitudes of 1,001 feet or more above sea level, add 1 minute simmering time for each additional 1,000 feet above sea level. (See The Boiling Point of Water by Altitude, page 28, for information on how to find out the altitude of your canning location.) Leave the lids and bands in the hot water until ready for placement on the jars. If the water covering the lids and bands in the saucepan cools before placement on filled jars, reheat the water to a simmer.

A magnetic lid wand, specifically made for the purpose, may be used to handily lift lids and bands from the hot water for placement on filled jars . Tongs also work well if care is exercised not to dent the sealing compound on the lids.

## FILLING THE JARS

### HOT PACKING AND RAW PACKING

There are two styles of packing foods into jars: hot packing and raw packing.

*Hot packing* means filling jars with hot foods that have been boiled 2 to 5 minutes or cooked for a longer period of time. Liquid used to cover solid foods in the jars is heated to boiling before being added.

*Raw packing* means filling jars with unheated, uncooked foods. As in hot packing, liquid used to cover raw-packed foods in the jars is heated to boiling before being added.

Hot packing is the preferred style for packing foods to be processed in a boiling-water canner. Raw packing is more suitable for vegetables to be processed in a pressure canner.

Many fresh foods contain from 10 percent to more than 30 percent air. The longevity of quality in canned foods is affected by the amount of air removed from the foods prior to sealing the jars. Raw-packed fruits often float in the jars. The air trapped in and around foods that have been raw packed may cause discoloration and adversely affect the flavor of the foods within a short storage period.

Raw packing is appropriate and useful for canning foods that quickly lose their shape when heated in boiling liquid; for example, Grapes (page 60) and Kiwis (page 61). The recipes for canning Blueberries (page 53) and Gooseberries (page 58) call for these fruits to be blanched only for a short time before being packed into the jars. Raw-packed fruits should be packed tightly because of shrinkage during processing. Raw-packed foods often require a longer processing time than the same foods hot packed.

It is often difficult to retain the shape of vine-ripened tomatoes in the jars when they are hot packed. If shape retention is desired, whole or halved tomatoes may be raw packed. The recipe for canning Tomatoes (page 95) includes procedures and processing times for both hot packing and raw packing.

Use the style(s) of packing specified in the recipe. Consult the USDA *Complete Guide to Home Canning* (see Canning Safety, page 14) or call the local Extension Service office serving your county for information before raw packing a food when the recipe you have specifies only hot packing. It is necessary to find out whether or not the food can be safely raw packed and, if so, what the processing time should be.

## PROCEDURES FOR FILLING AND CAPPING JARS

Follow recipe instructions for filling jars, heeding the headspace requirements to the letter. Headspace is the unfilled space in a jar between the top of the food (or the liquid covering it) and the bottom of the lid. Use a ruler to assure proper measurement of headspace.

Headspace is required for the expansion of food during processing and for forming a vacuum in cooled jars. Air content of the food and processing temperature determine the amount of expansion. Air heated to high temperatures expands greatly; the higher the temperature, the greater the expansion. Too little headspace may cause food to boil out of the jar during processing, thus causing food on the lid compound to prevent sealing of the jar. Too much headspace may not allow the extra air in the top of the jar to be driven out during the time period specified for processing. This could prevent a good vacuum seal. In addition, air left in the jar may cause discoloration of the food.

Solid foods packed into jars should be surrounded and covered with liquid (syrup, juice, or water, depending upon the food product and recipe). Solid foods left uncovered by liquid at the top of the jar usually darken and develop an off flavor.

A widemouthed funnel, designed especially for home canning, makes efficient and tidy work of filling jars with liquids; jams, jellies, and other sweet spreads; relishes; and small-sized solid foods, such as corn, peas, and berries.

During the filling process, air is often trapped in jars, especially when solid foods are packed into jars and then are covered with a liquid. To remove air bubbles trapped in a filled jar, run a plastic knife or a narrow, rubber spatula into the jar between the food and the side of the jar. Turn the jar and carefully move the knife or spatula up and down and against the food to release the air bubbles, allowing them to rise to the top of the jar and disperse.

After the release of air bubbles, often it is necessary to add a small amount of additional liquid or food to the jar to maintain the prescribed headspace (and to fully cover solid foods with liquid). Air generally is not trapped in jars filled with liquids alone; therefore, the procedure of removing air bubbles usually may be eliminated when canning these products. Recipes in *Blue Ribbon Country Canning* indicate when air bubbles should be removed from filled jars.

Just before capping the jars, wipe the rim and the threads of each jar with a clean, damp sponge to assure that they are free from syrup or other food residue. To achieve a tight seal, jar rims must be perfectly clean. Rinse the sponge in clean, running water several times during the wiping procedure.

Remove one lid and band at a time from the hot water. Place the lid squarely on the jar rim and screw the band firmly onto the jar with your hand. Then, proceed to cap the next jar. Do not use a jar tightener to tighten the bands. Extreme overtightening prevents air from venting during processing and may cause the lids to buckle and the jars to break. However, bands not screwed tightly enough may allow liquid to escape from the jars during processing, resulting in sealing failures.

## Processing Fundamentals

Two methods of processing home-canned foods meet the USDA guidelines for safe canning: (1) the boiling-water bath method, and (2) the pressure canner method. The acidity of the food product to be canned determines which of the two methods is employed for safe canning.

### ACIDITY

Acid foods are foods having a pH value of 4.6 or less (pH is a measure of acidity). Low-acid foods are foods having a pH value higher than 4.6

### SAFE PROCESSING

*Clostridium botulinum* and other bacteria are of central importance and concern when home canning foods. *Clostridium botulinum* is a common soil microorganism that produces a toxin or poison called botulism, a deadly form of food poisoning. While *Clostridium botulinum* vegetative cells are killed at boiling-water temperature sustained for a scientifically determined time in acid foods, *Clostridium botulinum* spores can survive boiling-water temperature under the same circumstances. Acid foods contain sufficient acidity to block the germination of *Clostridium botulinum* spores

into vegetative cells. Therefore, acid foods are safely processed using the boiling-water bath method. The time required to safely process acid foods using the boiling-water bath method ranges from 5 to 85 minutes.

*Clostridium botulinum* spores can germinate into vegetative cells in the conditions of low acidity and absence of air, such as a sealed canning jar. *Clostridium botulinum* spores can be destroyed at a temperature of 240°F, or above, maintained for a specified length of time. This is achievable in a pressure canner. The time required to destroy *Clostridium botulinum* spores in low-acid foods processed in a pressure canner operating at 10 to 15 pounds per square inch of pressure measure by gauge (PSIG) at 240° to 250°F ranges from 20 to 100 minutes, depending upon the kind of food, the size of jars, and the way the jars are packed.

Therefore, it is critically important to follow canning recipes, processing procedures, and processing times that adhere to the USDA guidelines for safe canning.

### HIGH-ACID FOODS

The natural acidity in most fruits is high enough to safely can these foods at boiling-water temperature. The acid added to pickles and relishes also allows safe canning of many of these products at boiling-water temperature. In addition, fermented sauerkraut, jellies, jams, preserves, conserves, marmalades, and fruit butters are safely processed at boiling-water temperature.

## LOW-ACID FOODS

Foods falling into the low-acid category include all fresh vegetables (except tomatoes; see Note, below), meats, poultry, fish, shellfish, wild game, and milk. These low-acid foods must be processed in a pressure canner.

**NOTE:** Although tomatoes are botanically a fruit, in 1893 the United States Supreme Court officially declared tomatoes a vegetable due to a tariff dispute. The paragraph that follows, entitled *Tomatoes and Figs,* contains important information about the safe canning of these foods.

## TOMATOES AND FIGS

While tomatoes and figs are considered to be acid foods, some of them have pH values slightly above 4.6. Therefore, if tomatoes and figs are processed using the boiling-water bath method, they must be further acidified with *bottled* lemon juice (5 percent acidity) or citric acid to ensure a safe pH level. *Bottled* lemon juice must be used because the acidity is at a consistent level and is high enough to be safe. The recipes in *Blue Ribbon Country Canning* for Tomatoes (page 95) and Tomato Juice (page 97) call for processing in a boiling-water canner and for the addition of 2 tablespoons of bottled lemon juice to each quart of these products (1 tablespoon to each pint) in accordance with the USDA guidelines. (If citric acid is used, add ½ teaspoon to each quart or ¼ teaspoon to each pint of these products. Food-grade citric acid is available at some supermarkets and at pharmacies. Do not substitute ascorbic acid for citric acid.)

## LOW-TEMPERATURE PASTEURIZATION

Certain approved recipes for cucumber pickles permit processing in simmering water sustained at 180 to 185°F for 30 minutes (see Bread and Butter Pickles, page 110, Fermented Dill Pickles, page 134, and Fermented Kosher Dill Pickles, page 136). The advantage of this procedure, known as "low-temperature-pasteurization," is that it results in crisper pickles.

When canning by this procedure, it is very important to attach a candy thermometer to the canner and to continually monitor the temperature of the water. A temperature of 180°F must be maintained for a full 30 minutes to avoid the possibility of spoilage. A temperature higher than 185°F may cause the pickles to soften. This procedure should be used only when it is indicated in an approved recipe. Low-temperature pasteurization should never be used to process reduced-sodium pickles.

*Asparagus Spears, Apples, and Mixed Pickled Vegetables*

# UNSAFE CANNING METHODS

Canning procedures and processes in *Blue Ribbon Country Canning* recipes conform to the USDA guidelines for safe canning as of the publication of this cookbook; therefore, it is highly important that other canning procedures and processes not be applied to recipes in this cookbook. The following are unsafe canning methods.

*Open-Kettle Canning*

Open-kettle canning, a former canning method in which foods were heated and packed into hot jars that were then sealed and not further processed, is no longer accepted as safe.

In open-kettle canning, bacteria, yeasts, and molds contaminating food in the jars are not destroyed by scientific processing, and lids are not reliably sealed. Botulism and spoilage are threats in food canned by the open-kettle method.

*Steam Canners*

Steam canners are not recommended because safe processing times for use with current models have not been adequately researched. Steam canners heat foods in a different way from boiling-water canners. Applying processing times used for boiling-water canners to steam canners may result in very underprocessed foods, risking the danger of food contamination and spoilage.

*Pressure Cookers*

Pressure cookers are not recommended for canning. Pressure canners are specially made for canning. They are heavy, with lids that close tightly to prevent steam from escaping. They should hold at least 4 quart-sized jars.

Pressure cookers are made with lighter-weight metal, and they are smaller in diameter than pressure canners, resulting in their use of less water than pressure canners. These factors result in a shorter period of time for the cooker to come up to the processing pressure and a shorter period of time for the cooker to cool to 0 pounds of pressure at the end of the canning time. The time required to come up to the processing pressure and the cool-down time were included in the total processing heat used to establish the USDA-recommended processing times for low-acid foods; therefore, reducing these times may result in underprocessed, unsafe foods with undestroyed targeted microorganisms.

### Conventional Ovens, Microwave Ovens, Slow Cookers, Crock-Pots, Dishwashers, and the Sun

Conventional Ovens, Microwave Ovens, Slow Cookers, Crock-Pots, Dishwashers, and the Sun are not recommended for safely processing canned foods; in fact, these processing modes may be very dangerous.

### Canning Powders

"Canning powders" are useless as preservatives, and they cannot be substituted for approved heat processing in canning foods.

### Canning by Inversion

Canning by the inversion method, whereby filled jars of jams, jellies, preserves, conserves, marmalades, and butters are inverted for a few minutes and then turned upright, but are not processed in a boiling-water canner, is unsafe and does not comply with the USDA guidelines for safe canning.

### Sealing Jars with Paraffin

Sealing filled jars of jams, jellies, preserves, conserves, marmalades, and butters with paraffin is not a safe canning procedure. These products must be processed in a boiling-water canner. Mycotoxins, which are known to cause cancer in animals, have been found in some jars of jelly having surface mold.

## The Boiling Point of Water by Altitude

You must know the altitude of the canning location in order to determine the proper processing time for a product to be canned by boiling-water bath canning, or the proper pounds of pressure for a product to be canned by pressure canning.

To find out the altitude of the location where you will can, contact the local Extension Service office serving your county or your local district conservationist with the United States Department of Agriculture, Natural Resources Conservation Service.

As altitude increases, atmospheric pressure decreases due to a thinner blanket of air. As the atmospheric pressure decreases, causing less weight of air on the surface of water, the boiling point of water also decreases. At sea level, water boils at 212°F. The following chart shows the boiling point of water at higher altitudes.

| Altitude | Boiling Point of Water |
|---|---|
| Sea Level | 212°F |
| 1,000 ft. | 210°F |
| 2,000 ft. | 208°F |
| 3,000 ft. | 206°F |
| 4,000 ft. | 204°F |
| 5,000 ft. | 203°F |
| 6,000 ft. | 201°F |
| 7,000 ft. | 199°F |
| 8,000 ft. | 197°F |

Weather conditions also affect the boiling point of water, but to a far less extent than altitude. At a given altitude, high barometric pressure causes water to boil at a somewhat higher temperature and low barometric pressure causes water to boil at a somewhat lower temperature.

Therefore, when recipes call for a mixture to be boiled to a certain number of degrees above the boiling point of water, it is a good practice to test the boiling point of water with an accurate candy thermometer just before boiling the mixture.

## Boiling-Water Bath Canning

### BOILING-WATER BATH CANNERS

A popular and reasonably priced style of boiling-water bath canner is made of a dark, speckled, porcelain finish over a steel core. A practical and very useable size holds up to 7 quart-sized, pint-sized, or half-pint-sized jars in a rack. The rack keeps the jars separated and off the bottom of the canner, allowing the water to circulate freely around the entirety of the jars. The rack also may be used for lowering and raising the jars into and out of the canner.

When boiling-water bath processing on an electric range, the diameter of the boiling-water bath canner should not exceed the diameter of the heat source on the range by more than 4 inches (that is, more than 2 inches on any side).

The boiling-water bath canner must be deep enough to allow for 1 to 2 inches of briskly boiling water over the tops of the jars during processing.

## PREPARING THE CANNER FOR PROCESSING

The water used to presterilize the jars in the boiling-water bath canner may be used to process the filled jars (see Preparing and Sterilizing Jars, page 19). After removing sterilized, empty jars from the canner immediately or shortly before filling them with food to be processed, it probably will be necessary to remove some of the water from the canner to accommodate the jars filled with food and ready for processing. Wearing rubber gloves, use a 4-cup glass measuring cup with a pouring spout to remove any necessary amounts of water from the canner.

Before loading filled jars into the canner, the water in the canner should be heated to 180°F for hot-packed foods and 140°F for raw-packed foods. (A candy thermometer may be attached to the canner to gauge the water temperature. Detach and remove the thermometer before placing the filled jars of food in the canner.) Filled jars should not be plunged into boiling water due to the chance of breakage.

## LOADING THE CANNER

To load the canner with filled jars fit with lids and bands, wear rubber gloves and use a jar lifter to place the jars in the rack resting on the bottom of the canner. Or, before loading the jars in the canner, the rack may be raised to a higher level in the canner by lifting the rack by its handles and hooking the handles over the rim of the canner. I prefer to leave the rack on the bottom of the canner during loading because the jars more easily can be maintained in a vertical position throughout the loading procedure.

During the entire canning process and later, in the storage of canned foods, special care should be taken to keep the jars vertical to prevent food and liquid from splashing against the side of the jars in the headspace and against the bottom of the lids, which could jeopardize sealing.

If the filled jars are loaded into the rack in its raised position, or if the processed jars will be unloaded from the rack in its raised position, it is important to load the jars in a manner that keeps their weight evenly distributed around the rack. This will help prevent the rack from tilting when in the raised position due to a disproportionate amount of weight on one side of the rack, causing the jars to lean and food to splash onto the headspace of the jars or the bottom of the jar lids.

When all the jars to be processed are loaded into the rack and the rack is resting on the bottom of the canner, there should be at least 1 inch of water covering the tops of the jars, except if the processing time will be 30 minutes or longer, in which case there should be at least 2 inches of water covering the tops of the jars. If necessary, add heated water to the canner.

Cover the canner.

## PROCESSING FILLED JARS IN THE CANNER

Turn the heat onto high under the covered canner containing filled jars ready for processing. Watch the canner closely.

When the water reaches a rapid boil, begin counting the processing time, using a timer. Lower the heat to maintain a gentle, but steady, boil throughout the processing time. Keep the canner covered for the processing time. If the water in the canner does not boil continuously throughout the entire processing time, for food safety it will be necessary to bring the water in the canner to a boil and commence the processing time from the beginning, even though this may jeopardize the quality of the processed food product.

### PROCESSING TIMES

Because the temperature at which water boils varies with the altitude above sea level, it is necessary to know the altitude of the canning location to determine the length of processing time required for a particular food product. See The Boiling Point of Water by Altitude (page 28) for a more complete explanation and for reliable sources to find out the altitude of your canning location. The recipes in *Blue Ribbon Country Canning* for canned foods processed by the boiling-water bath method each contain a chart showing the proper processing time by altitude of canning location and size of the jars to be processed.

*Processing times should be followed strictly.* Underprocessing jeopardizes food safety. Overprocessing adversely affects the quality of the canned product and is unnecessary.

### IMMEDIATELY AFTER CONCLUSION OF THE PROCESSING TIME

At the end of the processing time, turn off the heat under the canner. Before removing the jars from the canner, I usually lift the rack to its raised position in order to pull the jars out of the boiling water moments after the processing time has elapsed. However, if preferred, the rack may be left on the bottom of the canner while the jars are removed.

Immediately lift the jars from the canner, using a jar lifter and wearing rubber gloves. Keeping the jars vertical, transport them, one at a time, from the canner to a nearby dry, wooden board covered with two layers of a clean tea towel, away from drafts, and at room temperature. Place the jars at least 1 inch apart. Do not retighten the bands, possibly causing the hot lid gaskets to be cut through and the seals to fail. Do not touch the jars or lids, or move the jars for 12 to 24 hours. To destroy microorganisms in foods processed in a boiling-water canner, processed jars must be cooled at room temperature. As the jars cool, you will hear snapping sounds as the lids seal.

### CHECKING PROCESSED JARS FOR SEALING

12 to 24 hours after newly canned jars of food have stood undisturbed to cool, check the lid on each jar to make certain it has sealed as follows: The lid of a properly sealed jar is concave. To check a lid, press the middle of the lid with your finger. If the jar is properly sealed, the lid will not spring up when you release your finger.

Do not test a jar lid for sealing until the jar has completely cooled.

A jar of food that was processed in a boiling-water bath canner and did not seal after standing 12 to 24 hours at room temperature, may be reprocessed within 24 hours following processing. To reprocess a jar of food, remove the jar band and lid, and discard the lid. Check the jar sealing surface for any tiny nicks. If nicks are found, place the food in a different, sterilized jar. Place a new, properly prepared lid and a clean, properly prepared band on the jar (see Preparing Lids and Bands, page 20). Reprocess the jar of food using the same processing time as was used previously. Reprocessed food will be softer and will be lower in nutritional value.

A jar of food processed in a boiling-water bath canner that did not seal within 24 hours of processing may be refrigerated immediately and used within several days, or frozen within 24 hours of processing.

## Pressure Canning

### PRESSURE CANNERS

There are two acceptable types of pressure canners made for canning foods: weighted-gauge pressure canners and dial-gauge pressure canners. Only pressure canners made especially for canning foods should be used. The pressure canner must be large enough to hold at least 4 quart jars even though the canner may be used to process fewer than 4 quarts of food, or to process pint or half-pint jars of food. It is important to use a pressure canner that is in good condition and has the Underwriter's Laboratory (UL) approval to insure safety.

Steam canners and pressure cookers are not recommended for canning (see Unsafe Canning Methods, page 26).

The gauge on dial-gauge pressure canners should be checked for accuracy before use each year. Gauges may be checked at most county Extension Service offices or contact the pressure canner manufacturer for other options. Gauges that register high cause underprocessing and the risk of unsafe food, while gauges that register low cause overprocessing.

### HOW PRESSURE CANNERS WORK

For food safety, low-acid foods (see Low-Acid Foods, page 24) must be processed at 240 to 250°F (see Safe Processing, page 23). This temperature range, which is above the boiling point of water, can be achieved only in a pressure canner. Microorganisms are not destroyed by pressure, but by high temperatures sustained for a specified period of time. All microorganisms capable of growing in canned foods are successfully destroyed in pure steam, free of air, at 240 to 250°F sustained for a specified period of time.

The altitude of the canning location is a factor in pressure canning because at a given number of pounds of pressure, temperatures are lower in pressure canners at high altitudes. Therefore, the pounds of pressure at which canned foods are safely processed vary with the altitude of the canning location. See The Boiling Point of Water by Altitude (page 28) for reliable sources to find out the altitude of your canning location.

The type of canner—weighted-gauge or dial-gauge—also affects the pounds of pressure required to safely can specified foods at various altitudes. In *Blue Ribbon Country Canning*, each recipe for foods canned in a pressure canner contains a separate chart for dial-gauge pressure canners and weighted-gauge pressure canners, showing the processing time and pounds of pressure required at various altitudes for designated sizes of jars.

### FILLING THE CANNER

To fill the canner, place the rack on the bottom of the canner. Pour 2 to 3 inches of hot water into the canner. (Additional water is required for canning certain food products; however, none of the recipes in *Blue Ribbon Country Canning* require additional amounts of water.) Place the filled jars on the rack in the canner and fasten the lid securely.

### VENTING THE CANNER

Both weighted-gauge pressure canners and dial-gauge pressure canners should be vented for 10 minutes before being pressurized, as follows:

After securely locking the lid on the canner, leave the weight OFF the vent pipe if using a weighted-gauge pressure canner, or OPEN the petcock if using a dial-gauge pressure canner. Turn the heat on the highest setting under the canner. When the water in the canner comes to a full boil and steam emits freely from the open vent pipe or open petcock, set a timer for 10 minutes. After venting the canner 10 minutes, place the weight at the proper setting over the vent pipe if using a weighted-gauge pressure canner, or close the petcock if using a dial-gauge pressure canner to pressurize the canner. Continue to leave the heat under the canner at the highest setting.

The canner, whether weighted-gauge or dial-gauge, will pressurize in 3 to 10 minutes.

### PROCESSING

Begin to count the processing time when the prescribed pounds of pressure have been reached, as indicated by the jiggling of the weight on a weighted-gauge canner as described in the canner manufacturer's instructions or when the dial on a dial-gauge canner reaches the pressure prescribed in the recipe.

During the processing time, maintain the pressure as evenly as possible by finely regulating the heat under the canner. Fast and great fluctuations of pressure may cause liquid to be lost from the jars. Regulate the heat under the canner (1) per the manufacturer's directions for a weighted-gauge pressure canner, or (2) to maintain steady pressure as indicated on the gauge of a dial-gauge pressure canner.

*If, at any time, the pressure falls below the prescribed amount, it will be necessary to reestablish the prescribed pressure and start counting the processing time all over from the beginning. This is important for food safety.*

## WHEN THE PROCESSING TIME HAS ELAPSED

When the processing time has elapsed, turn off the heat under the canner. Do not remove the weight on a weighted-gauge canner or open the petcock on a dial-gauge canner. If the heating unit under the canner is electric, carefully lift the canner off the heating surface, if possible. Do not slide the canner. If the canner is too heavy to lift, possibly causing the jars in the canner to lean or fall over, it is satisfactory to leave the canner on the heating unit.

Let the pressure canner cool and depressurize naturally. Do not remove the weight on a weighted-gauge canner or open the petcock on a dial-gauge canner to hasten the reduction of pressure. Do not cool the canner with water or any other means of force cooling. The natural cooling time of the canner is a factor in the safe processing times prescribed in *Blue Ribbon Country Canning* recipes. It may take 30 to 45 minutes or more for the canner to cool depending upon the canner and the size and number of jars of food in it.

After the canner has completely depressurized, remove the weight if using a weighted-gauge canner or open the petcock if using a dial-gauge canner. Wait 10 minutes. Then, remove the canner lid, tilting the far side up to avoid being burned by escaping steam. If the canner lid does not open, do not force it. Follow the canner manufacturer's instructions.

Using a jar lifter and wearing rubber gloves, lift the jars from the canner. Keeping the jars vertical, transport them, one at a time, from the canner to a nearby dry, wooden board covered with two layers of a clean tea towel, away from drafts, and at room temperature. Place the jars at least 1 inch apart. Do not retighten the bands, possibly causing the hot lid gaskets to be cut through and the seals to fail. Do not touch the jars or lids, or move the jars for 12 to 24 hours. As the jars cool, you will hear snapping sounds as the lids seal.

## CHECKING PROCESSED JARS FOR SEALING

12 to 24 hours after newly canned jars of food have stood undisturbed to cool, check the lid on each jar to make certain it has sealed as follows: The lid of a properly sealed jar is concave. To check a lid, press the middle of the lid with your finger. If the jar is properly sealed, the lid will not spring up when you release your finger. Do not test a jar lid for sealing until the jar has completely cooled.

## DISPOSITION OF UNSEALED JARS

A jar of food that was processed in a pressure canner and did not seal after standing 12 to 24 hours at room temperature following processing, may be immediately refrigerated (see Checking Processed Jars for Sealing, above) and consumed within a few days.

# STORING AND HANDLING CANNED FOODS

After newly canned foods have stood, undisturbed, for 12 to 24 hours at room temperature, and they have been checked to verify that the lids have sealed (see Checking Processed Jars for Sealing, pages 30 and 33), they should be properly stored. For the proper handling of newly canned foods that did not properly seal after standing, undisturbed, for 12 to 24 hours at room temperature, see Reprocessing Unsealed Jars in the Boiling-Water Bath Canning section (page 31) and Disposition of Unsealed Jars in the Pressure Canning section (page 33).

Canned foods should be stored in a cool, dry, dark storage place, such as a clean cabinet in a dry basement. The best storage temperature for canned foods is 50 to 70°F. The maximum safe storage temperature for canned foods is 95°F. Do not store canned foods near a furnace, hot pipes, or a range, or under a sink, in direct sunlight, or in an uninsulated attic. A damp storage place should be avoided as it may cause jar lids to corrode and the seals to break. Jars of canned foods should be kept vertical, both as they are transported to the storage place and when they are stored.

It is best to consume canned foods within one year after processing, and it is a good idea to label canned foods with the date of canning before storing them.

## OPENING JARS OF CANNED FOODS

Before opening a jar of canned food for consumption, check the lid to make certain it has remained concave and sealed. Do not use or even taste canned food that is found to be unsealed upon removal from storage or canned food that shows any sign of spoilage, such as mold on the top of the food or on the underside of the lid, or an unnatural odor.

## DISPOSITION OF SUSPECT JARS OF CANNED FOODS

In the case of a sealed, but unopened jar of canned food that is suspected of spoilage, place the unopened jar in a heavy garbage bag, close the bag securely, and dispose of it in a regular trash container.

If a suspect jar is unsealed, open, or leaking, it should be detoxified before disposal. *When detoxifying a suspect jar, it is important to wear disposable rubber or heavy plastic gloves.* Contact with botulinum toxin can be fatal whether it is ingested or enters through the skin.

To detoxify a suspect jar of canned food, wear disposable rubber or heavy plastic gloves and carefully place the filled jar with the lid on the jar, on its side in an 8-quart or larger kettle or a boiling-water canner. Thoroughly wash your gloved hands. While avoiding splashing, carefully add water to the kettle or canner to at least 1 inch above the jar. Cover the kettle or canner. Over high heat, bring the water to a full boil. Boil 30 minutes. Then, cool the filled, lidded jar, including the food contents, place it in a heavy garbage bag, close the bag securely, and dispose of it in a regular trash container.

Wearing the disposable rubber or heavy plastic gloves and using a solution of 1 part unscented liquid household chlorine bleach (5 to 6 percent sodium hypochlorite) to 5 parts clean water, thoroughly scrub the counter or surface on which the jar was opened (if it was), the jar opener, and other equipment and clothing that may have come in contact with the suspect jar and food; let stand 30 minutes. Wearing the gloves, wipe the treated surfaces with paper towels. Place the paper towels in a plastic bag, close the bag securely, and dispose of it in a regular trash container.

Then, wearing the disposable rubber or heavy plastic gloves, repeat the application of the bleach solution to the counter or surface, equipment, and clothing; let stand 30 minutes; rinse. Thoroughly wash all detoxified surfaces, equipment, and clothing. Discard the rubber or heavy plastic gloves when the detoxification process has been completed.

# SPECIAL TECHNIQUES

## BLANCHING

To blanch (see Blanch, page 40) a food, over high heat bring water to a rapid boil in the bottom of a blancher or in a saucepan or kettle. If using a blancher, place the food in the top of the blancher and lower it into the boiling water. If using a saucepan or kettle, drop the food directly into the boiling water. Leave the blancher, saucepan, or kettle over the heat and use a timer to accurately time the blanching process. Follow the recipe for suggested blanching time (if given).

To blanch for peeling, tomatoes require approximately 45 seconds and peaches require approximately 1 minute in boiling water. Blanching times will vary somewhat, depending upon the ripeness and variety of the produce. During the blanching process, use a wooden mixing spoon to turn over foods that float so that the boiling water reaches all surfaces.

When the blanching time has been completed, *immediately* remove the food from the boiling water and immerse it in cold water to stop the cooking.

## CHOPPING NUTS

Most nuts can be chopped successfully in a hand-operated, rotary nut chopper that has metal (not plastic) blades (see illustration). For more finely chopped nuts, run the nuts through the chopper two or more times.

*Almonds* are very firm; therefore, the use of slivered almonds for chopping them simplifies the process and produces chopped pieces of more uniform size. Run slivered almonds through a hand-operated, rotary nut chopper (see illustration) twice if necessary.

*Whole almonds, Brazil nuts,* and *Hazelnuts* are too firm to chop in a hand-operated, rotary nut chopper (see illustration). Chop these nuts in a food processor.

*Rotary Nut Chopper*

## GRATING CITRUS RIND

Use unblemished fruit for grating (see Grate, page 40) citrus rind (see Rind, page 40). Wash the fruit well, removing any brand names or other markings that may be stamped on the surface. Leave the fruit whole. When finely grated rind is called for in a recipe, as is often the case, use a small, handheld, metal, finely pronged grater (see illustration) to grate the rind. Or, an ultra-fine Microplane® (see illustration) may be used. A Microplane® actually shreds (see Shred, page 41) extremely finely rather than grates; however, the planed citrus rind very closely resembles grated rind.

Grate only the thin, colored, outer part of the fruit's peel. Try not to include any of the white membrane beneath the colored, outer part of the peel. The white membrane has a bitter taste and is not the flavor desired when grated citrus rind is specified. Grate over waxed paper and use a paring knife or a tiny kitchen brush (such as a toothbrush reserved only for use as a kitchen tool) to help remove grated rind that does not fall onto the waxed paper and builds up between the tiny prongs.

One medium-sized lemon or 1 very small orange will yield about 1 teaspoon of finely grated or ultra-finely planed rind.

If grated citrus rind will not be used immediately, place it in a very small sauce dish, cover the dish securely with plastic wrap, and refrigerate it to retain the rind's moisture and color. Grated citrus rind may be satisfactorily stored in this manner up to 1 day.

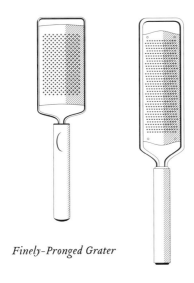

*Finely-Pronged Grater*

*Ultra-Fine Microplane®*

## GRINDING MOST FOODS OTHER THAN NUTS AND COFFEE BEANS

To grind (see Grind, page 40) most foods other than nuts and coffee beans, use a hand-cranked food grinder, generally called a "meat grinder," although it is used to grind many foods in addition to meats (see illustration, page 38). Meat grinders come with coarse- and fine-blade fittings for adaptation to specific uses.

Meat grinders reduce foods to small, quite uniform fragments. They do not shred or splinter food during grinding, and the ground food retains its original consistency quite well. For uniform size, shape, and texture, and for an attractive finished

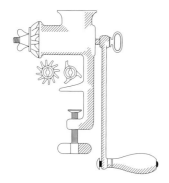

*Meat Grinder*

food, a meat grinder is a requisite tool in the preparation of many foods. For generations, meat grinders have not changed in appearance, function, and availability.

Although food processors often are used to chop foods, they generally are not well suited for grinding foods because often they do not cut foods into uniform sizes and shapes, and some foods may become paste-like or partially liquefy during processing.

## MAKING A CHEESECLOTH BAG FOR HERBS OR SPICES

A cheesecloth bag is often used to hold herbs or spices that are to be removed from a food after cooking and then discarded. To make such a cheesecloth bag, cut 4 layers of plain, *untreated* cheesecloth into a square large enough to hold the herbs or spices to be used (usually about 7 inches square). Draw the corners of the cheesecloth together and tie the bag very securely with white, cotton sewing thread. Do not pull the bag too tightly, leaving space for the liquid to flow freely through the herbs or spices.

## PEELING PEARL ONIONS

To peel pearl onions, place the onions in a saucepan; cover the onions with boiling water and let them stand 2 minutes. Then, drain the onions and immediately immerse them in cold water to halt the cooking process. Drain the onions in a colander.

Using a small paring knife, peel the onions.

## PREPARING MANGOS

The flesh of a mango adheres to its pit (seed), making it somewhat difficult to prepare. A good method of separating the flesh from a whole mango is as follows:

On a cutting board, hold the mango stem up, with one of the narrow sides of the mango facing you. Using a medium-sized, sharp knife, cut the mango, top to bottom, on both sides of the pit, cutting as closely to the pit as possible. Pare (see Pare, page 40) the skin from the flesh on the two mango pieces that have been cut away from the pit. Then, cut or slice the mango flesh as desired.

If useable flesh clings to the pit on the two narrow sides of the mango, cut it away from the pit and pare the skin.

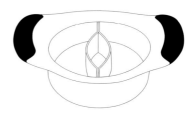

*Mango Splitter*

Note: If you are preparing a round species of mango, apply the above technique to all four sides of the mango.

There is a handy kitchen tool, called a "Mango Splitter" (see illustration, facing page), that greatly assists in cutting away mango flesh from the pit.

## SEEDING AND CORING TOMATOES

In general, when seeded and cored (see Core, page 40) tomatoes are used in food preparation, the tomatoes should be blanched (see Blanching, page 36) and peeled prior to seeding and coring.

To seed and core tomatoes, first quarter the tomatoes lengthwise. Then, using your thumb, remove and discard the seeds and the pouches containing them. Using a small paring knife, cut away and discard all white and greenish core and membrane. Only red tomato flesh should remain.

## USING FRESH GINGER

To use fresh ginger, purchase knobby, mature ginger that is firm, unwrinkled, and uncracked—indications of freshness. Pare (see Pare, page 40) the ginger, and then grate (see Grate, page 40), chop, or slice it.

Fresh, unpared ginger may stored in the refrigerator up to approximately 1 month. To prepare fresh ginger for refrigerator storage, wrap it tightly in paper toweling and place it in a zipper-seal plastic bag.

When fresh ginger is called for in recipes, do not substitute dried ginger because dried ginger is much more pungent and has a different flavor.

# GLOSSARY

BLANCH: *v.* To dip briefly in boiling water, generally for the purpose of loosening the skin of a food for peeling or for the purpose of cooking briefly.

BRINE: *n.* A strong salt and water solution used in pickling, curing, and fermenting food for the purpose of preserving it and/or imparting flavor.

CONDIMENT: *n.* A sauce, relish, or seasoning placed on or beside food, usually at the table, to enhance flavor.

CORE: *v.* To remove the central, often inedible, part of some fruits, such as apples.

CUBE: *v.* To cut food into chunks with 6 equal, square sides greater than ¼ inch square.

DICE: *v.* To cut food into small pieces with 6 equal, square sides ¼ inch square or less.

GRATE: *v.* To break down a semihard product to a texture resembling finely rolled cracker crumbs, usually by rubbing the product against a sharp, densely pronged, metal kitchen tool made for this purpose, or by processing it in a food processor or blender.

GRIND: *v.* To reduce food to small fragments with the use of a meat grinder or other kitchen implement or tool.

HULL: *v.* (1) To remove the green, leafy sepals at the stem end of a fruit, plus the pith (the central strand of tissue) of strawberries. (2) To remove the outer covering of a fruit or seed.

PARE: *v.* To cut the skin or outer layer off a tight-skinned product, such as an apple.

PECTIN: *n.* Water-soluble substances found in the cell walls and intercellular layers of fruits. Combined with sugar and acid in correct proportions, pectin forms a gel that is the basis for jellied sweet spreads, such as jelly and jam. Commercially packaged powdered or liquid fruit pectin is often used in making these jellied products.

PUREE: *v.* To whip, press, or mash a solid or semisolid food to a smooth, thick, consistency, but not liquefied. A blender, food processor, food mill, or sieve is often used to puree a food.

RIND: *n.* A usually tough outer layer; for example, the peel of a fruit.

ROLLING BOIL: *n.* A full, rapid boil, when water-vapor bubbles continuously and rapidly burst below the surface of the liquid, causing extreme agitation over the entire surface as they leave the liquid. A full rolling boil cannot be stirred down.

SAUTÉ: *v*. To cook food in a small amount of fat in an uncovered skillet or pan over direct heat.

SCALD: *v*. (1) To heat liquid to just under the boiling point. Milk reaches the scalding point when tiny bubbles appear at the edge of the pan. (2) To dip a food briefly in boiling water.

SHRED: *v*. To cut a semihard food into tiny or small strips, usually by rubbing it against a sharp, perforated, metal kitchen tool made for this purpose, or by cutting it very thinly with a knife.

SHUCK: *v*. (1) To remove the husks from some foods, such as corn. (2) To remove the shells from mollusks, such as oysters.

SIMMER: *n*. When liquid reaches a temperature just below the boiling point, at which time small water-vapor bubbles, which form principally on the bottom of the pan, slowly rise to the surface and break.

*Applesauce, Apple Butter, and Apples*

# CANNING RECIPES

*(Complete Recipe Index on page 8)*

*(Complete Recipe Index on page 8)*

Apples and Rhubarb

# Fruits and Spiced Fruits without Vinegar

Spiced Fruit without Vinegar: Fruit made with various spices and flavorings but not vinegar, which would classify it as a pickle. Served as an accompaniment to meals.

16 cups cold water

2 tablespoons white vinegar

2 tablespoons salt

8 pounds apples that hold their shape when cooked, such as Golden Delicious, Honeycrisp, or Jonathan

2½ cups sugar

10 cups water

* In a 16-quart kettle, place 16 cups water, vinegar, and salt; stir until the salt dissolves; set aside.

* Wash the apples. Pare (page 40) (see Note), cut in half, and core the apples. After each step of preparing the apples, drop them into the vinegar solution to prevent discoloration. Let the apples stand.

* In a 12-quart, heavy-bottomed, stainless steel kettle, place the sugar and 10 cups water; stir to combine. Over high heat, bring the sugar mixture to a boil, stirring until the sugar dissolves. Cover the kettle. Reduce the heat slightly and boil the sugar mixture (syrup) 5 minutes. Remove from the heat; let stand, covered.

* Meanwhile, secure a piece of damp cotton flannel, napped side up, in a sieve over a deep pan; set aside.

* After the syrup has boiled 5 minutes, drain and rinse the apples twice, using fresh, cold water. Drain the apples well. Place the apples in the boiled syrup.

Cover the kettle. Over high heat, return the syrup (with the apples) to a boil. Uncover the kettle. Reduce the heat and simmer the apples 7 minutes, stirring occasionally with a wooden mixing spoon. Remove from the heat; let stand, uncovered.

* Drain hot, sterilized (page 19), wide-mouthed, quart (or pint) jars, upside down, on a clean tea towel.

* Pack the hot apples (without syrup) into the drained jars, leaving ½-inch headspace; let stand.

* Pour the hot syrup (from the kettle) over the cotton flannel in the sieve to strain. Pour the strained syrup into a stainless steel saucepan. Over high heat, bring the syrup to a boil, stirring occasionally. Using a 1-cup measuring cup with a pouring spout, cover the apples in the jars with the hot syrup, maintaining ½-inch headspace. Using a plastic knife or a narrow, rubber spatula, remove the air bubbles in the jars. Then, check the headspace in each jar and if necessary, add additional hot syrup to maintain ½-inch headspace. Wipe the jar rims and threads. Place hot, metal lids on the jars and screw the bands firmly.

* Process in a boiling-water canner for the time shown in the PROCESSING TIMES chart at the end of this recipe.

✳ Remove the jars from the canner and place them on a dry, wooden board that has been covered with a tea towel. Let the jars stand, *undisturbed*, 12 hours to cool completely.

**NOTE:** *A Back to Basics® brand apple "peeler" (parer) (see illustration) helps accomplish this task expeditiously and efficiently.*

**YIELDS ABOUT 4 QUARTS (OR 8 PINTS)**

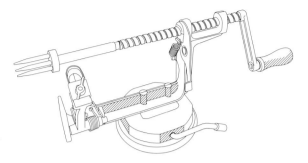

*Apple Peeler (Parer)*

| Processing Times | | | | |
|---|---|---|---|---|
| *Jar Size* | *Altitude of Canning Location* | | | |
| | 0 to 1,000 ft | 1,001 to 3,000 ft | 3,001 to 6,000 ft | Above 6,000 ft |
| Pints & Quarts | 20 min | 25 min | 30 min | 35 min |

# APPLESAUCE

16 cups cold water

2 tablespoons white vinegar

2 tablespoons salt

15 pounds cooking apples

4 cups water

3½ cups sugar

2 tablespoons plus 1 teaspoon freshly squeezed, strained lemon juice

1 tablespoon plus ½ teaspoon ground cinnamon

✳ In a 16-quart kettle, place 16 cups water, vinegar, and salt; stir until the salt dissolves; set aside.

✳ Wash the apples. Pare (page 40) (see Note, page 48), quarter, and core the apples. After each step of preparing the apples, drop them into the vinegar solution to prevent discoloration.

✳ Drain and rinse the apples twice, using fresh, cold water. Drain the apples well. In a 12-quart, heavy-bottomed, stainless steel kettle, place the apples and 4 cups water. Cover the kettle. Over medium-high heat, bring the apples to a simmer. Reduce the heat and simmer the apples (covered) 15 to 20 minutes, or until tender, stirring occasionally.

*continues*

* Remove from the heat. Using a large, metal mixing spoon, stir the apples well. If the apples have not pureed (See Puree, page 40) during the cooking and stirring processes, press the apples (with all the liquid) through a food mill.

* Add the sugar, lemon juice, and cinnamon; stir until well combined. Over medium heat, heat the applesauce through, stirring constantly to prevent scorching. Remove from the heat; let stand, uncovered.

* Drain hot, sterilized (page 19), pint or quart jars, upside down, on a clean tea towel.

* Using a 1-cup measuring cup with a pouring spout, pour the hot applesauce into the drained jars, leaving ½-inch headspace. Using a plastic knife or a narrow, rubber spatula, remove the air bubbles in the jars. Then, check the headspace in each jar and if necessary, add additional applesauce to maintain ½-inch headspace. Wipe the jar rims and threads. Place hot, metal lids on the jars and screw the bands firmly.

* Process in a boiling-water canner for the time shown in the PROCESSING TIMES chart at the end of this recipe.

* Remove the jars from the canner and place them on a dry, wooden board that has been covered with a tea towel. Let the jars stand, *undisturbed*, 12 hours to cool completely.

NOTE: *A Back to Basics® brand apple "peeler" (parer) (see illustration, page 47) helps accomplish this task expeditiously and efficiently.*

YIELDS ABOUT 7 PINTS (OR 3 QUARTS PLUS 1 PINT)

| PROCESSING TIMES | | | | |
|---|---|---|---|---|
| *Jar Size* | *Altitude of Canning Location* | | | |
| | 0 to 1,000 ft | 1,001 to 3,000 ft | 3,001 to 6,000 ft | Above 6,000 ft |
| Pints | 15 min | 20 min | 20 min | 25 min |
| Quarts | 20 min | 25 min | 30 min | 35 min |

# APRICOTS

16 cups cold water

2 tablespoons white vinegar

2 tablespoons salt

10 pounds apricots, divided*

2½ cups sugar

5 cups water

*Cooked apricots tend to fray quite easily and quickly. Therefore, it is important to heat them and place them in the jars in small batches, as described in the procedures, below, in order to maintain their shape.*

✶ In a 16-quart kettle, place 16 cups water, vinegar, and salt; stir until the salt dissolves; set aside.

✶ Wash 2½ pounds of the apricots; drain. Blanch the apricots (page 36) 30 seconds and immediately immerse them in cold water; drain. Peel, cut in half, and pit the apricots. As the apricots are prepared, drop them into the vinegar solution to prevent discoloration. Repeat the procedure 3 times to prepare the remaining apricots in 2½-pound batches. The apricots should be prepared in these small batches because they darken quickly in their skins after being blanched. Let the apricots stand.

✶ Secure a piece of damp cotton flannel, napped side up, in a sieve over a deep pan; set aside.

✶ In a 12-quart, heavy-bottomed, stainless steel kettle, place the sugar and 5 cups water; stir to combine. Over high heat, bring the sugar mixture to a boil, stirring until the sugar dissolves. Cover the kettle. Reduce the heat slightly and boil the sugar mixture (syrup) 5 minutes. Remove from the heat; let stand, covered.

✶ Drain hot, sterilized (page 19), wide-mouthed, pint or quart jars, upside down, on a clean tea towel; let stand.

✶ Return the covered kettle containing the sugar mixture (syrup) to high heat and return the sugar mixture (syrup) to a boil. Meanwhile, remove approximately ½ of the apricots from the vinegar solution. Rinse the apricots twice, using fresh, cold water. Drain the apricots well. Uncover the kettle containing the boiling syrup. Place ½ *of the rinsed and drained apricots* in the boiling syrup. Over high heat, heat the apricots through only. Do not overcook.

✶ Remove from the heat. Using a slotted mixing spoon, immediately pack the hot apricots (without syrup) into approximately ¼ of the drained jars, leaving ½-inch headspace; let stand.

✶ Cover the kettle containing the syrup. Over high heat, return the syrup to boiling. Uncover the kettle and place *the remaining ½ of the rinsed and drained apricots* in the boiling syrup. Repeat the previous process through packing the hot apricots into ¼ of the drained jars, leaving ½-inch headspace; let stand.

☀ Pour the hot syrup (from the kettle) over the cotton flannel in the sieve to strain. Then, pour the strained syrup into a stainless steel saucepan. Over high heat, bring the syrup to a boil, stirring occasionally. Using a 1-cup measuring cup with a pouring spout, cover the apricots in the jars with the hot, strained syrup, maintaining ½-inch headspace. Using a plastic knife or a narrow, rubber spatula, remove the air bubbles in the jars. Then, check the headspace in each jar and if necessary, add additional hot syrup to maintain ½-inch headspace. Wipe the jar rims and threads. Place hot, metal lids on the jars and screw the bands firmly. Let the jars of apricots stand.

☀ Pour the remaining hot syrup in the saucepan back into the 12-quart kettle.

Repeat the entire rinsing, draining, heating, packing, and final procedures, using the remaining ½ of the apricots.

☀ Process all the jars of apricots in a boiling-water canner for the time shown in the PROCESSING TIMES chart at the end of this recipe.

☀ Remove the jars from the canner and place them on a dry, wooden board that has been covered with a tea towel. Let the jars stand, *undisturbed*, 12 hours to cool completely.

YIELDS ABOUT 8 PINTS (OR 4 QUARTS)

VARIATION:
TO CAN UNPEELED APRICOTS

☀ Follow the Apricots recipe, above, eliminating the blanching and peeling procedures.

| Processing Times | | | | |
|---|---|---|---|---|
| *Jar Size* | *Altitude of Canning Location* | | | |
| | 0 to 1,000 ft | 1,001 to 3,000 ft | 3,001 to 6,000 ft | Above 6,000 ft |
| Pints | 20 min | 25 min | 30 min | 35 min |
| Quarts | 25 min | 30 min | 35 min | 40 min |

# BLUEBERRIES

1½ quarts blueberries*

½ cup sugar

2 cups water

*To maintain the shape of the blueberries, do not blanch and place in jars more than 1½ quarts of blueberries at a time (see procedures, below).*

* Place the blueberries in a flat-bottomed pan. Sort and stem the blueberries. Transfer the blueberries to a colander. Run cold water over the blueberries to wash; set aside.

* In a small, stainless steel saucepan, place the sugar and water; stir to combine. Over high heat, bring the sugar mixture to a boil, stirring until the sugar dissolves. Cover the saucepan. Reduce the heat slightly and boil the sugar mixture (syrup) 5 minutes. Remove from the heat; let stand, covered.

* Meanwhile, blanch the blueberries (page 36) 1½ minutes in fresh, boiling water. (*See asterisk (*) following the ingredients list, above.*) Immediately drain the blueberries; set aside.

* Drain 2 hot, sterilized (page 19), pint jars (or 1 hot, sterilized quart jar), upside down, on a clean tea towel.

* Using a 1-cup measuring cup with a pouring spout, pour ½ cup of the hot syrup into each of the 2 pint jars (or the 1 quart jar). Add ½ of the blueberries to each pint jar (or all of the blueberries to the quart jar), shaking the jars (or jar) intermittently as the blueberries are added to achieve close packing without crushing the blueberries. Leave ½-inch headspace.

* Using the 1-cup measuring cup with a pouring spout, cover the blueberries in the jars (or jar) with additional hot syrup, maintaining ½-inch headspace. Using a plastic knife or a narrow, rubber spatula, remove the air bubbles in the jars (or jar). Then, check the headspace in each jar (or the 1 jar) and if necessary, add additional hot syrup to maintain ½-inch headspace. Wipe the jar rims (or rim) and threads. Place hot, metal lids on the jars (or jar) and screw the bands (or band) firmly.

* Process in a boiling-water canner for the time shown in the PROCESSING TIMES chart at the end of this recipe.

* Remove the jars (or jar) from the canner and place them (or it) on a dry, wooden board that has been covered with a tea towel. Let the jars (or jar) stand, *undisturbed*, 12 hours to cool completely.

YIELDS ABOUT 2 PINTS (OR 1 QUART)

*continues*

- Use drained blueberries canned in either syrup (as in the above recipe) or water (see Variation, below), in muffins and pancakes.
- Spoon drained blueberries over vanilla ice cream.

**VARIATION:**
**TO CAN BLUEBERRIES IN WATER**

Follow the Blueberries recipe on page 53, substituting fresh, boiling water for the boiling syrup.

## PROCESSING TIMES

| Jar Size | Altitude of Canning Location | | | |
|---|---|---|---|---|
| | 0 to 1,000 ft | 1,001 to 3,000 ft | 3,001 to 6,000 ft | Above 6,000 ft |
| Pints & Quarts | 15 min | 20 min | 20 min | 25 min |

# WHITE CHERRIES

13 pounds Rainier (white) cherries

3 cups sugar

8 cups water

＊ Wash the cherries; drain. Remove the stems. Prick each cherry twice (on opposite sides) with a large, sterilized needle or hat pin to prevent bursting; set aside.

＊ In a 12-quart, heavy-bottomed, stainless steel kettle, place the sugar and water; stir to combine. Over high heat, bring the sugar mixture to a boil, stirring until the sugar dissolves. Cover the kettle. Reduce the heat slightly and boil the sugar mixture (syrup) 5 minutes.

＊ Then, place the cherries in the boiling syrup. Cover the kettle. Over high heat, return the syrup (with the cherries) to a boil. Uncover the kettle. Reduce the heat and cook the cherries at a low boil 4 minutes. Remove from the heat; let stand, uncovered.

＊ Drain hot, sterilized (page 19), quart or pint jars, upside down, on a clean tea towel.

＊ Using a large, slotted mixing spoon, pack the hot cherries (without syrup) into the drained jars, shaking the jars intermittently as the cherries are added to achieve close packing without crushing the cherries. Leave ½-inch headspace.

✳ Using a 1-cup measuring cup with a pouring spout, cover the cherries in the jars with the hot syrup, maintaining ½-inch headspace. Using a plastic knife or a narrow, rubber spatula, remove the air bubbles in the jars. Using a teaspoon, skim any foam off the syrup at the top of the jars. Then, check the headspace in each jar and if necessary, add additional hot syrup to maintain ½-inch headspace. Wipe the jar rims and threads. Place hot, metal lids on the jars and screw the bands firmly.

✳ Process in a boiling-water canner for the time shown in the PROCESSING TIMES chart at the end of this recipe.

✳ Remove the jars from the canner and place them on a dry, wooden board that has been covered with a tea towel. Let the jars stand, *undisturbed*, 12 hours to cool completely.

YIELDS ABOUT 6 QUARTS (OR 12 PINTS)

| PROCESSING TIMES | | | | |
|---|---|---|---|---|
| *Jar Size* | *Altitude of Canning Location* | | | |
| | 0 to 1,000 ft | 1,001 to 3,000 ft | 3,001 to 6,000 ft | Above 6,000 ft |
| Pints | 15 min | 20 min | 20 min | 25 min |
| Quarts | 20 min | 25 min | 30 min | 35 min |

# FRUIT COCKTAIL

16 cups cold water

2 tablespoons white vinegar

2 tablespoons salt

1½ cups sugar

4 cups water

2 pineapples

3½ pounds Bartlett pears

3½ pounds Colorado, Michigan, Missouri, or Idaho peaches

1½ pounds stemmed, seedless, whole white grapes

1 10-ounce commercial jar, red maraschino cherries

✳ In a 16-quart kettle, place 16 cups water, vinegar, and salt; stir until the salt dissolves. Half fill 2 large mixing bowls with the vinegar solution; set aside. Leave the remaining solution in the kettle; set aside. (The vinegar solution will be used to prevent discoloration of the uncooked fruit.)

✳ In a 12-quart, heavy-bottomed, stainless steel kettle, place the sugar and 4 cups water; stir to combine. Over high heat, bring the sugar mixture to a boil,

*continues*

stirring until the sugar dissolves. Cover the kettle. Reduce the heat slightly and boil the sugar mixture (syrup) 5 minutes. Remove from the heat; let stand, covered.

✳ Secure a piece of damp cotton flannel, napped side up, in a sieve over a deep pan; set aside.

✳ Pare (page 40) and core the pineapples; cut into ½-inch cubes (page 40). Weigh 1¾ pounds cubed pineapple. Place the pineapple cubes in the boiled syrup. Cover the kettle. Over high heat, bring the syrup (with the pineapple cubes) to a simmer. Uncover the kettle. Reduce the heat and simmer the pineapple cubes 3 minutes.

✳ Remove from the heat. Using a slotted spoon, remove the pineapple cubes from the syrup and place them in a very large, clean, mixing bowl (not one of the large mixing bowls containing the vinegar solution); set aside.

✳ Pour the hot syrup (from the kettle) over the cotton flannel in the sieve to strain. Pour the strained syrup back into the kettle; cover and set aside.

✳ Wash, cut in half, core, and pare the pears. As the pears are prepared, drop them into the kettle containing the vinegar solution. Then, cut the prepared pears into ½-inch cubes. As the cubes are cut, drop them into one of the mixing bowls containing the vinegar solution.

✳ Drain and rinse the pear cubes twice, using fresh, cold water. Drain the pear cubes well; let stand. Over high heat, bring the syrup in the kettle to a boil. Uncover the kettle and add the pear cubes. Cover the kettle. Over high heat, bring the syrup (with the pear cubes) to a simmer. Uncover the kettle. Reduce the heat and simmer the pear cubes 2 minutes.

✳ Remove from the heat. Using a slotted spoon, remove the pear cubes from the syrup and place them in the mixing bowl with the pineapple cubes; set aside.

✳ Pour the hot syrup (from the kettle) over the cotton flannel in the sieve to strain. Pour the strained syrup back into the kettle; cover and set aside.

✳ Wash the peaches. Blanch the peaches (page 36) 30 seconds and immediately immerse them in cold water; drain. Peel, quarter lengthwise, and pit the peaches. Cut away the frayed flesh that surrounded the pits. As the peaches are prepared, drop them into the 16-quart kettle containing the vinegar solution. Then, cut the prepared peaches into ½-inch cubes. As the cubes are cut, drop them into the remaining mixing bowl containing the vinegar solution.

✳ Drain and rinse the peach cubes twice, using fresh, cold water. Drain the peach cubes well; let stand. Over high heat, bring the syrup in the kettle to a boil. Uncover the kettle and add the peach cubes. Cover the kettle. Over high heat, bring the syrup (with the peach cubes) to a simmer. Uncover the kettle. Reduce the heat and simmer the peach cubes 2 minutes.

✳ Remove from the heat. Using a slotted spoon, remove the peach cubes from the syrup and place them in the mixing bowl with the pineapple and pear cubes; set aside.

✳ Pour the hot syrup (from the kettle) over the cotton flannel in the sieve to strain. Pour the strained syrup into a stainless steel saucepan; set aside.

✳ Wash the grapes and drain them well. Add the uncooked grapes to the mixing bowl containing the cooked fruit; set aside.

✳ In a colander, drain the maraschino cherries and rinse them very well. Place the rinsed cherries between a double layer of paper towels to further drain them. Cut the cherries in half lengthwise; add to the mixing bowl containing the prepared fruit.

✳ Using a large, wooden mixing spoon, *carefully* toss the fruit until evenly distributed, being cautious not to cut or crush the fruit. Let stand.

✳ Drain 8 hot, sterilized (page 19), pint jars, upside down, on a clean tea towel; let stand.

✳ Over high heat, bring the strained syrup to a boil. Using a 1-cup measuring cup with a pouring spout, pour ½ cup of the hot syrup into each of the 8 jars. Then, fill the jars with the fruit, leaving ½-inch headspace. Using a plastic knife or a narrow, rubber spatula, remove the air bubbles in the jars. Then, check the headspace in each jar and if necessary, add additional syrup to maintain ½-inch headspace. Wipe the jar rims and threads. Place hot, metal lids on the jars and screw the bands firmly.

✳ Process in a boiling-water canner for the time shown in the PROCESSING TIMES chart at the end of this recipe.

✳ Remove the jars from the canner and place them on a dry, wooden board that has been covered with a tea towel. Let the jars stand, *undisturbed*, 12 hours to cool completely.

YIELDS ABOUT 8 PINTS

| PROCESSING TIMES | | | |
|---|---|---|---|
| *Jar Size* | *Altitude of Canning Location* | | |
| | 0 to 1,000 ft | 1,001 to 3,000 ft | 3,001 to 6,000 ft | Above 6,000 ft |
| Pints | 20 min | 25 min | 30 min | 35 min |

# GOOSEBERRIES

2 quarts (about 2½ pounds) gooseberries

3 cups boiling water, divided

✳ Wash the gooseberries and drain them in a colander.

✳ Using a small, sharp paring knife, cut tiny portions off both ends of the gooseberries. Place the gooseberries in a large mixing bowl; set aside.

✳ Drain 2 hot, sterilized (page 19), pint jars or 1 hot, sterilized quart jar, upside down, on a clean tea towel; let stand.

✳ Blanch ½ of the gooseberries (page 36) 20 seconds. Immediately drain the blanched gooseberries in a colander; let stand.

✳ Using a 1-cup measuring cup with a pouring spout, pour ½ cup fresh, boiling water into 1 of the hot, sterilized pint jars or the hot, sterilized quart jar. Add the blanched gooseberries, shaking the jar intermittently as the gooseberries are added to achieve close packing without crushing the gooseberries. Leave ½-inch headspace in the pint jar (if used); let stand.

✳ Quickly blanch and drain the remaining ½ of the gooseberries; let stand.

✳ If using pint jars, pour ½ cup fresh, boiling water into the 1 empty, hot, sterilized (page 19), pint jar. If using a quart jar, do not add additional boiling water to the jar at this time. Repeat the procedure used for the first ½ of the gooseberries, packing the gooseberries into the pint jar containing the ½ cup boiling water or adding the gooseberries to the partially filled quart jar containing the first ½ of the gooseberries. Leave ½-inch headspace in the pint jars as well as the quart jar.

✳ Using the 1-cup measuring cup with a pouring spout, cover the gooseberries in the jars (or jar) with additional fresh, boiling water, maintaining ½-inch headspace. Using a plastic knife or a narrow, rubber spatula, remove the air bubbles in the jars (or jar). Then, check the headspace in each jar (or the 1 jar) and if necessary, add additional fresh, boiling water to maintain ½-inch headspace. Wipe the jar rims (or rim) and threads. Place hot, metal lids on the jars (or jar) and screw the bands (or band) firmly.

✳ Process in a boiling-water canner for the time shown in the PROCESSING TIMES chart at the end of this recipe.

✳ Remove the jars (or jar) from the canner and place them (or it) on a dry, wooden board that has been covered with a tea towel. Let the jars (or jar) stand, *undisturbed*, 12 hours to cool completely.

YIELDS ABOUT 2 PINTS (OR 1 QUART)

## VARIATION:
### TO CAN GOOSEBERRIES IN SYRUP

In a saucepan, place 1 cup sugar and 4 cups water; stir to combine. Over medium heat, bring the sugar mixture to a boil, stirring until the sugar dissolves. Cover the saucepan. Reduce the heat slightly and boil the sugar mixture (syrup) 5 minutes.

Follow the Gooseberries recipe on the facing page with the following exceptions: Blanch the gooseberries in the syrup. Using a slotted spoon, immediately remove the blanched gooseberries from the syrup and place them in a colander over a mixing bowl. Add ½ cup of the boiling syrup (instead of boiling water) to the jars (jar) prior to adding the gooseberries. Cover the gooseberries in the jars (jar) with the boiling syrup instead of the boiling water.

| PROCESSING TIMES | | | |
|---|---|---|---|
| *Jar Size* | *Altitude of Canning Location* | | |
| | 0 to 1,000 ft | 1,001 to 6,000 ft | Above 6,000 ft |
| Pints & Quarts | 15 min | 20 min | 25 min |

# GRAPES

6 pounds seedless white or red grapes

1 cup sugar

4 cups water

✳ Wash the grapes, remove them from the stems, and place them in a bowl; set aside.

✳ In a medium-large, stainless steel saucepan, place the sugar and water; stir to combine. Over high heat, bring the sugar mixture to a boil, stirring until the sugar dissolves. Cover the saucepan. Reduce the heat slightly and boil the sugar mixture (syrup) 5 minutes. Remove from the heat; let stand, covered.

✳ Drain hot, sterilized (page 19) pint or quart jars, upside down, on a clean tea towel.

✳ Fill the jars with the raw grapes, leaving ½-inch headspace.

✳ Using a 1-cup measuring cup with a pouring spout, cover the grapes in the jars with the hot syrup, maintaining ½-inch headspace. Using a plastic knife or a narrow, rubber spatula, remove the air bubbles in the jars. Then, check the headspace in each jar and if necessary,

add additional hot syrup to maintain ½-inch headspace. Wipe the jar rims and threads. Place hot, metal lids on the jars and screw the bands firmly.

✳ Process in a boiling-water canner for the time shown in the PROCESSING TIMES chart at the end of this recipe.

✳ Remove the jars from the canner and place them on a dry, wooden board that has been covered with a tea towel. Let the jars stand, *undisturbed*, 12 hours to cool completely.

YIELDS ABOUT 6 PINTS (OR 3 QUARTS)

*SERVING SUGGESTIONS*

• Use in mixed or molded fruit salads.

• Combine with fresh and/or poached fruits in dessert fruit compotes.

| PROCESSING TIMES | | | | |
|---|---|---|---|---|
| *Jar Size* | *Altitude of Canning Location* | | | |
| | 0 to 1,000 ft | 1,001 to 3,000 ft | 3,001 to 6,000 ft | Above 6,000 ft |
| Pints | 15 min | 20 min | 20 min | 25 min |
| Quarts | 20 min | 25 min | 30 min | 35 min |

# KIWIS

4 pounds kiwis (about 15 large kiwis)

1 cup sugar

4 cups water

✳ Trim off both ends of the kiwis and carefully cut away the core at the stem end. Pare (page 40) the kiwis, slice them widthwise ¼ inch thick, and place them in a bowl; set aside.

✳ In a medium-large, stainless steel saucepan, place the sugar and water; stir to combine. Over high heat, bring the sugar mixture to a boil, stirring until the sugar dissolves. Cover the saucepan. Reduce the heat slightly and boil the sugar mixture (syrup) 5 minutes. Remove from the heat; let stand, covered.

✳ Drain hot, sterilized (page 19), wide-mouthed, pint jars, upside down, on a clean tea towel.

✳ Arrange the sliced kiwis in the jars, leaving ½-inch headspace.

✳ Using a 1-cup measuring cup with a pouring spout, cover the kiwis in the jars with the hot syrup, maintaining ½-inch headspace. Using a plastic knife or a narrow, rubber spatula, remove the air bubbles in the jars. Then, check the headspace in each jar and if necessary, add additional hot syrup to maintain ½-inch headspace. Wipe the jar rims and threads. Place hot, metal lids on the jars and screw the bands firmly.

✳ Process in a boiling-water canner for the time shown in the PROCESSING TIMES chart at the end of this recipe.

✳ Remove the jars from the canner and place them on a dry, wooden board that has been covered with a tea towel. Let the jars stand, *undisturbed*, 12 hours to cool completely.

YIELDS ABOUT 4 PINTS

*SERVING SUGGESTION*

● Use in fruit salads and compotes.

| PROCESSING TIMES | | | | |
|---|---|---|---|---|
| *Jar Size* | *Altitude of Canning Location* | | | |
| | 0 to 1,000 ft | 1,001 to 3,000 ft | 3,001 to 6,000 ft | Above 6,000 ft |
| Pints | 15 min | 20 min | 20 min | 25 min |

# MIXED FRUIT

16 cups cold water

2 tablespoons white vinegar

2 tablespoons salt

12 small Bartlett pears,* halved lengthwise, cored, and pared

8 medium Golden Delicious apples,* pared,** quartered, and cored

8 Colorado, Michigan, Missouri, or Idaho peaches,* blanched (page 36), peeled, halved lengthwise, and pitted

4 cups stemmed, seedless, whole white grapes*

1½ cups sugar

4 cups water

*Approximately 3 pears, 2 apples, 2 peaches, and 1 cup of grapes will be used in each quart of mixed fruit.*

**A Back to Basics® brand apple " peeler" (parer) (see illustration, page 47) helps accomplish this task expeditiously and efficiently.*

❋ In a large kettle, place 16 cups water, vinegar, and salt; stir until the salt dissolves. Pour the vinegar solution evenly into 3 large mixing bowls; set aside. (The vinegar solution will be used to prevent discoloration of the uncooked fruit.)

❋ Prepare the fruit, as indicated in the ingredients list, above, dropping the pears, apples, and peaches separately into the 3 bowls of the vinegar solution as they are prepared; set aside.

❋ In a clean, 12-quart, heavy-bottomed, stainless steel kettle, place the sugar and 4 cups water; stir to combine. Over high heat, bring the sugar mixture to a boil,

stirring until the sugar dissolves. Cover the kettle. Reduce the heat slightly and boil the sugar mixture (syrup) 5 minutes.

❋ After the syrup has boiled 5 minutes, drain and rinse the pears twice, using fresh, cold water. Drain the pears well. Place the pears in the boiling syrup. Cover the kettle. Over high heat, bring the syrup (with the pears) to a simmer. Uncover the kettle. Reduce the heat and simmer the pears 4 minutes.

❋ Remove from the heat. Using a slotted spoon, remove the pears from the syrup and place them in a clean mixing bowl; set aside. Cover the kettle containing the syrup; set aside.

❋ Drain and rinse the apples twice, using fresh, cold water. Drain the apples well; let stand momentarily. Over high heat, bring the syrup in the kettle (the same syrup used for simmering the pears) to a boil. Uncover the kettle and add the apples. Cover the kettle. Over high heat, bring the syrup (with the apples) to a simmer. Uncover the kettle. Reduce the heat and simmer the apples 5 minutes.

❋ Remove from the heat. Using the slotted spoon, remove the apples from the syrup and place them in a separate, clean mixing bowl; set aside. Cover the kettle containing the syrup; set aside.

❋ Drain and rinse the peaches twice, using fresh, cold water. Drain the peaches well; let stand momentarily.

Over high heat, bring the syrup in the kettle (the same syrup used for simmering the pears and apples) to a boil. Uncover the kettle and add the peaches. Cover the kettle. Over high heat, heat the peaches through. *Do not overcook.*

✳ Remove from the heat. Using the slotted spoon, remove the peaches from the syrup and place them in a separate, clean mixing bowl; set aside.

✳ Wash the grapes; do not cook or heat. Place the grapes in a separate, clean mixing bowl; set aside.

✳ Secure a piece of damp cotton flannel, napped side up, in a sieve over a deep pan. Pour the hot syrup (from the kettle) over the cotton flannel in the sieve to strain. Pour the strained syrup into a stainless steel saucepan; set aside.

✳ Drain hot, sterilized (page 19), wide-mouthed, preferably quart jars (pint jars may be used), upside down, on a clean tea towel.

✳ Pack the fruit in layers by type of fruit, or pack the fruit mixed, into the jars, leaving ½-inch headspace; let stand.

✳ Over high heat, bring the strained syrup in the saucepan to a boil, stirring occasionally. Using a 1-cup measuring cup with a pouring spout, cover the fruit in the jars with the hot syrup, maintaining ½-inch headspace. Using a plastic knife or a narrow, rubber spatula, remove the air bubbles in the jars. Then, check the headspace in each jar and if

necessary, add additional syrup to maintain ½-inch headspace. Wipe the jar rims and threads. Place hot, metal lids on the jars and screw the bands firmly.

✳ Process in a boiling-water canner for the time shown in the PROCESSING TIMES chart at the end of this recipe.

✳ Remove the jars from the canner and place them on a dry, wooden board that has been covered with a tea towel. Let the jars stand, *undisturbed*, 12 hours to cool completely.

YIELDS ABOUT 4 QUARTS (OR 8 PINTS)

VARIATIONS: Other fruit of choice, such as plums and apricots, may be added or substituted.

| PROCESSING TIMES | | | | |
|---|---|---|---|---|
| Jar Size | Altitude of Canning Location | | | |
| | 0 to 1,000 ft | 1,001 to 3,000 ft | 3,001 to 6,000 ft | Above 6,000 ft |
| Pints | 20 min | 25 min | 30 min | 35 min |
| Quarts | 25 min | 30 min | 35 min | 40 min |

# PEACHES

32 cups (8 quarts) cold water

¼ cup white vinegar

¼ cup salt

15 pounds peaches*

2 cups sugar

8 cups water

*Colorado, Michigan, Missouri, or Idaho peaches are preferable.*

✳ In a 16-quart kettle, place 32 cups (8 quarts) water, vinegar, and salt; stir until the salt dissolves; set aside.

✳ Wash the peaches. In batches, blanch the peaches (page 36) 1 minute and immediately immerse them in cold water; drain. Peel, cut in half lengthwise, and pit the peaches. As the peaches are prepared, drop them into the vinegar solution to prevent discoloration. Let the peaches stand.

✳ In a 12-quart, heavy-bottomed, stainless steel kettle, place the sugar and 8 cups water; stir to combine. Over high heat, bring the sugar mixture to a boil, stirring until the sugar dissolves. Cover the kettle. Reduce the heat slightly and boil the sugar mixture (syrup) 5 minutes.

✳ After the syrup has boiled 5 minutes, remove approximately ⅓ of the peaches from the vinegar solution. Rinse the peaches twice, using fresh, cold water. Drain the peaches well. Place the drained

peaches in the boiling syrup. Cover the kettle. Over high heat, bring the syrup (with the peaches) to a simmer. Uncover the kettle. Reduce the heat and simmer the peaches 6 minutes. Do not overcook.

✳ Meanwhile, drain hot, sterilized (page 19), widemouthed, quart (or pint) jars, upside down, on a clean tea towel.

✳ Remove the peaches from the heat. Pack the hot peaches (without syrup) into the jars, leaving ½-inch headspace; let stand.

✳ Repeat the rinsing, draining, simmering, and packing procedures 2 additional times, using the remaining ⅔ of the peaches; let stand.

✳ Secure a piece of damp cotton flannel, napped side up, in a sieve over a deep pan. Pour the hot syrup (from the kettle) over the cotton flannel in the sieve to strain. Pour the strained syrup into a stainless steel saucepan. Over high heat, bring the syrup to a boil, stirring occasionally. Using a 1-cup measuring cup with a pouring spout, cover the peaches in the jars with the hot syrup, maintaining ½-inch headspace. Using a plastic knife or a narrow, rubber spatula, remove the air bubbles in the jars. Then, check the headspace in each jar and if necessary, add additional syrup to maintain ½-inch headspace. Wipe the jar rims and threads. Place hot, metal lids on the jars and screw the bands firmly.

✳ Process in a boiling-water canner for the time shown in the PROCESSING TIMES chart at the end of this recipe.

✳ Remove the jars from the canner and place them on a dry, wooden board that has been covered with a tea towel. Let the jars stand, *undisturbed*, 12 hours to cool completely.

YIELDS ABOUT 7 QUARTS (OR 14 PINTS)

### PROCESSING TIMES

| Jar Size | Altitude of Canning Location | | | |
|---|---|---|---|---|
| | 0 to 1,000 ft | 1,001 to 3,000 ft | 3,001 to 6,000 ft | Above 6,000 ft |
| Pints | 20 min | 25 min | 30 min | 35 min |
| Quarts | 25 min | 30 min | 35 min | 40 min |

# PEARS AMARETTO

16 cups cold water

2 tablespoons white vinegar

2 tablespoons salt

7 pounds firm and not overripe Bartlett pears

⅓ cup blanched whole almonds

1½ cups sugar

3 cups water

½ cup Amaretto*

*An almond-flavored liqueur, although apricot pits are often used to flavor it rather than almonds. Amaretto di Saronno, the original Amaretto, comes from Saronno, Italy.*

✳ In a 16-quart kettle, place 16 cups water, vinegar, and salt; stir until the salt dissolves; set aside.

✳ Wash, cut in half lengthwise, core, and pare (page 40) the pears. As the pears are prepared, drop them into the vinegar solution to prevent discoloration. Let the pears stand.

✳ Fill a 12-quart, heavy-bottomed, stainless steel kettle about ⅓ full of fresh water. Cover the kettle. Over high heat, bring the water to a boil.

✳ Meanwhile, drain and rinse the pears twice, using fresh, cold water. Drain the pears well. Place the pears, one layer at a time, in the boiling water in the kettle. Cover the kettle. Over high heat, bring the water (with the pears) to a simmer. Uncover the kettle. Reduce the heat

*continues*

and simmer the pears 3 minutes. *Do not overcook.*

✳ Remove from the heat. Using a slotted spoon, immediately remove the pears from the kettle and place them in a colander over a mixing bowl. Let stand briefly.

✳ Drain hot, sterilized (page 19), wide-mouthed, quart (or pint) jars, upside down, on a clean tea towel.

✳ Pack the hot pears into the jars, sprinkling 2 tablespoons of almonds evenly throughout each quart jar as it is packed. (Use 1 tablespoon of almonds in each pint jar.) Leave ½-inch headspace. Let the pears stand.

✳ In a large, stainless steel saucepan, place the sugar and 3 cups water (not the same water used to cook the pears); stir to combine. Over high heat, bring the sugar mixture to a boil, stirring until the sugar dissolves. Cover the saucepan. Reduce the heat slightly and boil the sugar mixture (syrup) 5 minutes. Remove from the heat. Add the Amaretto and stir to blend. Cover and let stand.

✳ Slightly spread the fingers of one of your hands and place them over the top of one of the filled jars. Invert the jar briefly over a bowl to drain away most of the liquid that has accumulated around the pears and almonds. Then, place the jar, right side up, on the work surface. Make certain that the pears settle back into the jar in order to retain ½-inch

headspace. Repeat the procedure with the remaining jars. (Draining the jars allows more of the Amaretto-flavored syrup to be added to the pears.)

✳ Using a 1-cup measuring cup with a pouring spout, cover the pears in the jars with the hot syrup, maintaining ½-inch headspace. Using a plastic knife or a narrow, rubber spatula, remove the air bubbles in the jars. Then, check the headspace in each jar and if necessary, add additional syrup to maintain ½-inch headspace. Wipe the jar rims and threads. Place hot, metal lids on the jars and screw the bands firmly.

✳ Process in a boiling-water canner for the time shown in the PROCESSING TIMES chart at the end of this recipe.

✳ Remove the jars from the canner and place them on a dry, wooden board that has been covered with a tea towel. Let the jars stand, *undisturbed*, 12 hours to cool completely.

YIELDS ABOUT 3 QUARTS (OR 6 PINTS)

*PLAIN PEARS:* Follow the Pears Amaretto recipe on page 65, omitting the almonds and Amaretto.

| PROCESSING TIMES | | | | |
|---|---|---|---|---|
| Jar Size | Altitude of Canning Location | | | |
| | 0 to 1,000 ft | 1,001 to 3,000 ft | 3,001 to 6,000 ft | Above 6,000 ft |
| Pints | 20 min | 25 min | 30 min | 35 min |
| Quarts | 25 min | 30 min | 35 min | 40 min |

# PLUMS IN PORT WINE

*Awarded first place overall among all canned fruits (nineteen classes) at the 1990 Iowa State Fair.*

8 pounds Italian prune plums

4 cups sugar

4 cups water

4 tablespoons coarsely shredded (page 41) orange rind

2 3-inch pieces stick cinnamon

2⅔ cups good port wine

✳ Wash the plums; drain. Prick each plum once with a large, sterilized needle or hat pin to prevent bursting; set aside. Pricking will not prevent the skins from cracking, but it will help prevent bursting.

✳ In a 12-quart, heavy-bottomed, stainless steel kettle, place the sugar, water, orange rind, and stick cinnamon; stir to combine. Over high heat, bring the sugar mixture to a boil, stirring until the sugar dissolves. Cover the kettle. Reduce the heat slightly and boil the sugar mixture (syrup) 5 minutes.

✳ Then, place the plums in the boiling syrup. Remove the kettle from the heat 3 minutes after adding the plums. Cover the kettle and let the plums stand 20 minutes.

✳ Meanwhile, secure a piece of damp cotton flannel, napped side up, in a sieve over a deep pan; set aside.

✳ Drain hot, sterilized (page 19), preferably widemouthed, quart (or pint) jars, upside down, on a clean tea towel.

✳ Pack the plums (without syrup) into the drained jars, leaving ½-inch headspace; let stand.

✳ Remove and discard the stick cinnamon from the syrup in the kettle. Then, pour the syrup (from the kettle) over the cotton flannel in the sieve to strain. Pour the strained syrup into a stainless steel saucepan. Over high heat, bring the syrup to a boil, stirring occasionally. Remove from the heat. Add the wine; stir to blend.

✳ Cover the plums in the jars with the hot syrup, maintaining ½-inch headspace. Using a plastic knife or a narrow, rubber spatula, remove the air bubbles in the jars. Then, check the headspace in each jar and if necessary, add additional hot syrup to maintain ½-inch headspace. Wipe the jar rims and threads. Place hot, metal lids on the jars and screw the bands firmly.

✳ Process in a boiling-water canner for the time shown in the PROCESSING TIMES chart at the end of this recipe.

✳ Remove the jars from the canner and place them on a dry, wooden board that has been covered with a tea towel. Let the jars stand, *undisturbed*, 12 hours to cool completely.

*continues*

*VARIATION:* The plum skins may be peeled immediately following the 3 minutes of cooking. Eliminate letting the plums stand 20 minutes and proceed to pack the plums in the jars.

*PLAIN PLUMS:* Follow the Plums in Port Wine recipe on page 67, omitting the orange rind, cinnamon, and wine.

### PROCESSING TIMES

| Jar Size | Altitude of Canning Location | | | |
|----------|-------------------|-------------------|-------------------|--------------|
| | 0 to 1,000 ft | 1,001 to 3,000 ft | 3,001 to 6,000 ft | Above 6,000 ft |
| Pints | 20 min | 25 min | 30 min | 35 min |
| Quarts | 25 min | 30 min | 35 min | 40 min |

# RASPBERRIES (RED OR BLACK)

*Blue ribbon awarded for red raspberries.*

1½ quarts raspberries (red or black)

½ cup sugar

1 cup water

✳ Place ½ of the raspberries (3 cups) in a colander. Run cold water over the raspberries to wash them; set aside.

✳ In a small, stainless steel saucepan, place the sugar and water; stir to combine. Over high heat, bring the sugar mixture to a boil, stirring until the sugar dissolves. Cover the saucepan. Reduce the heat slightly and boil the sugar mixture (syrup) 5 minutes. Remove from the heat; let stand, covered.

✳ Carefully transfer the raspberries to the top of a blancher. Blanch the raspberries (page 36) *exactly 10 seconds* (no longer: see Note) in fresh, boiling water. Immediately drain the raspberries; set aside.

✳ Drain 2 hot, sterilized (page 19) pint jars, upside down, on a clean towel.

✳ Using a 1-cup measuring cup with a pouring spout, pour ½ cup of the hot syrup into 1 of the pint jars. Add ½ of the blanched raspberries, shaking the jar intermittently as the raspberries are added to achieve close packing without crushing the raspberries. Leave ½-inch headspace. Let stand.

✳ Repeat the procedure, using ½ cup of the hot syrup and the remaining ½ of the raspberries.

✳ Using the 1-cup measuring cup with a pouring spout, cover the raspberries in the jars with additional hot syrup, maintaining ½-inch headspace. Using a plastic knife or a narrow, rubber spatula, carefully remove the air bubbles in the jars. Then, check the headspace in each jar and if necessary, add additional hot syrup to maintain ½-inch headspace. Wipe the jar rims and threads. Place hot, metal lids on the jars and screw the bands firmly.

✳ Process in a boiling-water canner for the time shown in the PROCESSING TIMES chart at the end of this recipe.

✳ Remove the jars from the canner and place them on a dry, wooden board that has been covered with a tea towel. Let the jars stand, *undisturbed*, 12 hours to cool completely.

NOTE: *Raspberries are very soft and fragile. To maintain their wholeness, handle the raspberries very gently and take extreme caution not to blanch them longer than the specified 10 seconds. Due to their vulnerability to crushing, it is recommended that raspberries be canned only in pints, not quarts.*

YIELDS ABOUT 2 PINTS

*VARIATION:*
TO CAN RASPBERRIES IN WATER

Follow the Raspberries (Red or Black) recipe, above, substituting fresh, boiling water for the boiling syrup.

| PROCESSING TIMES | | | |
|---|---|---|---|
| *Jar Size* | *Altitude of Canning Location* | | |
| | 0 to 1,000 ft | 1,001 to 6,000 ft | Above 6,000 ft |
| Pints | 15 min | 20 min | 25 min |

# RHUBARB

4½ pounds rhubarb

1½ cups sugar

✳ Wash the rhubarb and cut it into
2-inch lengths. Measure 12 cups of cut
rhubarb and place them in a 12-quart,
heavy-bottomed, stainless steel kettle.
Add the sugar; stir lightly. Cover the
kettle. Let stand 4 hours to draw juice
out of the rhubarb.

✳ Then, drain hot, sterilized (page 19),
pint or quart jars, upside down, on a
clean tea towel. Let stand.

✳ Over medium-high heat, bring the
rhubarb mixture to a boil, stirring continuously. Boil the rhubarb *10 seconds
only*.

✳ Remove from the heat. Using a slotted
spoon, pack the hot rhubarb (without
syrup) into the prepared jars, leaving
½-inch headspace.

✳ Using a 1-cup measuring cup with a
pouring spout, cover the rhubarb in the
jars with the hot syrup, maintaining

½-inch headspace. Using a plastic knife
or a narrow, rubber spatula, remove the
air bubbles in the jars. Then, check the
headspace in each jar and if necessary,
add additional syrup to maintain ½-inch
headspace. Wipe the jar rims and threads.
Place hot, metal lids on the jars and
screw the bands firmly.

✳ Process in a boiling-water canner for
the time shown in the PROCESSING TIMES
chart at the end of this recipe.

✳ Remove the jars from the canner and
place them on a dry, wooden board that
has been covered with a tea towel. Let
the jars stand, *undisturbed*, 12 hours to
cool completely.

**YIELDS ABOUT 6 PINTS (OR 3 QUARTS)**

| PROCESSING TIMES | | | |
|---|---|---|---|
| *Jar Size* | *Altitude of Canning Location* | | |
| | 0 to 1,000 ft | 1,001 to 6,000 ft | Above 6,000 ft |
| Pints & Quarts | 15 min | 20 min | 25 min |

# STRAWBERRIES

4 quarts firm strawberries, divided

2 cups sugar

✳ **THE FIRST DAY:** Place 1 quart of the strawberries in a colander. Run cold water over the strawberries to wash them. Using a strawberry huller (see illustration), remove only the green, leafy sepals at the stem of the strawberries. *Do not remove the center pith of the strawberries.*

*Strawberry Huller*

✳ Place the prepared strawberries in a flat-bottomed pan. Using a potato masher, crush the strawberries. Press the crushed strawberries and juice through a food mill (see illustration).

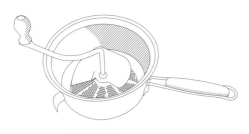

*Food Mill*

✳ Then, strain the pressed strawberries and juice through a sieve to remove the pulp. (Use a spoon to stir the pulp and expedite draining the juice through the sieve.) (Reserve the pulp for other uses, such as ice cream topping.)

✳ Measure 1 cup strained strawberry juice and pour it into a medium, stainless steel saucepan. Add the sugar; stir to combine. Over medium-high heat, bring the strawberry mixture to a boil, stirring constantly. Remove from the heat. Using tableware tablespoons and teaspoons, skim the foam off the strawberry mixture (syrup). Cover and let stand to cool.

✳ Meanwhile, wash the remaining 3 quarts of the strawberries in the colander, one quart at a time to avoid bruising or crushing the strawberries. Using the strawberry huller, remove the green, leafy sepals at the stem of the strawberries. *Do not remove the center pith of the strawberries.*

✳ Place the 3 quarts of prepared strawberries in an 8-quart, heavy-bottomed, stainless steel kettle. Pour the cooled strawberry syrup over the strawberries. Over medium-high heat, bring the strawberry syrup (with the strawberries) to a boil. Reduce the heat and cook the strawberries, uncovered, at a low boil, 4 minutes, stirring occasionally.

* Remove from the heat. Cover the kettle and let the strawberries stand, in a cool place, overnight or at least 8 hours.

* THE NEXT DAY: Secure a piece of damp cotton flannel, napped side up, in a sieve over a deep pan; set aside.

* Drain 2 hot, sterilized (page 19), pint jars or 1 hot, sterilized quart jar, upside down, on a clean tea towel; let stand.

* Uncover the kettle containing the strawberries. Over medium heat, gently bring the strawberries and syrup to a low boil, stirring often. Boil the strawberries and syrup only 30 seconds. Remove from the heat.

* Using a slotted spoon, pack the hot strawberries (without syrup) into the 2 pint jars or 1 quart jar, shaking the jars (or jar) intermittently as the strawberries are added to achieve close packing without crushing the strawberries. Leave ½-inch headspace. Let the strawberries stand.

* Pour the hot syrup from the kettle over the cotton flannel in the sieve to strain. Pour the strained syrup into a stainless steel saucepan. Over high heat, bring the syrup to a boil, stirring occasionally.

Cover the strawberries in the jars (or jar) with the hot syrup, maintaining ½-inch headspace. Using a plastic knife or a narrow, rubber spatula, remove the air bubbles in the jars (or jar). Then, check the headspace in each jar (or the 1 jar) and if necessary, add additional hot syrup to maintain ½-inch headspace. Wipe the jar rims (or rim) and threads. Place hot, metal lids on the jars (or jar) and screw the bands (or band) firmly.

* Process in a boiling-water canner for the time shown in the PROCESSING TIMES chart at the end of this recipe.

* Remove the jars (or jar) from the canner and place them (or it) on a dry, wooden board that has been covered with a tea towel. Let the jars (or jar) stand, *undisturbed*, 12 hours to cool completely.

YIELDS ABOUT 2 PINTS (OR 1 QUART)

| PROCESSING TIMES | | | |
|---|---|---|---|
| *Jar Size* | *Altitude of Canning Location* | | |
| | 0 to 1,000 ft | 1,001 to 6,000 ft | Above 6,000 ft |
| Pints & Quarts | 15 min | 20 min | 25 min |

# SPICED APPLE RINGS

16 cups cold water

2 tablespoons white vinegar

2 tablespoons salt

5 pounds bright red apples that hold their shape
   when cooked, such as Jonathan* (about 10 large
   apples)

6 cups sugar

8 cups water

4 3-inch pieces stick cinnamon

1 tablespoon red liquid food coloring

*Select uniform apples with a diameter that will
allow the stacked apple rings to fit nicely in the canning jars. Use widemouthed, pint canning jars with
straight sides.*

✳ In a 16-quart kettle, place 16 cups
water, vinegar, and salt; stir until the
salt dissolves; set aside.

✳ Wash the apples. Using a serrated-type
apple corer (see illustration), core the
apples; do not pare (page 40) them. As
the apples are cored, drop them into the
vinegar solution to prevent discoloration.

*Serrated-Type Apple Corer*

✳ Using a sharp, thin-bladed knife, slice
the cored apples, evenly, ¼-inch thick.
Be careful not to slice the apples too
thinly. Reserve the end slices for other
uses. Drop the apple rings back into the
vinegar solution as each apple is sliced.
Let the apple rings stand.

✳ In a 12-quart, heavy-bottomed,
stainless steel kettle, place the sugar,
8 cups water, stick cinnamon, and food
coloring; stir to combine. Over high
heat, bring the sugar mixture to a boil,
stirring until the sugar dissolves. Cover
the kettle. Reduce the heat slightly and
boil the sugar mixture (syrup) 5 minutes. Remove from the heat; let stand,
covered.

✳ Drain and rinse the apple rings twice,
using fresh, cold water. Drain the apple
rings well. Place the apple rings in the
hot syrup (removed from the heat).
Cover the kettle and let the apple rings
stand 10 minutes. This will help to firm
the apples.

✳ Then, over medium-high heat, bring
the apple rings to a boil in the covered
kettle. Uncover the kettle. Reduce the
heat and simmer the apple rings 10 minutes. Remove from the heat and let the
apple rings stand in the syrup, uncovered, until cool. The apple rings will
deepen in red color during the cooling
period. A plate weighted with a small

*continues*

bowl of water may be carefully placed on top of the apple rings to keep them all fully submerged in the red syrup during the cooling period.

* When the apple rings are cool, secure a piece of damp cotton flannel, napped side up, in a sieve over a deep pan; set aside.

* Drain hot, sterilized (page 19), wide-mouthed, pint jars with straight sides, upside down, on a clean tea towel.

* Stack the apple rings (without syrup) in the jars, leaving ½-inch headspace; let stand.

* Pour the syrup (in the kettle) over the cotton flannel in the sieve to strain. Pour the strained syrup into a stainless steel saucepan. Over high heat, bring the syrup to a boil, stirring occasion-ally. Using a 1-cup measuring cup with a pouring spout, cover the apple rings in the jars with the hot syrup, maintaining ½-inch headspace. Using a plastic knife or a narrow, rubber spatula, carefully remove the air bubbles in the jars. Then, check the headspace in each jar and if necessary, add additional hot syrup to maintain ½-inch headspace. Wipe the jar rims and threads. Place hot, metal lids on the jars and screw the bands firmly.

* Process in a boiling-water canner for the time shown in the PROCESSING TIMES chart at the end of this recipe.

* Remove the jars from the canner and place them on a dry, wooden board that has been covered with a tea towel. Let the jars stand, *undisturbed*, 12 hours to cool completely.

YIELDS 4 TO 5 PINTS

| PROCESSING TIMES | | | | |
|---|---|---|---|---|
| *Jar Size* | *Altitude of Canning Location* | | | |
| | 0 to 1,000 ft | 1,001 to 3,000 ft | 3,001 to 6,000 ft | Above 6,000 ft |
| Pints | 20 min | 25 min | 30 min | 35 min |

# PEPPERMINT PEARS

16 cups cold water

2 tablespoons white vinegar

2 tablespoons salt

7 pounds firm and not overripe Bartlett pears

4½ cups sugar

6 cups water

2 teaspoons peppermint extract

2 teaspoons green liquid food coloring

2¼ cups sugar

3 cups water

1 teaspoon peppermint extract

½ teaspoon green liquid food coloring

* In a 16-quart kettle, place 16 cups water, vinegar, and salt; stir until the salt dissolves; set aside.

* Wash, cut in half lengthwise, core, and pare (page 40) the pears. As the pears are prepared, drop them into the vinegar solution to prevent discoloration. Let the pears stand.

* In a 12-quart, heavy-bottomed, stainless steel kettle, place 4½ cups sugar and 6 cups water; stir to combine. Over high heat, bring the sugar mixture to a boil, stirring until the sugar dissolves. Cover the kettle. Reduce the heat slightly and boil the sugar mixture (syrup) 5 minutes.

* Remove from the heat. Add 2 teaspoons peppermint extract and 2 teaspoons food coloring; stir well to blend. Cover the kettle. Over medium-high heat, return

the syrup mixture to a boil. Remove from the heat; let stand, covered.

* Drain and rinse the pears twice, using fresh, cold water. Drain the pears well. Place the pears in the hot syrup. Cover the kettle. Over high heat, bring the syrup (with the pears) to a simmer. Uncover the kettle. Reduce the heat and simmer the pears 3 minutes. Remove from the heat. Let the pears stand in the syrup, uncovered, until cool.

* Then, in a large, heavy-bottomed, stainless steel saucepan, make another batch of the syrup, using 2¼ cups sugar, 3 cups water, 1 teaspoon peppermint extract, and ½ teaspoon green liquid food coloring, following the previous procedure through removing the syrup from the heat and letting it stand, covered.

* Drain hot, sterilized (page 19) , wide-mouthed, quart or pint jars, upside down, on a clean tea towel; let stand.

* In a colander, carefully drain the pears. Pack the pears into the jars, leaving ½-inch headspace. Using a 1-cup measuring cup with a pouring spout, cover the pears in the jars with the second batch of hot syrup, maintaining ½-inch headspace. (The second batch of syrup contains proportionately less food coloring, making it more attractive in the jars.) Using a plastic knife or a

narrow, rubber spatula, carefully remove the air bubbles in the jars. Then, check the headspace in each jar and if necessary, add additional hot syrup to maintain ½-inch headspace. Wipe the jar rims and threads. Place hot, metal lids on the jars and screw the bands firmly.

✳ Process in a boiling-water canner for the time shown in the PROCESSING TIMES chart at the end of this recipe.

✳ Remove the jars from the canner and place them on a dry, wooden board that has been covered with a tea towel. Let the jars stand, *undisturbed*, 12 hours to cool completely.

YIELDS ABOUT 3 QUARTS (OR 6 PINTS)

*SERVING SUGGESTIONS*

- Peppermint Pears complement the flavor of lamb, roast pork, and poultry.
- Pair bright-green Peppermint Pears with festive, red Spiced Apple Rings (page 75) on a divided serving dish and place it on the holiday dinner table near the turkey.

### PROCESSING TIMES

| Jar Size | Altitude of Canning Location | | | |
|---|---|---|---|---|
| | 0 to 1,000 ft | 1,001 to 3,000 ft | 3,001 to 6,000 ft | Above 6,000 ft |
| Pints | 20 min | 25 min | 30 min | 35 min |
| Quarts | 25 min | 30 min | 35 min | 40 min |

*Green Beans and Dilly Beans*

# Vegetables

# ASPARAGUS SPEARS

**6 pounds medium-diameter asparagus spears**

✳ Use widemouthed, pint or quart jars with straight sides. Measure the height of the pint or quart canning jars to be used and deduct 1¼ inches (1 inch for headspace plus ¼-inch allowance for liquid to cover the asparagus spears). This measurement will be the exact length to cut the asparagus spears. Measure 1 asparagus spear and cut it at the stem end. Use this spear as a pattern to cut the spears. Carefully place the cut spears in a colander. Run cold water over the spears to wash them; let stand.

✳ Secure a piece of damp cotton flannel, napped side up, in a sieve over a deep pan; set aside.

✳ Place the asparagus spears in the top of a blancher. Drop the top of the blancher into the blancher pan containing boiling water over high heat. Cover the blancher and return the water to boiling. Reduce the heat and pressure and cook the asparagus spears at a low boil 3½ minutes. Immediately remove the top of the blancher from the blancher pan to drain the asparagus spears; reserve the cooking liquid. Set the asparagus spears aside.

✳ Pour the hot cooking liquid in the blancher pan over the cotton flannel in the sieve to strain.

✳ Meanwhile, drain hot, sterilized (page 19), widemouthed pint or quart jars with straight sides, upside down, on a clean tea towel.

✳ Pack the asparagus spears vertically (with the tips up) and decoratively into the drained jars, leaving 1-inch headspace; let stand.

✳ Pour the strained cooking liquid into a stainless steel saucepan. Over high heat, bring the cooking liquid to a boil. Using a 1-cup measuring cup with a pouring spout, cover the asparagus spears in the jars with the hot cooking liquid, maintaining 1-inch headspace. Using a plastic knife or a narrow, rubber spatula, remove the air bubbles in the jars. Then, check the headspace in each jar and if necessary, add additional hot cooking liquid to maintain 1-inch headspace. Wipe the jar rims and threads. Place hot, metal lids on the jars and screw the bands firmly.

✳ Process in a pressure canner for the time and pressure shown in the PROCESSING TIMES AND POUNDS OF PRESSURE chart at the end of this recipe.

✳ Remove the jars from the canner and place them on a dry, wooden board that has been covered with a tea towel. Let the jars stand, *undisturbed*, 12 hours to cool completely.

*continues*

*CUT ASPARAGUS*: Follow the Asparagus Spears recipe on page 82 with the following exceptions: Cut the asparagus spears into 1½-inch lengths. Pack the cut spears randomly into pint or quart jars, leaving 1-inch headspace.

### PROCESSING TIMES AND POUNDS OF PRESSURE

**Dial-Gauge Pressure Canner**

| Jar Size | Processing Time | Altitude of Canning Location | | | |
|---|---|---|---|---|---|
| | | 0 to 2,000 ft | 2,001 to 4,000 ft | 4,001 to 6,000 ft | 6,001 to 8,000 ft |
| Pints | 30 min | 11 lbs | 12 lbs | 13 lbs | 14 lbs |
| Quarts | 40 min | 11 lbs | 12 lbs | 13 lbs | 14 lbs |

**Weighted-Gauge Pressure Canner**

| Jar Size | Processing Time | Altitude of Canning Location | |
|---|---|---|---|
| | | 0 to 1,000 ft | Above 1,000 ft |
| Pints | 30 min | 10 lbs | 15 lbs |
| Quarts | 40 min | 10 lbs | 15 lbs |

# GREEN AND WAX BEANS

*The ribbon was awarded for a pint of green and wax beans packed vertically and alternately. (See TO CAN GREEN AND/OR WAX BEANS VERTICALLY, on facing page.)*

**6 pounds green and/or wax beans***

**Green beans and wax beans may be canned separately or mixed.*

✴ Using a vegetable brush, wash the beans well. Cut off the ends; then, cut the beans into 1- to 2-inch lengths, depending upon your preference. Let the beans stand.

✴ Secure a piece of damp cotton flannel, napped side up, in a sieve over a deep pan; set aside.

✴ Place the beans in a 12-quart, heavy-bottomed, stainless steel kettle. Cover the beans with boiling water. Cover the kettle. Over high heat, bring the beans to a boil. Reduce the heat and cook the beans at a low boil for 5 minutes. Remove from the heat. Using a slotted mixing spoon, remove the beans from the cooking liquid, and place them in 1 or more stainless steel or glass pans or bowls; let stand.

✴ Pour the hot cooking liquid in the kettle over the cotton flannel in the sieve to strain; let stand.

* Meanwhile, drain hot, sterilized (page 19), pint or quart jars, upside down, on a clean tea towel.

* Pack the hot beans (without cooking liquid) loosely into the drained jars, leaving 1-inch headspace; let stand.

* Pour the strained cooking liquid into a stainless steel saucepan. Over high heat, bring the cooking liquid to a boil. Using a 1-cup measuring cup with a pouring spout, cover the beans in the jars with the hot cooking liquid, maintaining 1-inch headspace. Using a plastic knife or a narrow, rubber spatula, remove the air bubbles in the jars. Then, check the headspace in each jar and if necessary, add additional hot cooking liquid to maintain 1-inch headspace. Wipe the jar rims and threads. Place hot, metal lids on the jars and screw the bands firmly.

* Process in a pressure canner for the time and pressure shown in the PROCESSING TIMES AND POUNDS OF PRESSURE chart at the end of this recipe.

* Remove the jars from the canner and place them on a dry, wooden board that has been covered with a tea towel. Let the jars stand, *undisturbed*, 12 hours to cool completely.

YIELDS ABOUT 6 PINTS (OR 3 QUARTS)

---

## PROCESSING TIMES AND POUNDS OF PRESSURE

### Dial-Gauge Pressure Canner

| Jar Size | Processing Time | Altitude of Canning Location | | | |
|---|---|---|---|---|---|
| | | 0 to 2,000 ft | 2,001 to 4,000 ft | 4,001 to 6,000 ft | 6,001 to 8,000 ft |
| Pints | 20 min | 11 lbs | 12 lbs | 13 lbs | 14 lbs |
| Quarts | 25 min | 11 lbs | 12 lbs | 13 lbs | 14 lbs |

### Weighted-Gauge Pressure Canner

| Jar Size | Processing Time | Altitude of Canning Location | |
|---|---|---|---|
| | | 0 to 1,000 ft | Above 1,000 ft |
| Pints | 20 min | 10 lbs | 15 lbs |
| Quarts | 25 min | 10 lbs | 15 lbs |

---

*VARIATION:*
**TO CAN GREEN AND/OR WAX BEANS VERTICALLY (see Note, page 86)**

* After washing the beans, cut off the stem ends and trim the blossom ends, leaving about ⅛ inch of the "tails" intact. Let the beans stand.

* Use widemouthed, pint jars with straight sides. Measure the height of the jars and deduct 1¼ inches (1 inch for headspace plus ¼-inch allowance for liquid to cover the beans [and "tails"]). This measurement will be the exact length to cut the beans. Measure 1 bean and cut it at the stem end. Use this bean as a pattern to cut the beans. Let the beans stand.

* Secure a piece of damp, cotton flannel, napped side up, in a sieve over a deep pan; set aside.

*continues*

✳ Carefully place the beans in a 12-quart, heavy-bottomed, stainless steel kettle. Cover the beans with boiling water. Cover the kettle. Over high heat, bring the beans to a boil. Reduce the heat and cook the beans at a low boil for 5 minutes. Remove from the heat. Using a slotted mixing spoon, remove the beans from the cooking liquid and place them in 1 or more stainless steel or glass pans or bowls; let stand.

✳ Pour the hot cooking liquid in the kettle over the cotton flannel in the sieve to strain; let stand.

✳ Meanwhile, drain hot, sterilized (page 19), widemouthed, pint jars with straight sides, upside down, on a clean tea towel.

✳ Pack the hot beans (without cooking liquid) vertically (with the "tails" up) into the drained jars; let stand.

✳ Pour the strained cooking liquid into a stainless steel saucepan. Over high heat, bring the cooking liquid to a boil. Using a 1-cup measuring cup with a pouring spout, cover the beans in the jars with the hot cooking liquid, maintaining 1-inch headspace. Using a plastic knife or a narrow, rubber spatula, remove the air bubbles in the jars. Then, check the headspace in each jar and if necessary, add additional hot cooking liquid to maintain 1-inch headspace. Wipe the jar rims and threads. Place hot, metal lids on the jars and screw the bands firmly.

✳ Process and cool the jars following the *Green and Wax Beans* recipe, on the preceding pages.

NOTE: *For a very showy jar, pack green and wax beans alternately around the inside of the jar against the side glass. Evenly mix the green and wax beans in the center of the jar.*

YIELDS ABOUT 6 PINTS

# CARROTS

7½ pounds carrots (weighed without the green tops)

✳ Wash the carrots. Cut off the ends, pare (page 40), and wash again. Drain the carrots. Slice the carrots widthwise and/or lengthwise, or leave them whole. Let the carrots stand.

✳ Secure a piece of damp cotton flannel, napped side up, in a sieve over a deep pan; set aside.

✳ Place the carrots in a 12-quart, heavy-bottomed, stainless steel kettle. Cover the carrots with boiling water. Cover the kettle. Over high heat, bring the carrots to a boil. Reduce the heat and simmer the carrots 5 minutes. Remove from the heat. Using a slotted mixing spoon, remove the carrots from the cooking liquid and place them in 1 or more stainless steel or glass pans or bowls; let stand.

✳ Pour the hot cooking liquid in the kettle over the cotton flannel in the sieve to strain; let stand.

✳ Meanwhile, drain hot, sterilized (page 19), pint or quart jars, upside down, on a clean tea towel.

✳ Pack the hot carrots (without cooking liquid) into the drained jars, leaving 1-inch headspace; let stand.

✳ Pour the strained cooking liquid into a stainless steel saucepan. Over high heat, bring the cooking liquid to a boil. Using a 1-cup measuring cup with a pouring spout, cover the carrots in the jars with the hot cooking liquid, maintaining 1-inch headspace. Using a plastic knife or a narrow, rubber spatula, remove the air bubbles in the jars. Then, check the headspace in each jar and if necessary, add additional hot cooking liquid to maintain 1-inch headspace. Wipe the jar rims and threads. Place hot, metal lids on the jars and screw the bands firmly.

✳ Process in a pressure canner for the time and pressure shown in the PROCESSING TIMES AND POUNDS OF PRESSURE chart at the end of this recipe.

✳ Remove the jars from the canner and place them on a dry, wooden board that has been covered with a tea towel. Let the jars stand, *undisturbed*, 12 hours to cool completely.

YIELDS ABOUT 10 PINTS (OR 5 QUARTS)

### PROCESSING TIMES AND POUNDS OF PRESSURE

**Dial-Gauge Pressure Canner**

| Jar Size | Processing Time | Altitude of Canning Location | | | |
|---|---|---|---|---|---|
| | | 0 to 2,000 ft | 2,001 to 4,000 ft | 4,001 to 6,000 ft | 6,001 to 8,000 ft |
| Pints | 25 min | 11 lbs | 12 lbs | 13 lbs | 14 lbs |
| Quarts | 30 min | 11 lbs | 12 lbs | 13 lbs | 14 lbs |

**Weighted-Gauge Pressure Canner**

| Jar Size | Processing Time | Altitude of Canning Location | |
|---|---|---|---|
| | | 0 to 1,000 ft | Above 1,000 ft |
| Pints | 25 min | 10 lbs | 15 lbs |
| Quarts | 30 min | 10 lbs | 15 lbs |

# WHOLE-KERNEL CORN

22 pounds unshucked (see "shuck," page 41) corn
   (about 34 medium ears)

\* Shuck the corn and carefully remove all the silk. Wash the corn; set aside.

\* Fill a 12-quart, heavy-bottomed, stainless steel kettle ½ to ⅔ full of water. Cover the kettle. Over high heat, bring the water to a rapid boil. Uncover the kettle.

\* In small batches, drop the ears of corn into the boiling water and boil the corn 3 minutes. Immediately remove the ears of corn from the water and place them, single layer, on a folded tea towel spread on the kitchen counter or spread on a large wooden board; let stand. Return the water to a rapid boil before adding each batch of corn to the kettle.

\* Using a medium-sized, sharp knife, cut the kernels from the cobs at approximately ⅔ the depth of the kernels, leaving on the cobs any small, undeveloped kernels at the ends of the cobs. Do not scrape the cobs. Place the kernels in one or more large mixing bowls; let stand.

\* Drain hot, sterilized (page 19), pint or quart jars, upside down, on a clean tea towel.

\* Fill the jars with the corn, leaving 1-inch headspace. Do not shake the jars to pack the corn or press the corn into the jars. Using a 1-cup measuring cup with a pouring spout, cover the corn in the jars with fresh, boiling water, maintaining 1-inch headspace. Using a plastic knife or a narrow, rubber spatula, remove the air bubbles in the jars. Then, check the headspace in each jar and if necessary, add additional hot water to maintain 1-inch headspace. Wipe the jar rims and threads. Place hot, metal lids on the jars and screw the bands firmly.

\* Process in a pressure canner for the time and pressure shown in the PROCESSING TIMES AND POUNDS OF PRESSURE chart at the end of this recipe.

\* Remove the jars from the canner and place them on a dry, wooden board that has been covered with a tea towel. Let the jars stand, *undisturbed*, 12 hours to cool completely.

YIELDS ABOUT 10 PINTS (OR 5 QUARTS)

| PROCESSING TIMES AND POUNDS OF PRESSURE | | | | | |
|---|---|---|---|---|---|
| **Dial-Gauge Pressure Canner** | | | | | |
| Jar Size | Processing Time | Altitude of Canning Location | | | |
| | | 0 to 2,000 ft | 2,001 to 4,000 ft | 4,001 to 6,000 ft | 6,001 to 8,000 ft |
| Pints | 55 min | 11 lbs | 12 lbs | 13 lbs | 14 lbs |
| Quarts | 85 min | 11 lbs | 12 lbs | 13 lbs | 14 lbs |
| **Weighted-Gauge Pressure Canner** | | | | | |
| Jar Size | Processing Time | Altitude of Canning Location | | | |
| | | 0 to 1,000 ft | | Above 1,000 ft | |
| Pints | 55 min | 10 lbs | | 15 lbs | |
| Quarts | 85 min | 10 lbs | | 15 lbs | |

# CORN WITH RED PEPPERS AND BASIL

13 pounds unshucked (see "shuck," page 41) corn
(about 20 medium ears)

¾ pound red bell peppers (about 2 large peppers)

1 tablespoon dried leaf basil

✳ Shuck the corn and carefully remove all the silk. Wash the corn; set aside.

✳ Fill a 12-quart, heavy-bottomed, stainless steel kettle ½ to ⅔ full of water. Cover the kettle. Over high heat, bring the water to a rapid boil. Uncover the kettle.

✳ In small batches, drop the ears of corn into the boiling water and boil the corn 3 minutes. Immediately remove the ears of corn from the water and place them, single layer, on a folded tea towel spread on the kitchen counter or spread on a large wooden board. Return the water to a rapid boil before adding each batch of corn to the kettle.

✳ Using a medium-sized, sharp knife, cut the kernels from the cobs at approximately ⅔ the depth of the kernels, leaving on the cobs any small, undeveloped kernels at the ends of the cobs. Do not scrape the cobs. Place the kernels in one or more large mixing bowls; set aside

✳ Cut the red peppers lengthwise into 24 ¾-x-3-inch strips. Cut away any protruding flesh from the backs of the strips. Using a small, sharp knife, trim the ends of the strips to simulate ribbons (see illustration).

*Ribbon*

✳ Carefully place the red pepper ribbons in a saucepan and cover with boiling water; let stand 3 minutes to soften the ribbons slightly. Remove the ribbons from the water and place them, flat and single layer, on paper towels; set aside.

✳ Drain 6 hot, sterilized (page 19), wide-mouthed, preferably straight-sided, pint jars, upside down, on a clean tea towel.

✳ Place about ½ inch of corn in the bottom of each of the drained jars. Arrange 4 red pepper ribbons, shiny side out, decoratively around the inside of each jar against the side glass. Carefully fill the jars with corn, leaving 1-inch headspace. Do not shake the jars to pack the corn or press the corn into the jars. Then, sprinkle ½ teaspoon basil in each jar.

✳ Using a 1-cup measuring cup with a pouring spout, cover the corn in the jars with fresh, boiling water, maintaining 1-inch headspace. Using a plastic knife or a narrow, rubber spatula, carefully remove the air bubbles in the jars. Then, check the headspace in each jar and if necessary, add additional fresh, boiling water to maintain 1-inch headspace. Wipe the jar rims and threads. Place hot, metal lids on the jars and screw the bands firmly.

✳ Process in a pressure canner for the time and pressure shown in the PROCESSING TIMES AND POUNDS OF PRESSURE chart at the end of this recipe.

✳ Remove the jars from the canner and place them on a dry, wooden board that has been covered with a tea towel. Let the jars stand, *undisturbed*, 12 hours to cool completely.

**YIELDS ABOUT 6 PINTS**

---

### PROCESSING TIMES AND POUNDS OF PRESSURE

Dial-Gauge Pressure Canner

| Jar Size | Processing Time | Altitude of Canning Location | | | |
|---|---|---|---|---|---|
| | | 0 to 2,000 ft | 2,001 to 4,000 ft | 4,001 to 6,000 ft | 6,001 to 8,000 ft |
| Pints | 55 min | 11 lbs | 12 lbs | 13 lbs | 14 lbs |

Weighted-Gauge Pressure Canner

| Jar Size | Processing Time | Altitude of Canning Location | |
|---|---|---|---|
| | | 0 to 1,000 ft | Above 1,000 ft |
| Pints | 55 min | 10 lbs | 15 lbs |

# CREAM-STYLE CORN

20 pounds unshucked (see "shuck," page 41) corn
(about 31 medium ears)

* Shuck the corn and carefully remove all the silk. Wash the corn; set aside.

* Fill a 12-quart, heavy-bottomed, stainless steel kettle ½ to ⅔ full of water. Cover the kettle. Over high heat, bring the water to a rapid boil. Uncover the kettle.

* In small batches, drop the ears of corn into the boiling water and boil the corn 3 minutes. Immediately remove the ears of corn from the water and place them, single layer, on a folded tea towel spread on the kitchen counter or spread on a large wooden board; let stand. Return the water to a rapid boil before adding each batch of corn to the kettle.

* Using a medium-sized, sharp knife, cut the kernels from the cobs at approximately ½ the depth of the kernels, leaving on the cobs any small, undeveloped kernels at the ends of the cobs. Place the kernels in a large mixing bowl. Then, with the knife at a 90-degree angle to the cob, scrape the cobs using a downward motion. Add the scrapings to the bowl containing the kernels; stir to combine; let stand.

* Drain hot, sterilized (page 19) pint (see Note) jars, upside down, on a clean tea towel.

* Fill the jars with the corn, leaving 1-inch headspace. Do not shake the jars to pack the corn or press the corn into the jars. Using a 1-cup measuring cup with a pouring spout, cover the corn in the jars with fresh, boiling water, maintaining 1-inch headspace. Using a plastic knife or a narrow, rubber spatula, remove the air bubbles in the jars. Then, check the headspace in each jar and if necessary, add additional hot water to maintain 1-inch headspace. Wipe the jar rims and threads. Place hot, metal lids on the jars and screw the bands firmly.

* Process in a pressure canner for the time and pressure shown in the PROCESSING TIMES AND POUNDS OF PRESSURE chart at the end of this recipe.

* Remove the jars from the canner and place them on a dry, wooden board that has been covered with a tea towel. Let the jars stand, *undisturbed*, 12 hours to cool.

**NOTE:** *For processing safety, do not can Cream-Style Corn in quart jars because of the denseness of this product.*

YIELDS ABOUT 9 PINTS

## PROCESSING TIMES AND POUNDS OF PRESSURE

Dial-Gauge Pressure Canner

| Jar Size | Processing Time | Altitude of Canning Location | | | |
|---|---|---|---|---|---|
| | | 0 to 2,000 ft | 2,001 to 4,000 ft | 4,001 to 6,000 ft | 6,001 to 8,000 ft |
| Pints | 95 min | 11 lbs | 12 lbs | 13 lbs | 14 lbs |

Weighted-Gauge Pressure Canner

| Jar Size | Processing Time | Altitude of Canning Location | |
|---|---|---|---|
| | | 0 to 1,000 ft | Above 1,000 ft |
| Pints | 95 min | 10 lbs | 15 lbs |

# TOMATOES

## WHOLE OR HALVED TOMATOES HOT-PACKED IN WATER

**CAUTION:** Because tomatoes are somewhat low in acid (see page 23), they must be canned carefully to insure safety from possible toxins. Add *bottled* lemon juice to the jars (see page 24), as specified in this recipe, to increase acidity. Follow processing times and procedures strictly. Do not use tomatoes from dead or frost-killed vines.

3 gallons firm, vine-ripened tomatoes

½ cup plus 2 tablespoons bottled lemon juice, divided

* Wash the tomatoes. In batches, blanch the tomatoes (page 36) 45 seconds and immediately immerse them in cold water; drain. Remove the stem ends (see Note, page 96) and peel the tomatoes. Carefully remove the tiny blossom ends. Leave the tomatoes whole or cut them in half, according to your preference.

* Carefully place the tomatoes in a 16-quart, heavy-bottomed, stainless steel kettle. Cover the tomatoes with water. Cover the kettle. Over high heat, bring the tomatoes to a low boil. Reduce the heat and simmer the tomatoes gently for 5 minutes. Remove from the heat; uncover and let stand.

* Drain hot, sterilized (page 19), wide-mouthed, quart (or pint ) jars, upside down, on a clean tea towel.

* Pour 2 tablespoons *bottled* lemon juice into each drained quart jar (or 1 tablespoon *bottled* lemon juice into each drained pint jar).

* Pack the hot tomatoes into the jars, leaving ½-inch headspace.

* Using a 1-cup measuring cup with a pouring spout, cover the tomatoes in the jars with the hot cooking liquid, maintaining ½-inch headspace.

* Using a plastic knife or a narrow, rubber spatula, remove the air bubbles in the jars. Then, check the headspace in each jar and if necessary, add additional hot cooking liquid to maintain ½-inch headspace. Wipe the jar rims and threads. Place hot, metal lids on the jars and screw the bands firmly.

* Process in a boiling-water canner for the time shown in the PROCESSING TIMES chart at the end of this recipe.

* Remove the jars from the canner and place them on a dry, wooden board that has been covered with a tea towel. Let the jars stand, *undisturbed*, 12 hours to cool completely.

*continues*

*Tomato "Corer"*

**NOTE:** *A kitchen tool commonly known as a "tomato corer" (see illustration) is a handy, inexpensive kitchen tool to use for this task.*

**YIELDS ABOUT 5 QUARTS (OR 10 PINTS)**

## PROCESSING TIMES

| Jar Size | Altitude of Canning Location | | | |
|---|---|---|---|---|
| | 0 to 1,000 ft | 1,001 to 3,000 ft | 3,001 to 6,000 ft | Above 6,000 ft |
| Pints | 40 min | 45 min | 50 min | 55 min |
| Quarts | 45 min | 50 min | 55 min | 60 min |

## WHOLE OR HALVED TOMATOES RAW-PACKED WITHOUT ADDED LIQUID

**CAUTION:** Because tomatoes are somewhat low in acid (see page 23), they must be canned carefully to insure safety from possible toxins. Add *bottled* lemon juice to the jars (see page 24), as specified in this recipe, to increase acidity. Follow processing times and procedures strictly. Do not use tomatoes from dead or frost-killed vines.

3 gallons firm, vine-ripened tomatoes

½ cup plus 2 tablespoons bottled lemon juice, divided

✳ Wash the tomatoes. In batches, blanch the tomatoes (page 36) 45 seconds and immediately immerse them in cold water; drain. Remove the stem ends (see Note, above) and peel the tomatoes. Carefully remove the tiny blossom ends. Leave the tomatoes whole or cut them in half, according to your preference, and place them in a large mixing bowl or kettle; set aside.

✳ Drain hot, sterilized (page 19), wide-mouthed, quart (or pint) jars, upside down, on a clean tea towel.

✳ Pour 2 tablespoons *bottled* lemon juice into each drained quart jar (or 1 tablespoon *bottled* lemon juice into each drained pint jar).

✳ Pack the raw tomatoes *tightly* into the jars, leaving ½-inch headspace. Using a wooden spoon, press the tomatoes in the jars until the spaces between the tomatoes fill with juice. Leave ½-inch headspace. If necessary, add to the jars additional juice from other fresh tomatoes to maintain ½-inch headspace.

✳ Using a plastic knife or a narrow, rubber spatula, remove the air bubbles in the jars. Then, check the headspace in each jar and if necessary, add additional fresh, hot water or additional juice from other fresh tomatoes to maintain ½-inch headspace. Wipe the jar rims and threads. Place hot, metal lids on the jars and screw the bands firmly.

* Process in a boiling-water canner for the time shown in the PROCESSING TIMES chart at the end of this recipe.

* Remove the jars from the canner and place them on a dry, wooden board that has been covered with a tea towel. Let the jars stand, *undisturbed*, 12 hours to cool completely.

YIELDS ABOUT 5 QUARTS (OR 10 PINTS)

| Jar Size | Altitude of Canning Location | | | |
|---|---|---|---|---|
| | 0 to 1,000 ft | 1,001 to 3,000 ft | 3,001 to 6,000 ft | Above 6,000 ft |
| Pints & Quarts | 85 min | 90 min | 95 min | 100 min |

PROCESSING TIMES

# TOMATO JUICE

**CAUTION:** Because tomatoes are somewhat low in acid (see page 23), they must be canned carefully to insure safety from possible toxins. Add *bottled* lemon juice to the jars (see page 24), as specified in this recipe, to increase acidity. Follow processing times and procedures strictly. Do not use tomatoes from dead or frost-killed vines.

14 pounds firm, vine-ripened tomatoes (16 cups juice; see recipe procedures, following)

3 tablespoons onion juice (see recipe procedures, following)

2 tablespoons green bell pepper juice (see recipe procedures, following)

2 tablespoons red bell pepper juice (see recipe procedures, following)

1½ teaspoons salt

1 tablespoon sugar

5 drops Tabasco pepper sauce

½ cup bottled lemon juice, divided

* Wash the tomatoes. In batches, blanch the tomatoes (page 36) 1 minute and immediately immerse them in cold water; drain. Remove the stem ends (see Note, page 96) and peel the tomatoes. Remove the tiny blossom ends. Quarter the tomatoes lengthwise (or cut them into eighths, lengthwise, if the tomatoes are quite large). Using a paring knife, cut away and discard all the white core.

*continues*

* In batches, process the tomatoes in a blender to make juice. Strain the juice through a sieve to remove the seeds. Measure 16 cups juice; set aside.

* If you do not have onion, green pepper, and red pepper juices reserved from previously making Bell Pepper Relish (page 142), Chili Sauce (page 143), or Zucchini Relish (page 154), make onion, green pepper, and red pepper juices by chopping the vegetables, processing them separately in the blender, and then straining them separately in the sieve.

* In an 8-quart, heavy-bottomed, stainless steel kettle, place the 16 cups tomato juice, onion juice, green pepper juice, red pepper juice, salt, sugar, and pepper sauce. Cover the kettle. Over medium-high heat, bring the tomato juice mixture to a simmer. Uncover the kettle. Reduce the heat and simmer the tomato juice mixture 5 minutes. Remove from the heat. Skim the foam off the tomato juice mixture, using tableware tablespoons and teaspoons; let stand.

* Drain hot, sterilized (page 19), quart (or pint) jars, upside down, on a clean tea towel.

* Pour 2 tablespoons *bottled* lemon juice into each drained quart jar (or 1 tablespoon *bottled* lemon juice into each drained pint jar.

* Using a measuring cup with a pouring spout, pour the hot Tomato Juice into the jars, leaving ½-inch headspace. Wipe the jar rims and threads. Place hot, metal lids on the jars and screw the bands firmly.

* Process in a boiling-water canner for the time shown in the PROCESSING TIMES chart at the end of this recipe.

* Remove the jars from the canner and place them on a dry, wooden board that has been covered with a tea towel. Let the jars stand, *undisturbed*, 12 hours to cool completely.

YIELDS 4 QUARTS (OR 8 PINTS)

| PROCESSING TIMES | | | | |
|---|---|---|---|---|
| Jar Size | Altitude of Canning Location | | | |
| | 0 to 1,000 ft | 1,001 to 3,000 ft | 3,001 to 6,000 ft | Above 6,000 ft |
| Pints | 35 min | 40 min | 45 min | 50 min |
| Quarts | 40 min | 45 min | 50 min | 55 min |

Tomato Juice and Tomatoes

# Meats and Fish

# CUBES, STRIPS, OR CHUNKS OF BONELESS MEAT

## Beef, Veal, Pork, Lamb, Venison, Elk, Moose

**IMPORTANT:** Whether domestic or wild, can only fresh, good-quality, refrigerated meat. Can the refrigerated meat within a few days; otherwise, freeze it at 0°F or lower until ready to can. If frozen, defrost the meat before canning. *Trim away all external fat.* If desired, prior to canning raw-packed meat or prior to precooking hot-packed meat, strongly flavored wild meat may be soaked for 1 hour in a brine containing 1 tablespoon of salt per quart of water. Rinse the meat under clear, running water.

### CUBES OF BONELESS MEAT – RAW PACKED

*See* **IMPORTANT**, *above.*

**NOTE:** *When canned meat is raw packed rather than hot packed, there is generally less fraying of the meat over the lengthy processing time required for the safe canning of meat.*

1 teaspoon salt per quart of canned meat (optional*)

2 pounds raw, boneless, 1-inch meat cubes** per quart of canned meat

*Omitting the addition of salt to the jars allows for complete seasoning options at the time the canned meat is utilized.*

**Remove all surface fat on the meat prior to cubing.*

✳ Drain hot, sterilized (page 19), wide-mouthed, pint or quart jars, upside down, on a clean tea towel.

✳ If used, place 1 teaspoon of salt in each quart jar or ½ teaspoon of salt in each pint jar. Pack the meat cubes tightly in the jars, leaving 1-inch headspace in both quart and pint jars. Do not add any liquid. Wipe the jar rims and threads. Place hot, metal lids on the jars and screw the bands firmly.

✳ Process in a pressure canner for the time shown in the PROCESSING TIMES AND POUNDS OF PRESSURE chart below.

| PROCESSING TIMES AND POUNDS OF PRESSURE | | | | | | |
|---|---|---|---|---|---|---|
| **Dial-Gauge Pressure Canner** | | | | | | |
| Style of Pack | Jar Size | Process-ing Time | Altitude of Canning Location | | | |
| | | | 0 to 2,000 ft | 2,001 to 4,000 ft | 4,001 to 6,000 ft | 6,001 to 8,000 ft |
| Raw | Pints | 75 min | 11 lbs | 12 lbs | 13 lbs | 14 lbs |
| | Quarts | 90 min | 11 lbs | 12 lbs | 13 lbs | 14 lbs |

| **Weighted-Gauge Pressure Canner** | | | | |
|---|---|---|---|---|
| Style of Pack | Jar Size | Processing Time | Altitude of Canning Location | |
| | | | 0 to 1,000 ft | Above 1,000 ft |
| Raw | Pints | 75 min | 10 lbs | 15 lbs |
| | Quarts | 90 min | 10 lbs | 15 lbs |

✳ Remove the jars from the canner and place them on a dry, wooden board that has been covered with a tea towel. Let the jars stand, *undisturbed*, 12 hours to cool completely.

**SERVING SUGGESTION**

● Use canned *Cubes of Beef Chuck – Raw Packed* for making quick and delicious beef stew.

## STRIPS OR CHUNKS OF BONELESS MEAT – RAW PACKED

✳ Follow the instructions, recipe, and procedures in *Cubes of Boneless Meat – Raw Packed*, facing page, substituting strips or chunks of boneless meat for cubes of boneless meat.

## CUBES OF BONELESS MEAT – HOT PACKED

See **IMPORTANT**, *facing page.*

About 2½ pounds raw, boneless, 1-inch meat cubes*
  per quart of canned meat

Water

1 teaspoon salt per quart of canned meat
  (optional**)

Strained, fat-free meat broth***

*Remove all surface fat on the meat prior to cubing.*

**Omitting the addition of salt to the jars allows for complete seasoning options at the time the canned meat is utilized.*

***Water or tomato juice may be substituted for meat broth.*

✳ Preheat the oven to 325°F.

✳ Place the raw meat cubes in a heavy roaster appropriate in size to the quantity of raw meat cubes. Add a small amount of water (½ cup water if using a large, 8-quart roaster filled with meat cubes). Cover the roaster and bake the meat cubes *only until rare* (approximately 1 hour). Baking the meat cubes beyond rare will cause excessive fraying of the meat during canning. Remove the roaster from the oven and leave it covered; let stand.

✳ Drain hot, sterilized (page 19), wide-mouthed, pint or quart jars, upside down, on a clean tea towel.

*continues*

* Pack the hot meat cubes (without liquid) in the jars, leaving 1-inch headspace in both quart and pint jars. If used, place 1 teaspoon of salt in each quart jar or ½ teaspoon of salt in each pint jar. Cover the hot meat cubes in the jars with boiling meat broth, boiling water, or boiling tomato juice, maintaining 1-inch headspace in both quart and pint jars.

* Using a plastic knife or a narrow, rubber spatula, remove the air bubbles in the jars. Then, check the headspace in each jar and if necessary, add additional hot meat broth, hot water, or hot tomato juice to maintain 1-inch headspace. Wipe the jar rims and threads. Place hot, metal lids on the jars and screw the bands firmly.

* Process in a pressure canner for the time and pressure shown in the PROCESSING TIMES AND POUNDS OF PRESSURE chart at the end of this recipe.

### PROCESSING TIMES AND POUNDS OF PRESSURE

**Dial-Gauge Pressure Canner**

| Style of Pack | Jar Size | Processing Time | Altitude of Canning Location | | | |
|---|---|---|---|---|---|---|
| | | | 0 to 2,000 ft | 2,001 to 4,000 ft | 4,001 to 6,000 ft | 6,001 to 8,000 ft |
| Hot | Pints | 75 min | 11 lbs | 12 lbs | 13 lbs | 14 lbs |
| | Quarts | 90 min | 11 lbs | 12 lbs | 13 lbs | 14 lbs |

**Weighted-Gauge Pressure Canner**

| Style of Pack | Jar Size | Processing Time | Altitude of Canning Location | |
|---|---|---|---|---|
| | | | 0 to 1,000 ft | Above 1,000 ft |
| Hot | Pints | 75 min | 10 lbs | 15 lbs |
| | Quarts | 90 min | 10 lbs | 15 lbs |

## STRIPS OR CHUNKS OF BONELESS MEAT – HOT PACKED

* Follow the instructions, recipe, and procedures in *Cubes of Boneless Meat – Hot Packed*, page 103, substituting strips or chunks of boneless meat for cubes of boneless meat.

# BRANDIED MINCEMEAT

4 pounds beef chuck neck meat cut into
   3-inch cubes or chunks

8 cups water

2½ cups raisins

2½ cups golden raisins

3½ cups currants

½ cup (4 ounces) diced candied citron

½ cup (4 ounces) diced candied lemon peel

½ cup (4 ounces) diced candied orange peel

2¼ cups granulated sugar

2 cups packed light brown sugar

1 tablespoon plus 1 teaspoon ground cinnamon

2 teaspoons ground mace

1 teaspoon ground cloves

1 teaspoon ground nutmeg

1 tablespoon salt

1 pound suet

6 pounds Golden Delicious apples, pared (page 40)
   (see Note, page 106), quartered, and cored

2 cups reserved meat broth

¼ cup freshly squeezed, strained lemon juice

4 cups (1 quart) apple cider

1 cup good brandy

✳ In a large kettle, place the neck meat and water. Cover the kettle. Over high heat, bring the meat to a boil. Reduce the heat and simmer the meat until tender (about 2 hours).

✳ Using a fork or slotted spoon, remove the meat from the kettle and place it in a large bowl; cover and refrigerate until cold. Reserve the hot meat broth and strain it through a piece of damp cotton flannel secured, napped side up, in a sieve over a deep bowl. Cover the strained broth and refrigerate.

✳ In a 12-quart, heavy-bottomed, stainless steel kettle, place the raisins, golden raisins, currants, citron, lemon peel, orange peel, granulated sugar, and brown sugar. Cover the kettle and set aside. In a small bowl, place the cinnamon, mace, cloves, nutmeg, and salt; stir to combine; cover and set aside.

✳ Grind coarsely (page 37) the cold meat, suet, and apples; add to the ingredients in the kettle. Add the cinnamon mixture, 2 cups strained meat broth, lemon juice, and apple cider to the ingredients in the kettle. Stir all the ingredients to combine.

✳ Cover the kettle. Over medium-high heat, bring the mixture to a simmer, stirring frequently. Reduce the heat to low. Uncover the kettle and simmer the mixture slowly for 1 hour, continuing to stir frequently.

✳ Remove from the heat. Add the brandy; stir well. Let stand.

✳ Drain hot, sterilized (page 19), quart jars, upside down, on a clean tea towel.

✳ Using a ladle or a 2-cup measuring cup with a pouring spout, pack the hot mincemeat into the drained jars, leaving 1-inch headspace. Using a plastic knife

*continues*

or a narrow, rubber spatula, remove the air bubbles in the jars. Then, check the headspace in each jar and if necessary, add additional hot mincemeat to maintain 1-inch headspace. Wipe the jar rims and threads. Place hot, metal lids on the jars and screw the bands firmly.

✳ Process in a pressure canner for the time and pressure shown in the PROCESSING TIMES AND POUNDS OF PRESSURE chart at the end of this recipe.

✳ Remove the jars from the canner and place them on a dry, wooden board that has been covered with a tea towel. Let the jars stand, *undisturbed*, 12 hours to cool completely.

YIELDS 7 QUARTS

NOTE: *A Back to Basics® brand apple "peeler" (parer) (see illustration, page 47) helps accomplish this task expeditiously and efficiently.*

<table>
<tr><td colspan="6">PROCESSING TIMES AND POUNDS OF PRESSURE</td></tr>
<tr><td colspan="6">Dial-Gauge Pressure Canner</td></tr>
<tr><td>Jar Size</td><td>Processing Time</td><td colspan="4">Altitude of Canning Location</td></tr>
<tr><td></td><td></td><td>0 to 2,000 ft</td><td>2,001 to 4,000 ft</td><td>4,001 to 6,000 ft</td><td>6,001 to 8,000 ft</td></tr>
<tr><td>Quarts</td><td>90 min</td><td>11 lbs</td><td>12 lbs</td><td>13 lbs</td><td>14 lbs</td></tr>
<tr><td colspan="6">Weighted-Gauge Pressure Canner</td></tr>
<tr><td>Jar Size</td><td>Processing Time</td><td colspan="2">Altitude of Canning Location</td><td></td><td></td></tr>
<tr><td></td><td></td><td>0 to 1,000 ft</td><td>Above 1,000 ft</td><td></td><td></td></tr>
<tr><td>Quarts</td><td>90 min</td><td>10 lbs</td><td>15 lbs</td><td></td><td></td></tr>
</table>

# SALMON IN PINT JARS

Also Trout, Mackerel, Blue, Steelhead, and Other Fatty Fish
*Except Tuna* in Pint Jars

**IMPORTANT:** *This recipe is for canning salmon and the other named fish in PINT JARS ONLY.* Bleed and eviscerate fish to be canned immediately after they are caught or never more than 2 hours after they are caught. Keep cleaned fish on ice or frozen until ready to can them.

8 pounds scaled salmon* fillets

*Any variety of salmon; i.e., Chinook (king), sockeye (red), coho (silver), pink (humpback), chum (dog), or Atlantic.*

✳ If frozen, thaw the salmon in a glass or other nonmetal-finish container in the refrigerator. Do not thaw the salmon unrefrigerated.

✳ Wash the salmon under cold, running water and place it between several layers of paper towels to dry. Then, using a very sharp knife, neatly cut the salmon into 1½ x 3½-inch strips (see Note 1). Do not remove the skin. The salmon will be canned unskinned.

✳ Drain hot, sterilized (page 19), wide-mouthed, straight-sided, pint jars, upside down, on a clean tea towel.

✳ Tightly pack the raw salmon strips into the jars, as follows: To fill each jar, start by snugly placing the salmon strips, skin-side out, around the inside of the jar against the side glass, leaving 1-inch headspace. Then, fill the center of the jar with very closely packed additional salmon strips, maintaining 1-inch headspace. Add no liquid to the jars.

✳ Wipe the jar rims and threads. Place hot, metal lids on the jars and screw the bands firmly.

✳ Process in a pressure canner for the time and pressure shown in the PROCESSING TIMES AND POUNDS OF PRESSURE chart at the end of this recipe.

✳ Remove the jars from the canner and place them on a dry, wooden board that has been covered with a tea towel. Let the jars stand, *undisturbed*, 12 hours to cool completely.

NOTE 1: *If starting with frozen salmon, remove it from the refrigerator when it is close to being thawed. The strips are more easily cut if the salmon is not quite thawed. Wash the salmon and place it between paper towels, following the procedures in the recipe. Cut the strips while the salmon is still very slightly frozen, and place the strips on several layers of paper towels. Let stand for a few minutes until the salmon is fully thawed. Then, blot the salmon strips with additional paper towels.*

NOTE 2: *Glass-like crystals of magnesium ammonium phosphate sometimes form in canned salmon. There is no way for the home canner to prevent these crystals from forming, but they usually dissolve when heated and are safe to eat.*

YIELDS 8 PINTS

| PROCESSING TIMES AND POUNDS OF PRESSURE | | | | | | |
| --- | --- | --- | --- | --- | --- | --- |
| **Dial-Gauge Pressure Canner** | | | | | | |
| Style of Pack | Jar Size | Processing Time | Altitude of Canning Location | | | |
| | | | 0 to 2,000 ft | 2,001 to 4,000 ft | 4,001 to 6,000 ft | 6,001 to 8,000 ft |
| Raw | Pints | 100 min | 11 lbs | 12 lbs | 13 lbs | 14 lbs |
| **Weighted-Gauge Pressure Canner** | | | | | | |
| Style of Pack | Jar Size | Processing Time | Altitude of Canning Location | | | |
| | | | 0 to 1,000 ft | Above 1,000 ft | | |
| Raw | Pints | 100 min | 10 lbs | 15 lbs | | |

Dilly Beans

# Pickles

Pickle: A food prepared in a seasoned vinegar mixture or a brine solution to preserve it and/or impart flavor.

# BREAD AND BUTTER PICKLES

5 pounds pickling cucumbers, 4 to 6 inches in length (about 1 gallon cucumbers)

1¼ pounds small, white onions, sliced ¹⁄₁₆ inch thick (about 8 small onions)

2½ cups green bell peppers cut lengthwise into fourths, then sliced widthwise ¹⁄₁₆ inch thick (about 2 large peppers)

½ cup canning salt (page 18)

1 quart crushed ice

5 cups sugar

1½ teaspoons ground turmeric

½ teaspoon ground cloves

2 tablespoons mustard seed

1 teaspoon celery seed

5 cups cider vinegar (5 percent acidity)

✳ Select fresh, crisp cucumbers. Wash the cucumbers; do not pare (page 40) them. Using a sharp, thin-bladed knife, slice the cucumbers widthwise ¹⁄₁₆ inch thick, *discarding the ends.*

✳ Place the cucumber slices in a 12-quart, heavy-bottomed, stainless steel kettle. Add the onions, peppers, and canning salt; stir to combine.

✳ Bury the ice throughout the cucumber mixture in the kettle. Place a dinner plate over the cucumber mixture in the kettle. Weight the plate with a water-filled, securely lidded quart jar. Cover the kettle and refrigerate 3 hours.

✳ Meanwhile, in a large mixing bowl, place the sugar, turmeric, cloves, mustard seed, and celery seed; stir to combine. Add the vinegar; stir to combine; cover and set aside.

✳ After 3 hours refrigeration, drain the pickle mixture thoroughly. Pour the vinegar mixture over the pickle mixture. Over medium-high heat, heat the mixture, uncovered, to scalding (page 41), but do not boil. Using a wooden spoon, paddle the mixture occasionally as it heats to scalding.

✳ Remove from the heat; let stand.

✳ Drain hot, sterilized (page 19), pint jars, upside down, on a clean tea towel; let stand.

✳ Pack the hot pickles (without liquid) into the drained jars, leaving ½-inch headspace. Using a 1-cup measuring cup with a pouring spout, cover the pickles in the jars with the hot pickle liquid, maintaining ½-inch headspace.

✳ Using a plastic knife or a narrow, rubber spatula, remove the air bubbles in the jars. Then, check the headspace in each jar and if necessary, add additional hot pickle liquid to maintain ½-inch headspace. The pickles should be covered with the hot pickle liquid. Wipe the jar rims and threads. Place hot, metal lids on the jars and screw the bands firmly.

✳ Process by low-temperature pasteurization (page 24), as follows: Place the filled jars in a boiling-water canner that is half full of 120° to 140°F water. Add 120° to 140°F water to a level 1 inch above the tops of the jars. Attach a candy thermometer to the canner. Cover the canner. Over medium to medium-high heat, heat the water in the canner to 180° to 185°F and maintain that temperature range for 30 minutes, regulating the heat under the canner as required. Make certain that a water temperature of at least 180°F is maintained for the full 30 minutes to avoid the possibility of spoilage.

Temperatures above 185°F may cause unnecessary softening of the pickles.

✳ Remove the jars from the canner and place them on a dry, wooden board that has been covered with a tea towel. Let the jars stand, *undisturbed*, 12 hours to cool completely.

YIELDS ABOUT 8 PINTS

# EASY REFRIGERATOR SWEET DILL PICKLES

NOTE: *These pickles are not canned, but their delicious flavor and ease of preparation earned them a place in this canning cookbook.*

1 46-ounce jar commercial unsliced, best-quality dill pickles (or 1 quart home-canned Fermented Dill Pickles, page 134)

3 cups sugar

1 cup cider vinegar (5 percent acidity)

1 cup water

2 small stalks celery hearts with leaves*

3 tablespoons mixed pickling spice, tied in a cheesecloth bag (page 38)

*Celery Hearts: The small, tender, pale green to nearly white celery stalks (and leaves) at the very center of a bunch of celery.*

✳ Drain the pickles. Rinse the pickles in fresh, cold water and drain them in a colander. Using a small, sharp knife, cut thin slices from the ends of the pickles and discard. Then, slice the pickles widthwise 5/16 inch thick and place the slices in a large, stainless steel mixing bowl; set aside.

✳ Wash the commercial pickle jar well; drain, upside down, and dry; let stand.

✳ In a large, heavy-bottomed, stainless steel saucepan, place the sugar, vinegar, and water; stir to combine. Add the celery hearts; briefly stir in. Over medium-high heat, bring the vinegar mixture to a boil, stirring constantly. Add the cheesecloth bag of pickling spice. Reduce the heat to medium and boil the mixture gently for 5 minutes.

✳ Remove from the heat and immediately pour the vinegar mixture

*continues*

(including the celery and cheesecloth bag) over the pickles; let stand, uncovered, until cool.

✳ When cool, pack the pickles, together with the celery, back into the pickle jar, placing the cheesecloth bag of pickling spice midway in the jar. Place the lid on the jar.

✳ Refrigerate the pickles and let stand in the refrigerator 10 days before serving. Remove the cheesecloth bag of pickling spice after 10 days standing in the refrigerator.

✳ The pickles will keep in the refrigerator for a long period of time.

YIELDS ONE 46-OUNCE JAR

# DILLY BEANS

4 pounds fresh green beans (see recipe procedures, below)

4 heads fresh dill

4 garlic cloves

1 teaspoon cayenne pepper, divided

2½ cups distilled water

2½ cups cider vinegar (5 percent acidity)

¼ cup canning salt (page 18)

✳ Using a vegetable brush, wash the beans well. Cut off the stem ends of the beans and trim the blossom ends, leaving about ⅛ inch of the "tails" intact. Let the beans stand.

✳ Use widemouthed, pint canning jars with straight sides. Measure the height of the jars and deduct ¾ inch (½ inch for headspace plus ¼-inch allowance for liquid to cover the beans [and "tails"]). This measurement will be the exact

length to cut the beans. Measure 1 bean and cut it at the stem end. Use this bean as a pattern to cut the beans.

✳ Carefully place the cut beans in a medium, heavy-bottomed, stainless steel kettle. Cover the beans with boiling water. Cover the kettle. Over high heat, bring the beans to a boil. Reduce the heat and cook the beans at a low boil for 5 minutes.

✳ Remove from the heat and drain the beans immediately; let stand.

✳ Drain 4 hot, sterilized (page 19), widemouthed, pint jars with straight sides, upside down, on a clean tea towel; let stand.

✳ Pack the beans vertically (with the "tails" up) into the jars, leaving ¾-inch headspace (½ inch for final headspace

*continues*

plus allowance for liquid to cover the beans [and "tails"]). To each jar, add 1 dill head, pushing the dill head into the jar decoratively against the side glass, and maintaining ¾-inch headspace. Then, to each jar, add 1 garlic clove. Sprinkle ¼ teaspoon cayenne pepper in each jar (see Note); set aside.

✳ In a stainless steel saucepan, place the distilled water, vinegar, and canning salt; stir to combine. Over high heat, bring the vinegar mixture to a boil, stirring intermittently. Remove from the heat.

✳ Using a 1-cup measuring cup with a pouring spout, cover the beans in the jars with the hot vinegar mixture, leaving ½-inch headspace.

✳ Using a plastic knife or a narrow, rubber spatula, remove the air bubbles in the jars. Then, check the headspace in each jar and if necessary, add additional hot vinegar mixture to maintain ½-inch headspace. The bean "tails" should be covered with the hot vinegar mixture. Wipe the jar rims and threads. Place hot, metal lids on the jars and screw the bands firmly.

✳ Process in a boiling-water canner for the time shown in the PROCESSING TIMES chart at the end of this recipe.

✳ Remove the jars from the canner and place them on a dry, wooden board that has been covered with a tea towel. Let the jars stand, *undisturbed*, 12 hours to cool completely.

NOTE: *For less spicy-hot Dilly Beans, sprinkle ⅛ teaspoon cayenne pepper in each jar.*

### SERVING SUGGESTIONS

- Serve these attractive, vertically canned, uncut green beans for an hors d'oeuvre right from the jar, letting nibblers pull out the beans with their fingers.

- These make an excellent picnic or tailgate lunch item because they're so easy to pack.

- Arrange on a dish and served on the table with just the right lunch or dinner.

| Processing Times | | | |
|---|---|---|---|
| *Jar Size* | *Altitude of Canning Location* | | |
| | 0 to 1,000 ft | 1,001 to 6,000 ft | Above 6,000 ft |
| Pints | 5 min | 10 min | 15 min |

YIELDS 4 PINTS

# PICKLED BEETS

5 pounds medium (about 1½ to 2 inches in diameter), trimmed, fresh beets (see recipe procedures, below)

2¼ cups sugar

3 cups cider vinegar (5 percent acidity)

1 cup distilled water

3 2-inch pieces stick cinnamon

1 teaspoon whole cloves

1 teaspoon whole allspice

✳ Trim away a portion of the stems and roots of the beets, leaving on the beets 1 inch of the stems and 1 inch of the roots to prevent bleeding. Using a vegetable brush, scrub the trimmed beets well.

✳ Place the beets in an 8-quart, heavy-bottomed, stainless steel kettle. Add fresh water to cover the beets. Cover the kettle. Over high heat, bring the beets to a boil. Reduce the heat and cook the beets at a low boil until just tender (about 25 minutes). *Drain the beets, discarding the cooking liquid.*

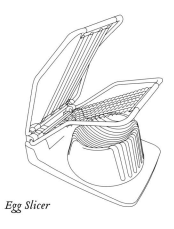

*Egg Slicer*

✳ When the beets are cool enough to handle, trim off the ends and slip off the skins. Using the fluted arm of an egg slicer (see illustration), slice the beets ¼ inch thick and place them in a flat-bottomed, glass dish; set aside.

✳ In a clean, 8-quart, heavy-bottomed, stainless steel kettle, place the sugar, vinegar, and distilled water; stir to combine. Add the stick cinnamon. Tie the cloves and allspice in a cheesecloth bag (page 38) and add to the vinegar mixture. Over medium-high heat, bring the vinegar mixture to a boil, stirring constantly. Add the sliced beets. Return the mixture to a simmer. Reduce the heat and simmer the sliced beets, uncovered, 5 minutes, stirring intermittently using a wooden mixing spoon to help prevent cutting the beets.

✳ Meanwhile, secure a piece of damp cotton flannel, napped side up, in a sieve over a deep pan; set aside.

✳ Remove the sliced beets from the heat. Remove and discard the stick cinnamon and cheesecloth bag; let stand.

✳ Drain hot, sterilized (page 19), pint jars, upside down, on a clean tea towel.

✳ Pack the sliced beets (without liquid) into the drained jars, leaving ½-inch headspace; let stand.

*continues*

* Pour the hot beet liquid (from the kettle) over the cotton flannel in the sieve to strain. Pour the strained beet liquid into a stainless steel saucepan. Over high heat, bring the beet liquid to a boil. Remove from the heat.

* Using a 1-cup measuring cup with a pouring spout, cover the sliced beets in the jars with the hot beet liquid, maintaining ½-inch headspace.

* Using a plastic knife or a narrow, rubber spatula, remove the air bubbles in the jars. Then, check the headspace in each jar and if necessary, add additional hot beet liquid to maintain ½-inch headspace. Wipe the jar rims and threads. Place hot, metal lids on the jars and screw the bands firmly.

* Process in a boiling-water canner for the time shown in the PROCESSING TIMES chart at the end of this recipe.

* Remove the jars from the canner and place them on a dry, wooden board that has been covered with a tea towel. Let the jars stand, *undisturbed*, 12 hours to cool completely.

YIELDS ABOUT 5 PINTS

*SERVING SUGGESTIONS*

- Tasty with informal sandwich lunches.
- A good accompaniment for beef dishes, such as Beef and Noodles, Chicken-Fried Steak, and Rib Roast.
- An excellent relish tray item.

*VARIATION:* Commercially canned, sliced beets may be substituted for fresh, cooked beets.

### PROCESSING TIMES

| Jar Size | Altitude of Canning Location | | | |
|---|---|---|---|---|
| | 0 to 1,000 ft | 1,001 to 3,000 ft | 3,001 to 6,000 ft | Above 6,000 ft |
| Pints | 30 min | 35 min | 40 min | 45 min |

# PICKLED MIXED VEGETABLES

1¼ pounds pickling cucumbers 3 to 4 inches in length, sliced ½-inch thick (cut off and discard both ends of the cucumbers)

2 cups fluted carrot slices cut ½ inch thick (use a fluted garnishing cutter, see illustration, page 120)

2 cups celery slices cut diagonally ½ inch thick

2 cups trimmed and peeled pearl onions (page 38)

20 strips red bell peppers cut ½ inch wide by 3 inches long (about 2 large peppers)

3 cups small cauliflower flowerets (about 1 small head of cauliflower)

16 cups cold, distilled water

1 cup canning salt (page 18)

2 cups sugar

¼ cup mustard seed

2 tablespoons celery seed

6½ cups white vinegar (5 percent acidity)

※ THE FIRST DAY: In an 8-quart, stainless steel kettle, place the prepared cucumbers, carrots, celery, onions, peppers, and cauliflower; set aside.

※ In a large mixing bowl, place the distilled water and canning salt; stir until the salt dissolves. Then, pour the salt water over the vegetables in the kettle. Cover the kettle; let stand, in a cool place, 12 to 18 hours.

※ 12 TO 18 HOURS LATER: Drain the vegetables thoroughly; set aside.

※ In a clean, 8-quart, heavy-bottomed, stainless steel kettle, place the sugar, mustard seed, celery seed, and vinegar;

stir to combine. Over medium-high heat, bring the vinegar mixture to a boil, stirring constantly. Cover the kettle. Reduce the heat and boil the vinegar mixture 3 minutes. Add the vegetables. Cover the kettle and return the mixture to a simmer. Simmer the vegetables, covered, 5 minutes. Remove from the heat; let stand.

※ Drain hot, sterilized (page 19), wide-mouthed, pint jars with straight sides, upside down, on a clean tea towel.

※ Decoratively arrange the vegetables (without liquid) in the jars, leaving ½-inch headspace.

※ Using a 1-cup measuring cup with a pouring spout, cover the vegetables in the jars with the hot vinegar mixture, maintaining ½-inch headspace.

※ Using a plastic knife or a narrow, rubber spatula, remove the air bubbles in the jars. Then, check the headspace in each jar and if necessary, add additional hot vinegar mixture to maintain ½-inch headspace. Wipe the jar rims and threads. Place hot, metal lids on the jars and screw the bands firmly.

※ Process in a boiling-water canner for the time shown in the PROCESSING TIMES chart at the end of this recipe.

※ Remove the jars from the canner and place them on a dry, wooden board that has been covered with a tea towel. Let

*continues*

the jars stand, *undisturbed*, 12 hours to cool completely.

**YIELDS ABOUT 5 PINTS**

**SERVING SUGGESTIONS**

- A lovely pickle accompaniment to pass at the table at meals featuring more plain-style entrées of beef, poultry, and fish.

- Nice for upscale picnics and tailgate lunches.

| Jar Size | Altitude of Canning Location | | |
|---|---|---|---|
| | 0 to 1,000 ft | 1,001 to 6,000 ft | Above 6,000 ft |
| Pints | 15 min | 20 min | 25 min |

PROCESSING TIMES

*Fluted Garnishing Cutter*

# MARINATED MUSHROOMS

2½ pounds (about 14 cups) petite-sized, whole mushrooms

1 cup commercial, bottled lemon juice

Water

3 cups white vinegar (5 percent acidity)

2 cups extra-virgin olive oil

1 tablespoon canning salt (page 18)

1 tablespoon dried leaf oregano

1 tablespoon dried leaf sweet basil

½ cup finely chopped onions

1 4-ounce jar diced pimientos, drained (about ¼ cup)

4 bay leaves

3½ garlic cloves cut in half lengthwise

21 whole black peppercorns

✳ Using a sharp paring knife, trim the stem of each mushroom, leaving up to ¼-inch stem on each mushroom; place in a large bowl. Then, using your fingers and where needed, a clean, soft-bristled toothbrush, thoroughly wash each mushroom under slow-running, cold water; place in a *clean*, large bowl.

✳ Place the mushrooms in an 8-quart, heavy-bottomed, stainless steel kettle. Add the lemon juice. Then, add enough water to cover the mushrooms about ½ inch. Note: The mushrooms will float, so using your hand, push them down to determine how much water to add to cover them about ½ inch if they were not floating. Cover the kettle. Over high heat, bring the mixture to a boil. Reduce the heat to medium and simmer the mushrooms, covered, for 5 minutes. Immediately remove from the heat and pour the mushrooms and water into a large sieve in the sink to drain the hot mushrooms; let stand.

✳ In a large, heavy-bottomed saucepan, place the vinegar, olive oil, canning salt, oregano, and basil; stir to blend and combine. Add the onions and pimientos; stir to combine. Add the bay leaves; stir in. Over high heat, bring the vinegar mixture to boiling; remove from the heat; set aside.

✳ Drain 7, hot, sterilized (page 19), half-pint jars, upside down, on a clean tea towel.

✳ In each of the drained jars, place ½ garlic clove and 3 peppercorns. Then, fill the jars with mushrooms, leaving ½-inch headspace; let stand. Stir the hot vinegar mixture to evenly combine the ingredients. Using a 1-cup measuring cup with a pouring spout, pour the hot vinegar mixture, including the evenly distributed ingredients, over the mushrooms in each jar, covering the mushrooms and maintaining ½-inch headspace.

✳ Using a plastic knife, remove the air bubbles in the jars. Then, check the headspace in each jar and if necessary, add additional hot vinegar mixture to maintain ½-inch headspace. The mushrooms should be covered with the hot vinegar mixture. Wipe the jar rims and threads. Place hot, metal lids on the jars and screw the bands firmly.

✳ Process in a boiling-water canner for the time shown in the PROCESSING TIMES chart at the end of this recipe.

✳ Remove the jars from the canner and place them on a dry, wooden board that has been covered with a tea towel. Let the jars stand, *undisturbed*, 12 hours to cool completely.

**YIELDS 7 HALF-PINTS**

| Style of Pack | Jar Size | Altitude of Canning Location | | | |
|---|---|---|---|---|---|
| | | 0 to 1,000 ft | 1,001 to 3,000 ft | 3,001 to 6,000 ft | Above 6,000 ft |
| Hot | Half-pints | 20 min | 25 min | 30 min | 35 min |

PROCESSING TIMES

# PICKLED OKRA

2 pounds okra pods about 4 inches in length

1 pound small okra pods

3 cups cider vinegar (5 percent acidity)

3 cups water

⅓ cup canning salt (page 18)

1 tablespoon dill seed*

7 garlic cloves

*Note: Dill seed, not dill weed.*

✳ In a sink filled with cold water, briefly wash the 4-inch okra pods; drain. Place the drained okra pods in a large bowl. Using a sharp paring knife, trim away a small portion of the stem end of each okra pod and place the trimmed okra pods in a large bowl; let stand.

✳ Refill the sink with cold water. In the cold water, briefly wash the small okra pods; drain. Place the small, drained okra pods in a medium bowl. Using the sharp paring knife, trim away a small portion of the stem end of each okra pod and place the trimmed okra pods in a separate, medium bowl; let stand.

✳ In a large, heavy-bottomed, stainless steel kettle, place the vinegar, water, canning salt, and dill seed; using a large mixing spoon, stir until the canning salt dissolves. Over medium-high heat, bring the vinegar mixture to a boil, stirring intermittently. Remove from the heat; let stand.

✳ Drain hot, sterilized (page 19), wide-mouthed, pint jars with straight sides, upside down, on a clean tea towel.

✳ Tightly pack the 4-inch-long okra pods *stem down* in the drained jars, leaving ½-inch headspace. Then, tightly pack the small pods *stem up* between the longer okra pods, maintaining ½-inch headspace. Press 1 garlic clove into each okra-packed jar; let stand.

✳ Over high heat, return the vinegar mixture to boiling. Remove from the heat. Using a 1-cup measuring cup with a pouring spout, pour the hot vinegar mixture over the okra pods in each jar, covering the okra pods and maintaining ½-inch headspace. As the okra pods heat from the vinegar mixture, thus becoming somewhat pliable, it may be possible to add additional okra pods to the jars. If the okra pods bounce up in the jars after the hot vinegar mixture is added, push the pods down to maintain ½-inch headspace.

✳ Using a plastic knife, remove the air bubbles in the jars. Then, check the headspace in each jar and if necessary, add additional hot vinegar mixture to maintain ½-inch headspace. The okra should be covered with the hot vinegar mixture. Wipe the jar rims and threads. Place hot, metal lids on the jars and screw the bands firmly.

* Process in a boiling-water canner for the time shown in the PROCESSING TIMES chart at the end of this recipe.

* Remove the jars from the canner and place them on a dry, wooden board that has been covered with a tea towel. Let the jars stand, *undisturbed*, 12 hours to cool.

* Due to the fact that the okra pods were raw-packed in the jars, they may unavoidably float in the jars. Sometimes, but not always, after a period of time in storage, the okra pods sink to the bottom of the jars.

YIELDS ABOUT 7 PINTS

| PROCESSING TIMES | | | | |
| --- | --- | --- | --- | --- |
| *Style of Pack* | *Jar Size* | *Altitude of Canning Location* | | |
| | | 0 to 1,000 ft | 1,001 to 6,000 ft | Above 6,000 ft |
| Hot | Pints | 10 min | 15 min | 20 min |

# MELON BALL PICKLES

20 pounds slightly underripe cantaloupes (about 6 cantaloupes)

4 cups cider vinegar (5 percent acidity)

3½ cups distilled water

6 3-inch pieces stick cinnamon

1½ teaspoons ground mace

2 tablespoons whole allspice

1 tablespoon whole cloves

5 cups sugar

* LATE IN THE DAY: Wash the cantaloupes. Cut the cantaloupes in half lengthwise and remove the seeds. Using a 1-inch melon baller, scoop whole melon balls. Measure 16 cups melon balls and place them in a large mixing bowl; set aside.

* In an 8-quart, heavy-bottomed, stainless steel kettle, place the vinegar, distilled water, stick cinnamon, and mace; stir to combine. Tie the allspice and cloves in a cheesecloth bag (page 38) and add to the vinegar mixture. Over medium-high heat, bring the vinegar mixture to a boil, stirring constantly. Reduce the heat and simmer the vinegar mixture, uncovered, 5 minutes.

* Remove the vinegar mixture from the heat. Add the melon balls. Cover the kettle; let stand, in a cool place, overnight.

* THE NEXT DAY: Remove the stick cinnamon and cheesecloth bag from the kettle, and reserve them. Using a slotted mixing spoon, remove the melon balls from the vinegar mixture and place them in a large mixing bowl; set aside.

*continues*

✴ Secure a piece of damp cotton flannel, napped side up, in a sieve over a deep pan. Pour the vinegar mixture over the cotton flannel in the sieve to strain.

✴ Pour the strained vinegar mixture into a clean, 8-quart, heavy-bottomed, stainless steel kettle. Add the sugar; stir to combine. Over medium-high heat, bring the vinegar mixture to a boil, stirring until the sugar dissolves. Add the melon balls, reserved stick cinnamon, and reserved cheesecloth bag. Reduce the heat and simmer the mixture, uncovered, until the melon balls are semi-translucent (about 45 minutes), stirring intermittently.

✴ Remove from the heat. Remove and discard the cheesecloth bag. Remove the stick cinnamon and reserve. Let stand.

✴ Drain hot, sterilized (page 19), pint jars, upside down, on a clean tea towel.

✴ Pack the melon balls (without syrup) into the jars, leaving ½-inch headspace. Place 1 piece of the reserved stick cinnamon against the side glass in each jar; let stand.

✴ Re-strain the syrup (from the kettle) through clean, damp cotton flannel, napped side up, in a clean sieve over a clean, deep pan. Pour the strained syrup into a stainless steel saucepan. Over high heat, bring the syrup to a boil, stirring occasionally. Remove from the heat.

✴ Using a 1-cup measuring cup with a pouring spout, cover the melon balls in the jars with the hot syrup, maintaining ½-inch headspace.

✴ Using a plastic knife or a narrow, rubber spatula, remove the air bubbles in the jars. Then, check the headspace in each jar and if necessary, add additional hot syrup to maintain ½-inch headspace. Wipe the jar rims and threads. Place hot, metal lids on the jars and screw the bands firmly.

✴ Process in a boiling-water canner for the time shown in the PROCESSING TIMES chart at the end of this recipe.

✴ Remove the jars from the canner and place them on a dry, wooden board that has been covered with a tea towel. Let the jars stand, *undisturbed*, 12 hours to cool completely.

YIELDS ABOUT 6 PINTS

*SERVING SUGGESTIONS*

● Melon Ball Pickles add a bit of zip and diversity to meals featuring more bland-tasting casseroles, such as Macaroni and Cheese and Tuna-Noodle Casserole.

● Place a small dish of Melon Ball Pickles on the lunch table when the fare is sandwiches and soup.

| PROCESSING TIMES | | | |
|---|---|---|---|
| *Jar Size* | *Altitude of Canning Location* | | |
| | 0 to 1,000 ft | 1,001 to 6,000 ft | Above 6,000 ft |
| Pints | 10 min | 15 min | 20 min |

# SPICED PEACHES

16 cups cold water

2 tablespoons white vinegar

2 tablespoons salt

8 pounds small peaches*

9 cups sugar

1 quart white vinegar (5 percent acidity)

2 cups water

3 3-inch pieces stick cinnamon

1 tablespoon whole allspice

Whole cloves (3 for each peach)

*Spiced peaches are nicest when canned and served whole, which generally necessitates your produce manager ordering a special lug of small-sized peaches for you.

* In a 16-quart kettle, place 16 cups cold water, 2 tablespoons vinegar, and salt; stir until the salt dissolves; set aside.

* Wash the peaches carefully. In batches, blanch the peaches (page 36) 1 minute and immediately immerse them in cold water; drain. Peel the peaches and leave them whole (unpitted) (or, if the peaches are too large, cut them in half and pit them). As the peaches are prepared, drop them into the vinegar solution to prevent discoloration. Let the peaches stand.

* In a 12-quart, heavy-bottomed, stainless steel kettle, place the sugar, 1 quart vinegar, and 2 cups water; stir to combine. Over high heat, bring the vinegar mixture to a boil, stirring until the sugar dissolves. Cover the kettle. Reduce the heat slightly and boil the vinegar mixture (syrup) 1 minute. Add the stick cinnamon and allspice. Cover the kettle and boil the syrup 4 additional minutes.

* Meanwhile, secure a piece of damp cotton flannel, napped side up, in a sieve over a deep pan; set aside.

* Remove the syrup from the heat. Remove and discard the stick cinnamon. Pour the hot syrup over the cotton flannel in the sieve to strain. Pour the strained syrup back into the kettle. Over high heat, bring the syrup to a boil. Remove from the heat; cover and let stand.

* Drain and rinse the peaches twice, using fresh, cold water. Drain the peaches well. Place 3 whole cloves randomly in each peach, and place the peaches in one or more large mixing bowls; let stand briefly. Over high heat, return the syrup in the kettle to a boil. Uncover the kettle and gently place the peaches in the boiling syrup. Cover the kettle and bring the syrup (with the peaches) to a simmer over high heat. Uncover the kettle. Reduce the heat and simmer the peaches until just tender (8 to 15 minutes, depending upon the size of the peaches.) Do not overcook.

* Remove from the heat; uncover and let stand. Do not remove the whole cloves from the peaches.

*continues*

* Drain hot, sterilized (page 19), wide-mouthed, quart (or pint) jars with straight sides, upside down, on a clean tea towel.

* Pack the hot peaches (without syrup) into the jars, leaving ½-inch headspace; let stand.

* Re-strain the syrup (from the kettle) through clean, damp cotton flannel, napped side up, in a clean sieve over a clean, deep pan. Pour the strained syrup into a stainless steel saucepan. Over high heat, bring the syrup to a boil, stirring occasionally. Remove from the heat.

* Using a 1-cup measuring cup with a pouring spout, cover the peaches in the jars with the hot syrup, maintaining ½-inch headspace.

* Using a plastic knife or a narrow, rubber spatula, remove the air bubbles in the jars. Then, check the headspace in each jar and if necessary, add additional hot syrup to maintain ½-inch headspace. Wipe the jar rims and threads. Place hot, metal lids on the jars and screw the bands firmly.

* Process in a boiling-water canner for the time shown in the PROCESSING TIMES chart at the end of this recipe.

* Remove the jars from the canner and place them on a dry, wooden board that has been covered with a tea towel. Let the jars stand, *undisturbed*, 12 hours to cool completely.

YIELDS ABOUT 4 QUARTS (OR 8 PINTS)

| Processing Times | | | | |
|---|---|---|---|---|
| *Jar Size* | *Altitude of Canning Location* | | | |
| | 0 to 1,000 ft | 1,001 to 3,000 ft | 3,001 to 6,000 ft | Above 6,000 ft |
| Pints | 20 min | 25 min | 30 min | 35 min |
| Quarts | 25 min | 30 min | 35 min | 40 min |

# SPICED SECKEL PEARS

**NOTE:** *Seckel is a variety of petite, reddish brown pears, perfect for making spiced pears because of their small size and their firmness, which allows them to hold their shape exceptionally well after cooking. Spiced Seckel Pears are canned and served whole, with the stem left in. Use a very sharp, tiny paring knife to fastidiously pare these miniature-like fruits.*

2 tablespoons mixed pickling spice

2 2-inch pieces gingerroot, pared (page 40) and cut in half lengthwise*

2 teaspoons whole cloves

6 cups sugar

1 quart white vinegar (5 percent acidity)

5 cups water

16 cups cold water

2 tablespoons white vinegar

2 tablespoons salt

11 pounds barely ripe Seckel pears

*See "Using Fresh Ginger," page 39.*

✳ **THE FIRST DAY:** Tie the pickling spice, gingerroot, and cloves in a cheesecloth bag (page 38); set aside.

✳ In an 8-quart, heavy-bottomed, stainless steel kettle, place the sugar, 1 quart vinegar, and 5 cups water; stir to combine. Over medium heat, bring the sugar mixture to a boil, stirring until the sugar dissolves. Add the cheesecloth bag. Cover the kettle. Reduce the heat and boil the sugar mixture (syrup) at a low boil for 5 minutes.

✳ Remove from the heat; let stand until the syrup cools slightly. Then, refrigerate the syrup in the covered kettle, leaving the cheesecloth bag in the syrup.

✳ **THE NEXT DAY:** In a 16-quart kettle, place 16 cups cold water, 2 tablespoons vinegar, and salt; stir until the salt dissolves; set aside.

✳ Remove the syrup from the refrigerator. Over medium-high heat, bring the syrup to a boil. Pour the hot syrup, including the cheesecloth bag, into a 12-quart, heavy-bottomed, stainless steel kettle; cover and set aside.

✳ Wash the pears carefully; drain. Using a very sharp, thin bladed, pointed paring knife, thinly pare the pears, leaving the pears whole with the stem in. As the pears are prepared, gently drop them into the cool vinegar solution in the 16-quart kettle to prevent discoloration.

✳ Remove approximately ⅓ of the pears from the vinegar solution. Rinse the pears twice, using fresh, cold water. Drain the pears well. Handle the pears carefully to avoid bruising or nicking them. Place the drained pears, single layer, in the kettle containing the syrup (and cheesecloth bag). Cover the kettle. Over medium-high heat, bring the pears to a low boil. Reduce the heat and boil the pears gently for 10 to 15 minutes, just until they are tender, yet firm.

*continues*

✴ Remove from the heat. Using a slotted spoon, remove the pears from the syrup and place them, no more than 2 layers deep, in a large, shallow dish (such as a baking dish); set aside, uncovered.

✴ Repeat the procedures 2 additional times for rinsing, draining, boiling, and placing the pears, no more than 2 layers deep, in 1 or more shallow dishes, using the remaining ⅔ of the pears.

✴ Remove the cheesecloth bag from the kettle and discard it. Let the kettle stand.

✴ Secure a piece of damp cotton flannel, napped side up, in a sieve over a deep pan. Pour the hot syrup in the kettle over the cotton flannel in the sieve to strain; let stand. Rinse and dry the kettle. Pour the strained syrup back into the kettle; set aside.

✴ Drain hot, sterilized (page 19), wide-mouthed, quart jars with straight sides, upside down, on a clean tea towel.

✴ Pack the pears (without syrup), upright, in the jars, leaving ½-inch headspace; let stand.

✴ Over medium-high heat, bring the syrup in the kettle to a boil. Using a 1-cup measuring cup with a pouring spout, cover the pears in the jars with the hot syrup, maintaining ½-inch headspace.

✴ Using a plastic knife or a narrow, rubber spatula, carefully remove the air bubbles in the jars. Then, check the headspace in each jar and if necessary, add additional hot syrup to maintain ½-inch headspace. Wipe the jar rims and threads. Place hot, metal lids on the jars and screw the bands firmly.

✴ Process in a boiling-water canner for the time shown in the PROCESSING TIMES chart at the end of this recipe.

✴ Remove the jars from the canner and place them on a dry, wooden board that has been covered with a tea towel. Let the jars stand, *undisturbed*, 12 hours to cool completely.

YIELDS ABOUT 5 QUARTS

### PROCESSING TIMES

| Jar Size | Altitude of Canning Location | | | |
|---|---|---|---|---|
| | 0 to 1,000 ft | 1,001 to 3,000 ft | 3,001 to 6,000 ft | Above 6,000 ft |
| Quarts | 25 min | 30 min | 35 min | 40 min |

# WATERMELON RIND PICKLES

1 25-pound watermelon

16 cups cold, distilled water

1 cup canning salt (page 18)

2 tablespoons whole cloves

2 tablespoons whole allspice

8 cups sugar

2⅓ cups white vinegar (5 percent acidity)

5 3-inch pieces stick cinnamon

✳ **EARLY THE FIRST DAY:** Wash the watermelon. Cut the watermelon in half widthwise. Then, cut each half into quarters, making lengthwise cuts. Cut each eighth of the watermelon widthwise into 1-inch-wide slices.

✳ Place each watermelon slice flat on a cutting board. Using a small, sharp paring knife, pare (page 40) the rind, cutting away the green. Then, cut away the fruit meat, leaving no pink on the rind. (Reserve the fruit meat for other uses.) Cut each rind slice into 1-inch-square pieces. Measure 16 cups rind pieces; set aside.

✳ In a 12-quart, stainless steel kettle, place the distilled water and canning salt; stir until the salt dissolves. Add the rind. Cover the kettle; let stand, in a cool place, 6 hours.

✳ Then, drain and rinse the rind twice, using fresh, cold water. Drain the rind well. Place the rind in a clean, 12-quart, heavy-bottomed, stainless steel kettle. Add fresh water to cover the rind. Over

high heat, bring the rind to a boil. Reduce the heat to medium-high. Cook the rind, uncovered, at a low boil, just until fork-tender (about 15 minutes), stirring intermittently.

✳ Drain the rind in a colander; let stand. Tie the cloves and allspice in a cheesecloth bag (page 38); set aside.

✳ In a clean, 12-quart, heavy-bottomed, stainless steel kettle, place the sugar and vinegar; stir to combine. Over medium-high heat, bring the vinegar mixture to a boil, stirring until the sugar dissolves. Add the cheesecloth bag and stick cinnamon. Reduce the heat to medium and boil the vinegar mixture (syrup), uncovered, 5 minutes, stirring occasionally.

✳ Remove from the heat. Add the drained rind. Cover the kettle; let stand, in a cool place, overnight.

✳ **THE NEXT DAY:** Over medium heat, bring the rind and syrup to a boil, stirring often. Cook the mixture, uncovered, at a low boil, until the rind is translucent (about 25 minutes), stirring intermittently.

✳ Remove from the heat. Remove and discard the cheesecloth bag. Remove the stick cinnamon and reserve. Let the mixture stand.

✳ Drain hot, sterilized (page 19), pint jars, upside down, on a clean tea towel.

*continues*

✳ Pack the rind (without syrup) in the jars, leaving ½-inch headspace. Place 1 piece of the reserved stick cinnamon in each jar against the side glass; let stand.

✳ Secure a piece of damp cotton flannel, napped side up, in a sieve over a deep pan. Pour the hot syrup (from the kettle) over the cotton flannel in the sieve to strain. Pour the strained syrup into a stainless steel saucepan. Over high heat, bring the syrup to a boil, stirring occasionally. Using a 1-cup measuring cup with a pouring spout, cover the rind in the jars with the hot syrup, maintaining ½-inch headspace.

✳ Using a plastic knife or a narrow, rubber spatula, remove the air bubbles in the jars. Then, check the headspace in each jar and if necessary, add additional hot syrup to maintain ½-inch headspace. Wipe the jar rims and threads. Place hot, metal lids on the jars and screw the bands firmly.

✳ Process in a boiling-water canner for the time shown in the PROCESSING TIMES chart at the end of this recipe.

✳ Remove the jars from the canner and place them on a dry, wooden board that has been covered with a tea towel. Let the jars stand, *undisturbed*, 12 hours to cool completely.

**YIELDS ABOUT 5 PINTS**

| PROCESSING TIMES | | | |
|---|---|---|---|
| *Jar Size* | *Altitude of Canning Location* | | |
| | 0 to 1,000 ft | 1,001 to 6,000 ft | Above 6,000 ft |
| Pints | 10 min | 15 min | 20 min |

# Fermented Foods

Fermented foods, such as Fermented Dill Pickles and Sauerkraut, are made by immersing the raw vegetables (cucumbers in the case of Fermented Dill Pickles and cabbage in the case of Sauerkraut) in a brine (salt and water) for several weeks. The brine draws sugar and moisture from the cucumbers or cabbage, and lactic acid is produced, which helps preserve the product and gives it a characteristic flavor, color, and texture.

It is important to carefully and precisely follow reliable recipes for making fermented foods to prevent spoilage. For example, use the kind of salt and full amount of salt called for.

# FERMENTED DILL PICKLES

20 pounds pickling cucumbers, 3 to 5 inches
in length (about ½ bushel cucumbers)

¾ cup mixed pickling spice

10 heads fresh dill

10 quarts distilled water

1¼ cups cider vinegar (5 percent acidity)

2½ cups canning salt (page 18)

1 quart distilled water (to fill jar used as a weight)

✳ Immediately prior to commencing
preparation of the pickles, wash a
5-gallon, stoneware crock in hot, soapy
water. Rinse the crock well; then, scald
(page 41) it with boiling water. Allow
the crock to dry 2 or 3 minutes and then
cover the top with plastic wrap. The least
exposure of the inside of the crock to air
after scalding, the better.

✳ Place the crock in a place where a temperature of 70 to 75°F can be maintained
during the fermentation period. While
temperatures of 55 to 65°F are acceptable, fermentation will take longer (5 to
6 weeks). Temperatures above 80°F will
cause the pickles to become too soft.

✳ Using a vegetable brush, scrub the
cucumbers thoroughly, making certain that all the soil particles have been
removed from the ends of the cucumbers. Cut a ¹⁄₁₆-inch slice off the blossom
end of the cucumbers and discard. It is
important that the blossom ends be fully
removed because the blossoms contain

enzymes that can cause the pickles to
soften. Set the cucumbers aside.

✳ Place ½ of the pickling spice and
5 heads of dill in the bottom of the crock.
Then, place the cucumbers in the crock,
filling the crock to within 3 to 4 inches
of the top. Place the remaining ½ of the
pickling spice and 5 heads of dill over
the cucumbers. Re-cover the crock with
plastic wrap; let stand.

✳ In a 16-quart, stainless steel kettle,
place the 10 quarts distilled water, vinegar, and canning salt; stir until the salt
dissolves and the mixture (brine, page
40) is thoroughly blended. Pour the
brine over the cucumbers.

✳ Select a dinner plate or glass pie plate
slightly smaller in diameter than the
crock. Wash the plate in soapy water
(rewash the plate even if clean); rinse
well. Then, scald the plate, dry it, and
allow it to cool briefly. Place the plate
over the cucumbers in the crock. Weight
the plate with a washed, scalded, and
securely lidded quart jar filled with
distilled water. The pickles should be
covered with 1 to 2 inches of brine.

✳ Cover the top of the crock with a
clean, unscented, heavy terry cloth
towel to help prevent contamination of
the pickles. Tie the towel with twine to
secure it to the crock.

✳ After a few days, scum will form on
the surface of the brine. Using a scalded,

stainless steel spoon, remove the scum and mold every day, as it will interfere with the desired fermentation and cause the pickles to be soft. Do not stir the pickles. Keep the pickles covered with the brine. If necessary, add more brine, using the ingredient proportions in this recipe. Change the terry cloth towel each week. *Caution:* If the pickles become soft or slimy, or develop a disagreeable odor, discard them.

✳ In about 3 to 4 weeks, the pickles will be olive green in color and should have achieved a desirable flavor.

✳ Drain hot, sterilized (page 19), wide-mouthed, quart jars, upside down, on a clean tea towel.

✳ Pack the pickles (without brine) into the jars, leaving ½-inch headspace. Add a whole or partial head of dill from the crock to each jar, pushing the dill heads into the jars decoratively against the side glass and maintaining ½-inch headspace; let stand.

✳ Pour the brine from the crock into a 16-quart, stainless steel kettle. Over medium-high heat, bring the brine to a boil. Reduce the heat and simmer the brine 5 minutes. Strain the brine through paper coffee filters to reduce cloudiness.

✳ Cover the pickles in the jars with the hot brine, maintaining ½-inch head-space. The brine will be cloudy due to yeast fermentation; however, it will give an added flavor to the pickles. (If preferred, cover the pickles with hot, fresh brine, using 16 cups distilled water, 4 cups cider vinegar [5 percent acidity], and ½ cup canning salt.)

✳ Using a plastic knife or a narrow, rubber spatula, remove the air bubbles in the jars. Then, check the headspace in each jar and if necessary, add additional hot brine to maintain ½-inch headspace. Wipe the jar rims and threads. Place hot, metal lids on the jars and screw the bands firmly.

✳ Process by low-temperature pasteurization (page 24), as follows: Place the filled jars in a boiling-water canner that is half full of 120 to 140°F water. Add to the canner 120 to 140°F water to a level 1 inch above the tops of the jars. Attach a candy thermometer to the canner. Cover the canner. Over medium to medium-high heat, heat the water in the canner to 180 to 185°F and maintain that temperature range for 30 minutes, regulating the heat under the canner as required. Make certain that a water temperature of at least 180°F is maintained for the full 30 minutes to avoid the possibility of spoilage. Temperatures above 185°F may cause unnecessary softening of the pickles.

✳ Remove the jars from the canner and place them on a dry, wooden board that has been covered with a tea towel. Let the jars stand, *undisturbed*, 12 hours to cool completely.

**YIELDS ABOUT 14 QUARTS, DEPENDING UPON THE SIZE OF THE PICKLES AND HOW THEY PACK IN THE JARS**

## FERMENTED KOSHER DILL PICKLES

6 garlic cloves, each garlic clove cut into fourths

✳ Follow the Fermented Dill Pickles recipe on page 134, placing 1 garlic clove cut into fourths in each canning jar before packing the pickles into the jars.

YIELDS ABOUT 14 QUARTS, DEPENDING UPON THE SIZE OF THE PICKLES AND HOW THEY PACK IN THE JARS

# SAUERKRAUT

6 quarts distilled water

½ cup plus 1 tablespoon canning salt (page 18)

25 pounds firm heads of fresh cabbage

¾ cup plus 3 tablespoons canning salt (page 18), divided

✳ Immediately prior to commencing preparation of the Sauerkraut, wash a 5-gallon, stoneware crock in hot, soapy water. Rinse the crock well; then, scald (page 41) it with boiling water. Allow the crock to dry 2 or 3 minutes and then cover the top with plastic wrap. The least exposure of the inside of the crock to air after scalding, the better. Place the crock in a location at 70 to 75°F, where it will be packed with salted cabbage and stored during fermentation.

✳ In an 8-quart, stainless steel kettle, place the distilled water and ½ cup plus 1 tablespoon canning salt (3 tablespoons canning salt to each 2 quarts distilled

water); stir to combine. Cover the kettle. Over high heat, bring the mixture (brine, page 40) to a boil.

✳ Remove from the heat. Uncover the kettle and let stand until the brine cools slightly. Then, cover the kettle and let it stand at room temperature until the brine cools to 70 to 75°F.

✳ Meanwhile, wash the cabbage heads under cold, running water; drain. Remove the outer leaves. Divide the cabbage into 5 approximately equal groups (about 5 pounds of cabbage per group). Prepare 1 group at a time, as follows:

✳ Quarter and core the cabbage heads. Using a sharp knife, cut the cabbage, as uniformly as possible, into ⅛- to 3/16-inch-wide shreds. Place the shreds in a large kettle or plastic container. Sprinkle 3 tablespoons canning salt over the shreds; using a large mixing spoon or your hands, combine well; let stand.

*continues*

* Prepare and shred the second group of cabbage. Place the shreds in a second kettle or plastic container. Sprinkle 3 tablespoons canning salt over the shreds and combine, repeating the procedure as for the first cabbage group; let stand.

* (Premixing the shredded cabbage and canning salt in a kettle or plastic container allows the cabbage to wilt slightly before placement in the crock, reducing breakage of the shreds when packed.)

* Place the first group of salted cabbage shreds in the crock. With your hands, press the cabbage shreds firmly into the bottom of the crock. Re-cover the crock with the plastic wrap.

* Prepare, shred, salt, and combine the third group of cabbage, using the kettle or plastic container used for the first group; set aside. Pack the second group of salted cabbage shreds into the crock, repeating the procedure as for the first cabbage group.

* Repeat the procedure until all 5 groups of cabbage have been packed into the crock. The rim of the crock must be at least 4 inches above the top of the cabbage shreds. If the liquid does not completely cover the cabbage when pressed down, add enough of the *cool* brine to cover it.

* Cover the packed cabbage directly with a clean, thin, white piece of cloth, such as muslin, and tuck it down around the inside edge of the crock. Wash a dinner plate in soapy water (rewash the plate even if clean); rinse well. Dry the plate and allow it to cool briefly. Then, place the plate on top of the cloth in the crock. The plate should be only slightly smaller in diameter than the crock. Let stand.

* Pour at least 1 gallon of the *cooled* brine into a 2-gallon, zipper-seal plastic bag; seal the bag securely. Place the filled and sealed bag in a second 2-gallon, zipper-seal plastic bag for extra protection; seal the second bag securely. Place the brine-filled bag on the plate in the crock as a weight to keep the cabbage covered with brine and to seal the fermented cabbage from the outside air. The cabbage should be covered with 1 to 2 inches of brine. Make certain that the brine-filled bag rests firmly against the entire inside edge of the crock. Then, cover the top of the crock with a double thickness of a clean, unscented, heavy, terry cloth towel.

* Let the cabbage ferment, *undisturbed*, 4 weeks. The terry cloth towel may be lifted intermittently to inspect the crock; however, the brine-filled bag should not be touched, in order to maintain the airtightness of the fermenting cabbage. If the crock is kept at a temperature of 60 to 65°F, fermentation may take 5 to 6 weeks. The cabbage may not ferment if stored at a temperature below 60°F. At temperatures above 75°F, the sauerkraut may become soft. Normal fermentation is complete when the bubbling ceases.

* To can fully fermented sauerkraut, place ½ of the sauerkraut and liquid in a 12-quart, heavy-bottomed, stainless steel kettle. Over medium-high heat, slowly bring the sauerkraut to a boil, stirring and turning the sauerkraut frequently. When the sauerkraut begins to boil, remove the kettle from the heat; let stand.

* Drain hot, sterilized (page 19), quart (or pint) jars, upside down, on a clean tea towel.

* Pack the hot sauerkraut fairly tightly into the jars, leaving ½-inch headspace. Cover the sauerkraut in the jars with the hot, sauerkraut liquid, maintaining ½-inch headspace.

* Using a plastic knife or a narrow, rubber spatula, remove the air bubbles in the jars. Then, check the headspace in each jar and if necessary, add additional hot, sauerkraut liquid to maintain ½-inch headspace. Wipe the jar rims and threads. Place hot, metal lids on the jars and screw the bands firmly.

* Process in a boiling-water canner for the time shown in the PROCESSING TIMES chart at the end of this recipe.

* Remove the jars from the canner and place them on a dry, wooden board that has been covered with a tea towel. Can the remaining ½ of the sauerkraut, repeating the procedure. Let the jars stand, *undisturbed*, 12 hours to cool completely.

YIELDS ABOUT 14 QUARTS (OR 28 PINTS)

NOTE: *Fully fermented, uncanned sauerkraut may be kept tightly covered in the refrigerator for several months.*

| PROCESSING TIMES | | | |
|---|---|---|---|
| *Jar Size* | *Altitude of Canning Location* | | |
| | 0 to 1,000 ft | 1,001 to 6,000 ft | Above 6,000 ft |
| Pints | 10 min | 15 min | 20 min |
| Quarts | 15 min | 20 min | 25 min |

*Corn Relish, Zucchini Relish, and Mango Salsa*

# Relishes and Salsas

Relish: (1) A chopped vegetable(s) and/or fruit(s) cooked in vinegar and seasonings; (2) Very small-sized pieces of a diced and/or thinly sliced and/or cut (not chopped) vegetable(s) and/or fruit(s) cooked in vinegar and seasonings.

Salsa: Spanish for "sauce." A Mexican food traditionally consisting of tomatoes, onions, chile peppers (hot to mild), spices, and other seasonings, but now may include a host of innovative food ingredients and combinations including fruits. Eaten dip-style or beside plated foods.

# BELL PEPPER RELISH

4¼ pounds green bell peppers (about 12 large peppers)

4¼ pounds red bell peppers (about 12 large peppers)

1½ pounds onions (about 3 large onions)

2 cups sugar

2 tablespoons canning salt (page 18)

1 teaspoon ground cinnamon

3½ cups cider vinegar (5 percent acidity)

✳ Wash the green and red peppers. Quarter the peppers lengthwise and cut away the seeds and white portions of the inner flesh. Cut the peppers into large pieces. Place the green and red peppers in separate mixing bowls; set aside.

✳ Cut off the ends and peel the onions. Cut the onions into large pieces and place in a separate mixing bowl; set aside.

✳ Coarsely grind (page 37), separately, the green peppers, red peppers, and onions, placing each of the ground vegetables in a separate mixing bowl. Drain the ground peppers and onions well, reserving the juices separately for use in making Tomato Juice (page 97).

✳ In an 8-quart, heavy-bottomed, stainless steel kettle, place the ground peppers and onions. Cover the ground vegetables with boiling water; let stand 10 minutes. Then, drain the vegetables well in a sieve. Return the vegetables to the kettle. Cover the vegetables, again, with boiling water. Over medium-high heat, bring the mixture to a boil.

✳ Remove from the heat. Drain the vegetables well in the sieve. Return the vegetables to the kettle; set aside.

✳ In a large mixing bowl, place the sugar, canning salt, and cinnamon; stir to combine. Add the vinegar; stir well to combine. Pour the vinegar mixture over the vegetables in the kettle; stir until the vegetables are evenly distributed. Over medium-high heat, bring the mixture to a simmer, stirring constantly. Reduce the heat and simmer the mixture, uncovered, 15 minutes, stirring occasionally.

✳ Remove from the heat; let stand.

✳ Drain hot, sterilized (page 19), pint jars, upside down, on a clean tea towel.

✳ Using a 1-cup measuring cup with a pouring spout, pour the hot relish into the drained jars, leaving ½-inch headspace. Using a plastic knife or a narrow, rubber spatula, remove the air bubbles in the jars. Then, check the headspace in each jar and if necessary, add additional hot relish to maintain ½-inch headspace. Wipe the jar rims and threads. Place hot, metal lids on the jars and screw the bands firmly.

✳ Process in a boiling-water canner for the time shown in the PROCESSING TIMES chart at the end of this recipe.

* Remove the jars from the canner and place them on a dry, wooden board that has been covered with a tea towel. Let the jars stand, *undistbed*, 12 hours to cool completely.

YIELDS ABOUT 8 PINTS

**SERVING SUGGESTIONS**

• Serve as a condiment with hamburger and wiener sandwiches in the same way you would serve sweet pickle relish.

• Pass Bell Pepper Relish at the table when serving ground beef patties, grilled hamburger steak, and hash.

| Processing Times | | | |
|---|---|---|---|
| *Jar Size* | *Altitude of Canning Location* | | |
| | 0 to 1,000 ft | 1,001 to 6,000 ft | Above 6,000 ft |
| Pints | 10 min | 15 min | 20 min |

# CHILI SAUCE

NOTE: *Chili Sauce is one of the best, most time-honored, homemade relishes. Quite different from commercial chili sauce, it is like a salsa in texture and flavor. It is used most often as a condiment (page 40), much in the same way and with the same foods as tomato catsup (see Serving Suggestion, page 145).*

**IMPORTANT:** Wear plastic or rubber gloves and do not touch your eyes or face when handling the jalapeño pepper called for in this recipe.

16 cups tomato pulp (about 8 gallons tomatoes) (see recipe procedures, below)

2 cups ground green bell peppers (about 4 large peppers) (see recipe procedures, below)

⅔ cup ground red bell peppers (about 2 large peppers) (see recipe procedures, below)

4 cups ground onions (about 5 large onions) (see recipe procedures, below)

1 small jalapeño pepper (see recipe procedures, below)

2 cups sugar

2 tablespoons canning salt (page 18)

½ teaspoon paprika

2½ cups cider vinegar (5 percent acidity)

3 4-inch pieces stick cinnamon

1 tablespoon plus 1 teaspoon whole cloves tied in a cheesecloth bag (page 38)

* Wash the tomatoes. In batches, blanch the tomatoes (page 36) 45 seconds and immediately immerse them in cold water; drain. Remove the stem ends (see Note 1, page 145), peel, remove the tiny blossom ends, quarter lengthwise, and seed and core the tomatoes (page 39). Pour off the

*continues*

surplus juice, reserving it for use in making Tomato Juice (page 97).

☀ Using a food processor fit with a steel blade, process the tomatoes in 1½-cup batches, using 5 quick on/off turns, to make pulp (see Note 2). Be careful not to overprocess the tomatoes and make juice.

☀ Measure 16 cups tomato pulp and pour it into a 12-quart, heavy-bottomed, stainless steel kettle; cover and set aside.

☀ Wash the green bell peppers and the red bell peppers. Quarter the peppers lengthwise and cut away the seeds and white portions of the inner flesh. Cut the peppers into large pieces. Place the green bell pepper and the red bell pepper pieces in separate mixing bowls; cover and set aside.

☀ Cut off the ends and peel the onions. Cut the onions into large pieces. Place the onion pieces in a separate mixing bowl; cover and set aside.

☀ Wearing plastic or rubber gloves, wash the jalapeño pepper. Using a sharp paring knife, cut off and discard the stem of the pepper. Cut the pepper in half, lengthwise; remove and discard the seeds and ribs. Cut the pepper halves into approximately 1-inch pieces. Place the pepper pieces in a small mixing bowl; cover and set aside.

☀ Coarsely grind (page 37) the green bell peppers. Drain the ground peppers,

reserving the juice for use in making Tomato Juice. Measure 2 cups ground and drained green bell peppers; place in a separate mixing bowl; cover and set aside.

☀ Following the same procedure as for the green bell peppers, coarsely grind and drain the red bell peppers, reserving the juice for use in making Tomato Juice. Measure ⅔ cup ground and drained red bell peppers; place in a separate mixing bowl; cover and set aside.

☀ Coarsely grind and drain the onions, reserving the juice for use in making Tomato Juice. Measure 4 cups ground and drained onions; place in a separate mixing bowl; cover and set aside.

☀ Grind and drain the jalapeño pepper; let stand.

☀ To the tomato pulp in the kettle, add the prepared green bell peppers, red bell peppers, onions, and jalapeño pepper. Then, add to the kettle the sugar, canning salt, paprika, and vinegar; stir to combine. Over medium-high heat, bring the mixture to a simmer, stirring constantly. Reduce the heat and cook the mixture, uncovered, at a low simmer, for 30 minutes, stirring frequently. Add the stick cinnamon and cheesecloth bag of cloves. Continue simmering the mixture very slowly, uncovered, an additional 1½ hours, or until the mixture reduces to the desired thickness (see Note 3), stirring frequently to prevent scorching.

✻ Remove from the heat. Remove and discard the stick cinnamon and cheese-cloth bag. Cover the kettle and let stand.

✻ Drain hot, sterilized (page 19), pint jars, upside down, on a clean tea towel.

✻ Using a 1-cup measuring cup with a pouring spout, pour the hot Chili Sauce into the drained jars, leaving ½-inch headspace. Using a plastic knife or a narrow, rubber spatula, remove any air bubbles in the jars. Then, check the headspace in each jar and if necessary, add additional hot Chili Sauce to maintain ½-inch headspace. Wipe the jar rims and threads. Place hot, metal lids on the jars and screw the bands firmly.

✻ Process in a boiling-water canner for the time shown in the PROCESSING TIMES chart at the end of this recipe.

✻ Remove the jars from the canner and place them on a dry, wooden board that has been covered with a tea towel. Let the jars stand, *undisturbed*, 12 hours to cool completely.

NOTE 1: *A kitchen tool commonly known as a tomato "corer" (see illustration, page 96) is a handy, inexpensive kitchen tool to use for this task.*

NOTE 2: *If a food processor is not available, a blender may be used. Process the tomatoes, in batches, for 1 to 2 seconds to make the pulp.*

NOTE 3: *To test for thickness, stir the mixture vigorously. Then, place a rounded tablespoonful of the mixture on a plate away from the heat. When little or no liquid separates from the mixture and runs onto the plate, the Chili Sauce has reached the optimum thickness. If you prefer thinner Chili Sauce, remove it from the heat before it reduces to this extent.*

### SERVING SUGGESTION

● Excellent on meat loaf and ground beef.

YIELDS ABOUT 6 PINTS

| PROCESSING TIMES | | | |
|---|---|---|---|
| *Jar Size* | *Altitude of Canning Location* | | |
| | 0 to 1,000 ft | 1,001 to 6,000 ft | Above 6,000 ft |
| Pints | 15 min | 20 min | 25 min |

# CORN RELISH

**NOTE:** *Homemade Heartland Corn Relish is usually made without flour thickening, which I definitely prefer. Commercially purchased corn relish is often gummy with thickener, which, to my palate, is ruinous to this delightful and refreshing relish.*

10 cups fresh whole-kernel corn (about 17 medium ears or 11 pounds unshucked corn) (see recipe procedures, below)

2½ cups diced (page 40) green bell peppers (about 3 large peppers) (see recipe procedures, below)

2½ cups diced (page 40) red bell peppers (about 3 large peppers) (see recipe procedures, below)

2½ cups diced (page 40) celery (see recipe procedures, below)

1¼ cups diced (page 40) onions (about 1 extra-large onion) (see recipe procedures, below)

2 cups sugar

2 tablespoons plus 1½ teaspoons canning salt (page 18)

2½ teaspoons celery seed

5 cups cider vinegar (5 percent acidity)

2 tablespoons plus 1½ teaspoons dry mustard

1¼ teaspoons ground turmeric

✳ Shuck the corn and carefully remove all the silk. Wash the corn; set aside.

✳ Fill a 12-quart, heavy-bottomed, stainless steel kettle ½ to ⅔ full of water. Cover the kettle. Over high heat, bring the water to a rapid boil. Uncover the kettle.

✳ In small batches, drop the ears of corn into the boiling water and boil exactly 5 minutes. Immediately remove the ears from the water and immerse them briefly in cold water to stop the cooking. Place the ears, single layer, on a folded tea towel spread on the kitchen counter or on a large wooden board. Bring the water to a rapid boil before boiling each batch of corn.

✳ Using a medium, sharp knife, cut the kernels from the cobs at about ⅔ the depth of the kernels, leaving on the cobs any small, undeveloped kernels at the ends of the cobs. Do not scrape the cobs. Measure 10 cups corn kernels and place them in a mixing bowl; cover and set aside.

✳ Dice the green bell peppers, red bell peppers, celery, and onions approximately ¼ inch square. Place each diced vegetable in a separate mixing bowl; set aside.

✳ In an 8-quart, heavy-bottomed, stainless steel kettle, place the sugar, canning salt, and celery seed; stir to combine. Add the vinegar; stir well to combine. Add the green peppers, red peppers, celery, and onions; stir to combine. Over medium-high heat, bring the mixture to a simmer, stirring constantly. Reduce the heat and gently simmer the mixture, uncovered, 5 minutes, stirring occasionally.

✳ Then, in a small mixing bowl, place the mustard, turmeric, and ½ cup of the simmered mixture from the kettle; stir well to combine. Add the mustard mixture to the hot mixture in the kettle; stir to combine. Gently simmer the mixture, uncovered, 5 additional minutes, stirring occasionally.

✳ Remove from the heat; let stand.

✳ Drain hot, sterilized (page 19), pint jars, upside down, on a clean tea towel.

✳ Using a 1-cup measuring cup with a pouring spout, pour the hot relish into the drained jars, leaving ½-inch headspace. Using a plastic knife or a narrow, rubber spatula, remove the air bubbles in the jars. Then, check the headspace in each jar and if necessary, add additional hot relish to maintain ½-inch headspace. Wipe the jar rims and threads. Place hot, metal lids on the jars and screw the bands firmly.

✳ Process in a boiling-water canner for the time shown in the PROCESSING TIMES chart at the end of this recipe.

✳ Remove the jars from the canner and place them on a dry, wooden board that has been covered with a tea towel. Let the jars stand, *undisturbed*, 12 hours to cool completely.

YIELDS ABOUT 9 PINTS

### SERVING SUGGESTIONS

● A wonderful accompaniment for ham, fresh pork, beef, poultry, or fish.

● Serve at lunch with sandwiches and soup.

| PROCESSING TIMES | | | |
|---|---|---|---|
| *Jar Size* | *Altitude of Canning Location* | | |
| | 0 to 1,000 ft | 1,001 to 6,000 ft | Above 6,000 ft |
| Pints | 15 min | 20 min | 25 min |

# JICAMA RELISH

**NOTE:** *Of Mexican and South American origin, jicama, pronounced HEE-ca-ma, is a thin-skinned, tuberous root vegetable that resembles a large, rather flat potato. Ranging in size from ½ to 6 pounds, jicama is juicy and somewhat sweet, and has a crunchy texture similar to water chestnuts. The flesh is white and does not discolor, making jicama a popular choice for addition to salads and for serving with dips. When stir-fried or sautéed, jicama retains its crisp texture.*

9 cups pared (page 40) and diced* jicama (about 4 pounds unpared jicama)

4 cups diced* red bell peppers (about 4 large peppers)

4 cups diced* yellow bell peppers (about 4 large peppers)

4 cups medium finely chopped yellow onions (about 3 medium to large onions)

2 tablespoons mixed pickling spice

2 3-inch pieces stick cinnamon

4 cups sugar

8 cups white vinegar (5 percent acidity)

1 teaspoon crushed red pepper (optional)

*Dice (page 40) ¼ inch square.*

*Available in the spice section at the supermarket. Include if a spicy hot dimension to the flavor is desired.*

✳ Using a very sharp, small knife, prepare the jicama; place in a bowl and cover with plastic wrap; set aside. Prepare the red bell peppers; place in a separate bowl and cover with plastic wrap; set aside. Prepare the yellow bell peppers; place in a separate bowl and cover with plastic wrap; set aside. Prepare the onions; place in a separate bowl and cover with plastic wrap; set aside.

✳ Tie the pickling spice and stick cinnamon in a cheesecloth bag (page 38); set aside.

✳ In a 12-quart, heavy-bottomed, stainless steel kettle, place the sugar, vinegar, and crushed red pepper if used; stir to combine. Over high heat, bring the vinegar mixture to a boil, stirring constantly until the sugar dissolves. Add the cheesecloth bag of spices; stir briefly. Remove from the heat. Add the jicama, red peppers, yellow peppers, and onions; stir to combine. Over high heat, bring the mixture to a boil, stirring constantly. Reduce the heat to medium low, cover, and simmer 25 minutes, stirring intermittently.

✳ Remove from the heat. Remove and discard the cheesecloth bag of spices. Cover the kettle; let stand.

✳ Drain hot, sterilized (page 19), pint jars, upside down, on a clean tea towel.

✳ Using a slotted mixing spoon, place the hot relish solids in the drained jars, leaving ½-inch headspace. Then, using a 1-cup measuring cup with a pouring spout, pour the hot vinegar mixture over the relish solids in each jar, covering the relish solids and maintaining ½-inch headspace.

✳ Using a plastic knife or a narrow, rubber spatula, remove the air bubbles in the jars. Then, check the headspace in each jar and if necessary, add additional hot vinegar mixture to maintain ½-inch headspace. The relish solids should be covered with the hot vinegar mixture. Wipe the jar rims and threads. Place hot, metal lids on the jars and screw the bands firmly.

✳ Process in a boiling-water canner for the time shown in the PROCESSING TIMES chart at the end of this recipe.

✳ Remove the jars from the canner and place them on a dry, wooden board that has been covered with a tea towel. Let the jars stand, *undisturbed*, 12 hours to cool completely.

✳ To serve, drain the relish in a sieve and serve without the vinegar mixture.

YIELDS ABOUT 7 PINTS

### *SERVING SUGGESTION*

● Particularly complements fish and poultry, but may be served happily with sundry dishes.

| Processing Times | | | | | |
|---|---|---|---|---|---|
| *Style of Pack* | *Jar Size* | *Altitude of Canning Location* | | | |
| | | 0 to 1,000 ft | 1,001 to 3,000 ft | 3,001 to 6,000 ft | Above 6,000 ft |
| Hot | Pints | 20 min | 25 min | 30 min | 35 min |

# PEACH CHUTNEY

**NOTE:** *Chutney is a highly spiced, thick relish containing fruits, spices (usually including ginger), vinegar, sugar (often brown sugar), often raisins, and often onions and/or garlic. Many kinds of chutney are made, using a variety of fruits and combinations of fruits; most notably, apple, peach, pear, mango, apricot, cranberry, and apple-tomato (ripe or green) chutney.*

*Emanating from India, chutney is used mainly as a condiment (page 40), but also, it is used as an ingredient in other dishes. For a guide to ways in which this unique-tasting relish may be used, see the Serving Suggestions at the end of this recipe.*

5 cups cider vinegar (5 percent acidity)

1 pound light brown sugar

1 pound dark brown sugar

2 cups (10 ounces) crystallized ginger diced (page 40) ³⁄₁₆ inch square

2 cups finely chopped onions (about 2 medium-large onions)

2 garlic cloves, pressed

3 tablespoons chili powder

¼ cup mustard seed

1 tablespoon plus 1 teaspoon canning salt (page 18)

16 cups water

2 tablespoons white vinegar

2 tablespoons table salt

16 cups peaches cut into approximately ½-inch cubes (page 40) (about 8 pounds peaches) (see recipe procedures, following)

✳ In a 12-quart, heavy-bottomed, stainless steel kettle, place the cider vinegar, light brown sugar, dark brown sugar, ginger, onions, garlic, chili powder, mustard seed, and canning salt; stir to combine. Cover the kettle and set aside.

✳ In a 16-quart kettle, place 16 cups water, white vinegar, and table salt; stir until the salt dissolves; set aside.

✳ Wash the whole peaches. In batches, blanch the peaches (page 36) 1 minute and immediately immerse them in cold water; drain. Peel, cut in half, and pit the peaches. As the peaches are prepared, drop them into the white vinegar solution in the 16-quart kettle to prevent discoloration.

✳ Drain and rinse the peaches twice, using fresh, cold water. Drain the peaches well. Cut the peaches into approximately ½-inch cubes.

✳ Measure 16 cups cubed peaches and add to the brown sugar mixture in the 12-quart kettle; stir to combine. Over medium heat, bring the mixture to a simmer, stirring constantly until the brown sugar dissolves. Reduce the heat slightly and simmer the mixture, uncovered, at least 1 hour, or until the mixture is dark and reduced to the desired thickness. Stir the mixture frequently during the first stages of cooking, and stir constantly as the mixture reduces and thickens to prevent sticking.

✳ Remove from the heat. Cover the kettle; let stand.

✳ Drain hot, sterilized (page 19), pint jars, upside down, on a clean tea towel.

✳ Using a 1-cup measuring cup with a pouring spout, pour the hot Peach Chutney into the drained jars, leaving ½-inch headspace. Using a plastic knife or a narrow, rubber spatula, remove the air bubbles in the jars. Then, check the headspace in each jar and if necessary, add additional hot Peach Chutney to maintain ½-inch headspace. Wipe the jar rims and threads. Place hot, metal lids on the jars and screw the bands firmly.

✳ Process in a boiling-water canner for the time shown in the PROCESSING TIMES chart at the end of this recipe.

✳ Remove the jars from the canner and place them on a dry, wooden board that has been covered with a tea towel. Let the jars stand, *undisturbed*, 12 hours to cool completely.

YIELDS ABOUT 9 PINTS

### SERVING SUGGESTIONS

- Serve as a condiment with curry dishes and roast pork.
- Use as an ingredient in dips.
- Use as an ingredient in cheese balls.

| Processing Times | | | |
|---|---|---|---|
| *Jar Size* | Altitude of Canning Location | | |
| | 0 to 1,000 ft | 1,001 to 6,000 ft | Above 6,000 ft |
| Pints | 10 min | 15 min | 20 min |

# PICCALILLI

**NOTE:** *Piccalilli is made with green tomatoes, cabbage, green and red bell peppers, onions, vinegar, salt, and spices, and is sweetened slightly with brown sugar. A favored relish with canners, there is always some acceptable variance in ingredients among recipes of this kind. Piccalilli is a down-home yet ultra-gourmet delicacy.*

5 cups chopped green tomatoes* (see recipe procedures, below)

7 cups finely shredded cabbage (if available, use a food processor fitted with a shredding disk)

2¼ cups chopped onions (if available, use a food processor fitted with a steel blade)

1⅔ cups green bell peppers uniformly hand-chopped into pieces approximately ¼ x ⅜ inch

1⅔ cups red bell peppers uniformly hand-chopped into pieces approximately ¼ x ⅜ inch

½ cup canning salt (page 18)

3¾ cups white vinegar (5 percent acidity)

2½ cups packed light brown sugar

2 tablespoons plus 1 teaspoon mixed pickling spice, tied in a cheesecloth bag (page 38)

*\*Do not use tomatoes from dead or frost-killed vines.*

✳ **AFTERNOON OF THE FIRST DAY:** Wash the tomatoes. In batches, blanch the tomatoes (page 36) 2 minutes and immediately immerse them in cold water; drain. Remove the stem ends (see Note) and peel the tomatoes. Remove the tiny blossom ends. Cut the tomatoes lengthwise into quarters or sixths, depending upon their size. Remove and discard as many of the seeds and as much of the pouches containing them as possible (page 39). (They are more difficult to remove in green tomatoes.) Cut away the cores (page 39).

✳ Chop the tomatoes. (If available, use a food processor fitted with a steel blade.)

✳ Measure 5 cups chopped tomatoes and place them in an 8-quart, stainless steel kettle. Add the cabbage, onions, green peppers, red peppers, and canning salt; stir to combine. Cover the kettle; let stand, at cool room temperature, overnight.

✳ **THE NEXT DAY:** Place ⅓ of the prepared vegetables in the center of a clean, thin tea towel. Pull the corners of the tea towel tautly over the vegetables. With your hands, wring the tea towel of vegetables and press it on the bottom of a colander to remove as much liquid as possible. Place the drained vegetables in a large mixing bowl; set aside. Repeat the procedure 2 more times to drain the remaining vegetables, adding them to the mixing bowl of drained vegetables; cover and set aside.

✳ In a clean, 8-quart, heavy-bottomed, stainless steel kettle, place the vinegar and brown sugar; stir to combine. Add the cheesecloth bag of pickling spice. Over medium-high heat, bring the vinegar mixture to a boil, stirring until the brown sugar dissolves. Reduce the heat to medium and boil the vinegar mixture (syrup) at a moderate rate, uncovered, 5 minutes, stirring frequently.

✳ Remove from the heat. Add the vegetables; stir to combine. Over medium-high heat, bring the mixture to a boil, stirring constantly. Reduce the heat slightly and boil the mixture, uncovered, 2 minutes, stirring intermittently.

✳ Remove from the heat. Remove and discard the cheesecloth bag. Cover the kettle; let stand.

✳ Drain hot, sterilized (page 19), pint jars, upside down, on a clean tea towel.

✳ Using a 1-cup measuring cup with a pouring spout, pack the hot Piccalilli into the drained jars, leaving ½-inch headspace. Pour the remaining syrup equally into the filled jars, maintaining ½-inch headspace. Using a plastic knife or a narrow, rubber spatula, remove any air bubbles in the jars. Then, check the headspace in each jar and if necessary, add additional hot Piccalilli to maintain ½-inch headspace. Wipe the jar rims and threads. Place hot, metal lids on the jars and screw the bands firmly.

✳ Process in a boiling-water canner for the time shown in the PROCESSING TIMES chart at the end of this recipe.

✳ Remove the jars from the canner and place them on a dry, wooden board that has been covered with a tea towel. Let the jars stand, *undisturbed*, 12 hours to cool completely.

NOTE: *A kitchen tool commonly known as a tomato "corer" (see illustration, page 96) is a handy, inexpensive kitchen tool to use for this task.*

YIELDS ABOUT 4 PINTS

| Processing Times | | | |
|---|---|---|---|
| *Jar Size* | *Altitude of Canning Location* | | |
| | 0 to 1,000 ft | 1,001 to 6,000 ft | Above 6,000 ft |
| Pints | 5 min | 10 min | 15 min |

# ZUCCHINI RELISH

6½ cups ground zucchini (about 3 pounds zucchini) (see recipe procedures, below)

3½ cups ground onions (about 5 medium onions) (see recipe procedures, below)

1½ cups ground green bell peppers (about 3 large peppers) (see recipe procedures, below)

1½ cups ground red bell peppers (about 3 large peppers) (see recipe procedures, below)

¼ cup plus 2 tablespoons canning salt (page 18)

Cold, distilled water

3 cups cider vinegar (5 percent acidity)

4 cups sugar

2 tablespoons celery seed

1 tablespoon mustard seed

✳ Wash the zucchini. Cut off and discard the ends of the zucchini. Do not pare (page 40). Cut the zucchini into large pieces and grind coarsely (page 37). Drain the ground zucchini. Measure 6½ cups ground and drained zucchini; place in a large, stainless steel mixing bowl; cover and set aside.

✳ Cut off the ends and peel the onions. Cut the onions into large pieces and grind coarsely. Drain the ground onions, reserving the juice for use in making Tomato Juice (page 97). Measure 3½ cups ground and drained onions; place in a separate mixing bowl; cover and set aside.

✳ Wash the green peppers. Quarter the peppers lengthwise and cut away the seeds and white portions of the inner

flesh. Cut the peppers into large pieces and grind coarsely. Drain the ground peppers, reserving the juice for use in making Tomato Juice. Measure 1½ cups ground and drained green peppers; place in a separate mixing bowl; cover and set aside.

✳ Prepare the red peppers, following the same procedure as for the green peppers.

✳ Redrain each of the vegetables. Add the onions, green peppers, and red peppers to the zucchini in the mixing bowl; stir until evenly distributed. Sprinkle the canning salt over the vegetables; stir to combine. Add distilled water to cover the vegetable mixture. Cover the mixing bowl with plastic wrap; let stand 2 hours at cool room temperature.

✳ Then, drain ½ of the vegetables in a sieve, pressing the vegetables with the back of a spoon to remove as much liquid as possible. Place the drained vegetables in a large mixing bowl; set aside. Drain and press the remaining ½ of the vegetables; add to the mixing bowl of drained vegetables; cover and set aside.

✳ In an 8-quart, heavy-bottomed, stainless steel kettle, place the vinegar, sugar, celery seed, and mustard seed; stir to combine. Over high heat, bring the vinegar mixture to a boil, stirring constantly. Reduce the heat to medium-high. Add the vegetables. Bring the mixture to a simmer, stirring constantly. Simmer the mixture, uncovered, 10 minutes, stirring frequently. (Reduce the heat slightly, if necessary.)

✳ Remove from the heat. Cover the kettle; let stand.

✳ Drain hot, sterilized (page 19), pint jars, upside down, on a clean tea towel.

✳ Using a 1-cup measuring cup with a pouring spout, pour the hot relish into the drained jars, leaving ½-inch headspace. Using a plastic knife or a narrow, rubber spatula, remove the air bubbles in the jars. Then, check the headspace in each jar and if necessary, add additional hot relish to maintain ½-inch headspace. Wipe the jar rims and threads. Place hot, metal lids on the jars and screw the bands firmly.

✳ Process in a boiling-water canner for the time shown in the PROCESSING TIMES chart at the end of this recipe.

✳ Remove the jars from the canner and place them on a dry, wooden board that has been covered with a tea towel. Let the jars stand, *undisturbed*, 12 hours to cool completely.

YIELDS ABOUT 5 PINTS

*SERVING SUGGESTIONS*

● Serve with hamburger and wiener sandwiches in the same way you would serve sweet pickle relish.

● Serve in meat loaf, roast beef, and roast pork sandwiches.

● Serve as a relish with Broiled Ground Beef Patties and Grilled Hamburger Steak.

| PROCESSING TIMES | | | |
|---|---|---|---|
| *Jar Size* | *Altitude of Canning Location* | | |
| | 0 to 1,000 ft | 1,001 to 6,000 ft | Above 6,000 ft |
| Pints | 10 min | 15 min | 20 min |

# MANGO SALSA

6 cups slightly underripe, pared (page 40) and diced mangos* (about 4 large mangos)

1½ cups diced** red bell peppers (about 1 extra-large red bell pepper)

½ cup finely chopped yellow onions

2 teaspoons very finely chopped garlic cloves

2 teaspoons finely grated fresh ginger (page 39)

½ teaspoon crushed red pepper***

1¼ cups cider vinegar (5 percent acidity)

½ cup distilled water

1 cup packed light brown sugar

*See Preparing Mangos, page 38. Dice (page 40) ¼ inch square. Wear plastic or rubber gloves when handling unripe mangos, as they may irritate the skin of some people in the same manner as poison ivy or poison oak. Mangos, poison ivy, and poison oak belong to the same plant family, Anacardiaceae or cashew family.*

**Dice (page 40) ¼ inch square.*

***Available in the spice section at the supermarket.*

✳ In a large mixing bowl, place the mangos, red bell peppers, onions, garlic, ginger, and crushed red pepper; stir to combine; using plastic wrap, cover and set aside.

✳ In an 8-quart, heavy-bottomed, stainless steel kettle, place the vinegar, distilled water, and brown sugar; stir to combine. Over medium-high heat, bring the mixture to a boil, stirring until the brown sugar dissolves.

✳ Remove from the heat. Add the mango mixture; stir to combine. Over medium-high heat, bring the mixture to a simmer, stirring constantly. Reduce the heat and simmer the mixture, uncovered, 5 minutes, stirring occasionally. Remove from the heat; cover and let stand.

✳ Drain hot, sterilized (page 19), half-pint jars, upside down, on a clean tea towel.

✴ Using a 1-cup measuring cup with a pouring spout, pour the hot salsa into the drained jars, leaving ½-inch headspace. Using a plastic knife or a narrow, rubber spatula, remove the air bubbles in the jars. Then, check the headspace in each jar and if necessary, add additional hot salsa to maintain ½-inch headspace. Wipe the jar rims and threads. Place hot, metal lids on the jars and screw the bands firmly.

✴ Process in a boiling-water canner for the time shown in the PROCESSING TIMES chart at the end of this recipe.

✴ Remove the jars from the canner and place them on a dry, wooden board that has been covered with a tea towel. Let the jars stand, *undisturbed*, 12 hours to cool completely.

YIELDS ABOUT 7 HALF-PINTS

*SERVING SUGGESTIONS*

● Serve as an appetizer/dip with white corn scoops.

● Pass at the table as a relish for spooning on pork, chicken, and wild game.

### PROCESSING TIMES

| Style of Pack | Jar Size | Altitude of Canning Location | | |
|---|---|---|---|---|
| | | 0 to 1,000 ft | 1,001 to 6,000 ft | Above 6,000 ft |
| Hot | Half-pints | 10 min | 15 min | 20 min |

# PEACH-APPLE SALSA

2¼ cups cider vinegar (5 percent acidity)

3¾ cups packed light brown sugar

1 tablespoon canning salt (page 18)

2 teaspoons crushed red pepper*

¼ cup mixed pickling spice tied in a 4-layer**
cheesecloth bag (page 38)

2½ cups yellow onions diced (page 40)
approximately ¼ inch square (about 2 extra-large
onions)

2 cups green bell peppers diced (page 40)
approximately ¼ inch square (about 2 large
peppers)

6 cups Roma tomatoes cubed (page 40)
approximately ½ inch square (about 4 pounds
large Roma tomatoes) (see recipe procedures,
below)

12 cups cold water

1 tablespoon plus 2 teaspoons white vinegar

1 tablespoon plus 2 teaspoons table salt

10 cups firm, underripe peaches cubed (page 40)
approximately ½ inch square (about 5 pounds
peaches) (see recipe procedures, below)

2 cups Granny Smith apples cubed (page 40)
approximately ½ inch square (about 1 pound
apples) (see recipe procedures, below)

*Available in the spice section at the supermarket.
For less spicy salsa, reduce the crushed red pepper to
1 teaspoon.

**Cut the layers 10 inches square.

✳ In an 8-quart, heavy-bottomed, stainless steel kettle, place the cider vinegar,
brown sugar, canning salt, and crushed
red pepper; stir to combine. Add the

cheesecloth bag of mixed pickling spice.
Over medium-high heat, bring the vinegar mixture to a boil, stirring until the
brown sugar dissolves. Remove from the
heat; cover and let stand.

✳ Prepare the diced onions and place in
a mixing bowl; cover and let stand. Prepare the diced green peppers and place
in a separate mixing bowl; cover and let
stand.

✳ Wash the whole tomatoes. In batches,
blanch the tomatoes (page 36) 1 minute
(not longer) and immediately immerse
them in cold water; drain. Remove the
stem ends (see Note 1, page 160), peel,
remove the tiny blossom ends, quarter,
and seed and core the tomatoes (page 39).
Using a knife (not a food processor), cut
the tomatoes into approximately ½-inch
cubes (page 40). (The cubes will be
irregular.) Measure 6 cups cubed tomatoes and place them in a separate mixing
bowl; cover and let stand.

✳ In a 12-quart, heavy-bottomed, stainless steel kettle, place 12 cups cold water,
1 tablespoon plus 2 teaspoons white vinegar, and 1 tablespoon plus 2 teaspoons
table salt; stir until the salt dissolves;
set aside.

✳ Wash the whole peaches. In batches,
blanch the peaches (page 36) 2 minutes
(not longer) and immediately immerse

*continues*

them in cold water; drain. Peel the peaches, cut them in half and pit them. As the peaches are cut in half and pitted, immediately drop them into the 12-quart kettle containing the white vinegar solution to prevent discoloration. Let the peaches stand.

✳ In the 8-quart kettle containing the brown sugar mixture, place the prepared onions, green peppers, and tomatoes; stir briefly to combine; cover and let stand.

✳ Remove the peaches from the kettle. Drain and rinse the peaches twice, using fresh, cold water. Drain the peaches well. Cut the peaches into approximately ½-inch cubes. (The cubes will be irregular.) Measure 10 cups cubed peaches and place them in the kettle containing the brown sugar mixture; stir briefly to combine; set aside.

✳ Wash, pare (page 40) (see Note 2), quarter, and core (page 40) the apples. Cut the apples into approximately ½-inch cubes. (The cubes will be irregular.) Measure 2 cups cubed apples and add to the kettle containing the brown sugar mixture; stir gently to combine.

✳ Over medium-high heat, bring the peach-apple mixture to a boil, uncovered, gently stirring intermittently. Reduce the heat to medium-low and gently simmer the mixture, uncovered, 30 minutes, stirring occasionally.

✳ Remove from the heat. Remove and discard the cheesecloth bag; cover and let stand.

✳ Drain hot, sterilized (page 19), pint jars, upside down, on a clean tea towel.

✳ Using a slotted spoon, place hot salsa solids in the drained jars, leaving 1¼-inches headspace. Then, using a 1-cup measuring cup with a pouring spout, cover the salsa solids in the jars with cooking liquid from the kettle, leaving ½-inch headspace. Using a plastic knife or a narrow, rubber spatula, remove the air bubbles in the jars. Then, check the headspace in each jar and if necessary, add additional cooking liquid to maintain ½-inch headspace. Wipe the jar rims and threads. Place hot, metal lids on the jars and screw the bands firmly.

✳ Process in a boiling-water canner for the time shown in the PROCESSING TIMES chart at the end of this recipe.

✳ Remove the jars from the canner and place them on a dry, wooden board that has been covered with a tea towel. Let the jars stand, *undisturbed*, 12 hours to cool completely.

NOTE 1: *A tomato corer (see illustration, page 96) is a handy, inexpensive kitchen tool to use for this task.*

NOTE 2: *A Back to Basics® brand apple "peeler" (parer) (see illustration, page 47) helps accomplish this task expeditiously and efficiently.*

YIELDS ABOUT 6 PINTS

- An avant-garde salsa that complements veal, pork, poultry, fish, and wild game birds.
- Serve with white corn scoops for an upscale hors d'oeuvre.

| PROCESSING TIMES | | | | |
|---|---|---|---|---|
| Style of Pack | Jar Size | Altitude of Canning Location | | |
| | | 0 to 1,000 ft | 1,001 to 6,000 ft | Above 6,000 ft |
| Hot | Pints | 15 min | 20 min | 25 min |

# TOMATO-CHILE SALSA

**IMPORTANT FOOD SAFETY ALERTS:** Do not alter the amounts of tomatoes, peppers, onions, and vinegar in this recipe. Do not thicken the salsa with flour, cornstarch, or other starches before canning. If a thicker salsa is desired, after opening the jar of canned salsa, pour off some of the liquid or add thickening ingredients.

The varieties of peppers may be altered to suit taste preference provided the measurement of 2½ cups total chopped peppers is not altered. See Varieties of Chile Peppers, page 163. Bell peppers may be substituted for part or all of the chile peppers. Canned chile peppers may be substituted for fresh chile peppers.

Wear plastic or rubber gloves and do not touch your eyes or face when handling hot chile peppers.

4 cups chopped Roma tomatoes* (about 4 pounds Roma tomatoes) (see recipe procedures, below)

2 cups chopped mild chile peppers** (see recipe procedures, below)

½ cup chopped jalapeño peppers*** (about 2 jalapeño peppers) (see recipe procedures, below)

¾ cup chopped onions (about 1 large onion) (see recipe procedures, below)

4 garlic cloves, pressed

2 cups cider vinegar (5 percent acidity)

1½ teaspoons canning salt (page 18)

1 tablespoon dried leaf oregano

1 teaspoon ground cumin

*Do not use tomatoes from dead or frost-killed vines.*

**Such as Anaheim peppers. See additional varieties of relatively mild chile peppers on page 163.*

***A different variety of hot chile peppers may be substituted. See additional varieties of hot chile peppers on page 163.*

✳ Wash the whole tomatoes. In batches, blanch the tomatoes (page 36) 1 minute (not longer) and immediately immerse them in cold water; drain. Remove the stem ends (see Note, page 163), peel,

*continues*

remove the tiny blossom ends, quarter lengthwise, and seed and core the tomatoes (page 39). Using a food processor fitted with a steel blade, chop the tomatoes in small batches, using 4 quick on/off turns. Measure 4 cups of chopped tomatoes and place them in an 8-quart, heavy-bottomed, stainless steel kettle; cover and set aside.

✱ Wearing plastic or rubber gloves, wash the mild chile peppers selected for use in this recipe. Using a sharp paring knife, cut off and discard the stems of the peppers. Cut the peppers in half, lengthwise; remove and discard the seeds and ribs. Then, cut the peppers into approximately 1-inch pieces. Using the food processor fitted with the steel blade, chop the peppers in small batches, using 4 quick on/off turns. Measure 2 cups chopped mild chile peppers and place them in the kettle containing the tomatoes; cover and set aside.

✱ Wearing plastic or rubber gloves, wash the jalapeño peppers (or other selected variety of hot peppers). Using a sharp paring knife, cut off and discard the stems of the peppers. Cut the peppers in half, lengthwise; remove and discard the seeds and ribs. Cut the pepper halves into approximately 1-inch pieces. Using the food processor fitted with the steel blade, chop the peppers using 4 quick on/off turns. Measure ½ cup chopped jalapeño (or other selected variety) peppers and

place them in the kettle containing the tomatoes; cover and set aside.

✱ Cut off the ends and peel the onion(s). Cut the onion(s) into approximately 1-inch pieces. Using the food processor fitted with the steel blade, chop the onions using 4 quick on/off turns. Measure ¾ cup chopped onions and place them in the kettle containing the tomatoes.

✱ Then, in the kettle containing the tomatoes, peppers, and onions, place the pressed garlic cloves, vinegar, canning salt, oregano, and cumin; stir to evenly combine all of the ingredients. Over medium-high heat, bring the tomato mixture to a simmer, stirring constantly. Reduce the heat and simmer the mixture, uncovered, 20 to 25 minutes, until the desired salsa consistency is reached, stirring occasionally. Remove from the heat; cover and let stand.

✱ Drain hot, sterilized (page 19), pint jars, upside down, on a clean tea towel.

✱ Using a 1-cup measuring cup with a pouring spout, pour the hot salsa into the drained jars, leaving ½-inch headspace. Using a plastic knife or a narrow, rubber spatula, remove the air bubbles in the jars. Then, check the headspace in each jar and if necessary, add additional hot salsa to maintain ½-inch headspace. Wipe the jar rims and threads. Place hot, metal lids on the jars and screw the bands firmly.

* Process in a boiling-water canner for the time shown in the PROCESSING TIMES chart at the end of this recipe.

* Remove the jars from the canner and place them on a dry, wooden board that has been covered with a tea towel. Let the jars stand, *undisturbed*, 12 hours to cool completely.

NOTE: *A kitchen tool commonly known as a tomato "corer" (see illustration, page 96) is a handy, inexpensive kitchen tool to use for this task.*

YIELDS ABOUT 3 PINTS

*VARIATION:* For less spicy salsa, eliminate the ½ cup seeded and chopped jalapeño peppers (hot chile peppers) and increase the seeded and chopped mild chile peppers to 2½ cups.

*SERVING OPTION:* If desired, 1 teaspoon snipped, fresh cilantro may be added to each pint of Tomato-Chile Salsa prior to serving (not before canning).

| PROCESSING TIMES | | | | |
|---|---|---|---|---|
| *Style of Pack* | *Jar Size* | *Altitude of Canning Location* | | |
| | | 0 to 1,000 ft | 1,001 to 6,000 ft | Above 6,000 ft |
| Hot | Pints | 15 min | 20 min | 25 min |

## VARIETIES OF CHILE PEPPERS

RELATIVELY MILD CHILE PEPPERS

Anaheim

Ancho

College

Colorado

Hungarian Yellow Wax

HOT CHILE PEPPERS

Cayenne

Habañero

Jalapeño

Serrano

Tabasco

# Savory and
# Sweet Sauces

# TOMATO CATSUP

ABOUT CATSUP: When most of us hear the word "catsup" or "ketchup" (either spelling is correct), we think of tomato catsup, perhaps America's best-loved (and some might say "overused") condiment (page 40). But many kinds of catsup besides tomato catsup were made with regularity in earlier days. Mushroom, walnut (made with green English walnuts), and celery catsup, as well as many fruit catsups, such as grape, plum, apple, and cranberry, were among the most popular. These interesting condiments would seem to be stylish enhancers for some of today's most popular foods like chicken breasts, broiled fish, and lean meats. Happily, some of these now-uncommon catsups sometimes turn up in gourmet stores and upscale restaurants for rediscovery.

Taking into account the broader horizon of catsup, it is defined as follows: A thick sauce consisting of a pureed food (often including onions), vinegar, spices, salt, and usually sugar, used as a condiment especially with meats, fish, poultry, eggs, and certain vegetables. It also is used as an ingredient in cooking.

1½ cups cider vinegar (5 percent acidity)

2 3-inch pieces stick cinnamon

1 tablespoon celery seed

2 teaspoons whole cloves

1 teaspoon whole allspice

12 pounds tomatoes

1½ cups chopped onions

1 garlic clove, pressed

1 cup sugar

2 tablespoons salt

⅛ teaspoon cayenne pepper

✳ THE FIRST DAY: In a small, stainless steel saucepan, place the vinegar, stick cinnamon, celery seed, cloves, and allspice; stir to combine. Cover the saucepan. Over high heat, bring the vinegar mixture to a boil. Remove from the heat. Cover and let stand at room temperature until incorporated into the recipe the next day. This allows time for the spices to steep in the vinegar and for the flavors to blend.

✳ THE NEXT DAY: Wash the tomatoes. In batches, blanch the tomatoes (page 36) 45 seconds and immediately immerse them in cold water; drain. Remove the stem ends (see Note 1), peel, remove the tiny blossom ends, quarter, and seed and core the tomatoes (page 39). As the tomatoes are prepared, drop them into an 8-quart, heavy-bottomed, stainless steel kettle.

✳ Using a potato masher, crush the tomatoes in the kettle; cover and set aside.

✳ In a blender beaker, place the chopped onions; using the blender, puree. Add the pureed onions and pressed garlic to the crushed tomatoes in the kettle; stir to combine. Cover the kettle. Over medium-high heat, bring the tomato mixture to a simmer, stirring frequently to prevent the mixture from scorching on the bottom of the kettle. Uncover the kettle. Reduce the heat and simmer the tomato mixture 20 minutes, stirring frequently. Remove from the heat.

✳ Press the tomato mixture through a food mill. Return the mixture to the kettle and cover. Over medium-high heat, bring the tomato mixture to a simmer, stirring frequently. Uncover the kettle. Reduce the heat and simmer the tomato mixture until the volume is reduced by one-half (about 1 hour), stirring very frequently to prevent scorching. Remove from the heat and set aside.

✳ Secure a piece of damp cotton flannel, napped side up, in a sieve over a deep pan; set aside.

✳ Over high heat, bring the vinegar mixture to a boil. Remove from the heat. Remove and discard the stick cinnamon. Pour the vinegar mixture over the cotton flannel in the sieve to strain.

✳ Add the strained vinegar mixture, sugar, salt, and cayenne pepper to the tomato mixture; stir to combine. Over medium-high heat, bring the tomato mixture to a simmer, stirring constantly. Reduce the heat and cook the mixture, uncovered, at a low simmer, until the catsup is reduced to the point that it will mound on a spoon without separation, stirring nearly constantly to prevent scorching. Remove from the heat; let stand.

✳ Drain hot, sterilized (page 19), pint jars, upside down, on a clean tea towel.

✳ Using a 1 cup measuring cup with a pouring spout, pour the hot catsup into the drained jars, leaving ⅛-inch headspace. Wipe the jar rims and threads. Place hot, metal lids on the jars and screw the bands firmly.

✳ Process in a boiling-water canner for the time shown in the PROCESSING TIMES chart at the end of this recipe.

✳ Remove the jars from the canner and place them on a dry, wooden board that has been covered with a tea towel. Let the jars stand, *undisturbed*, 12 hours to cool completely.

NOTE 1: *A kitchen tool commonly known as a tomato "corer" (see illustration, page 96) is a handy, inexpensive kitchen tool to use for this task.*

NOTE 2: *This recipe may be doubled.*

YIELDS ABOUT 3 PINTS

VARIATION: To prepare more spicy hot catsup, increase the cayenne pepper to ¼ teaspoon.

| PROCESSING TIMES | | | |
| --- | --- | --- | --- |
| *Jar Size* | *Altitude of Canning Location* | | |
| | 0 to 1,000 ft | 1,001 to 6,000 ft | Above 6,000 ft |
| Pints | 15 min | 20 min | 25 min |

# SPAGHETTI SAUCE

**IMPORTANT:** For food safety, do not increase the proportions of onions and green bell peppers in this recipe.

30 pounds tomatoes

2 tablespoons vegetable oil

1 cup medium finely chopped yellow onions* (about 1 medium to large onion)

1 cup medium finely chopped green bell peppers* (about 1 large pepper)

6 garlic cloves, pressed

2 tablespoons dried leaf sweet basil

2 tablespoons dried leaf oregano

2 tablespoons dried Italian herb seasoning**

1 tablespoon dried parsley

1 tablespoon plus 2 teaspoons salt

¼ cup packed light brown sugar

3 bay leaves

*Chop in batches in a food processor if available.*

**Available in the spice section at the supermarket.*

✳ Wash the tomatoes. In batches, blanch the tomatoes (page 36) 30 seconds and immediately immerse them in cold water; drain. Remove the stem ends (see Note), peel, remove the tiny blossom ends, quarter lengthwise, and seed and core the tomatoes (page 96). (Cut very large tomatoes into eighths, lengthwise, for easier seeding and coring.) Place the tomatoes in a 12-quart, heavy-bottomed, stainless steel kettle. Using a potato masher, crush the tomatoes.

✳ Over medium-high heat, bring the tomatoes to a simmer, stirring constantly to prevent the tomatoes from scorching on the bottom of the kettle. Reduce the heat and simmer the tomatoes 20 minutes, stirring nearly constantly to prevent scorching. Remove from the heat.

✳ In batches, press the tomatoes through a food mill, discarding any small amount of tomato pulp that may remain in the food mill after pressing each batch. Place the pressed tomatoes in 1 (or 2, if needed) large, stainless steel mixing bowls; let stand.

✳ Wash the 12-quart, heavy-bottomed, stainless steel kettle. Pour the pressed tomatoes into the kettle; cover and set aside.

✳ In a medium-sized, heavy-bottomed skillet, place the vegetable oil. Over medium-high heat, heat the vegetable oil. Tilt the skillet back and forth to spread the vegetable oil over the entire bottom of the skillet. Place the onions, green peppers, and garlic in the skillet; sauté (page 41) about 10 minutes until tender but not brown, turning often. Remove from the heat.

✴ Into the kettle containing the pressed tomatoes, place the sautéed onions, green peppers, and garlic; stir to combine. Then, add the basil, oregano, Italian herb seasoning, parsley, salt, and brown sugar; stir to evenly combine. Add the bay leaves; stir, briefly, to combine. Over medium-high heat, bring the mixture to a simmer, stirring constantly. Reduce the heat and cook the mixture, uncovered, at a low simmer, for about 1½ hours, or until the mixture reaches the desired consistency, stirring frequently to prevent scorching. (The mixture will be reduced by approximately one-half.) Remove from heat. Remove and discard the bay leaves; cover and let stand.

✴ Drain hot, sterilized (page 19), pint jars, upside down, on a clean tea towel.

✴ Using a 1-cup measuring cup with a pouring spout, pour the hot Spaghetti Sauce into the drained jars, leaving 1-inch headspace. Using a plastic knife or a narrow, rubber spatula, remove the air bubbles in the jars. Then, check the headspace in each jar and if necessary, add additional Spaghetti Sauce to maintain 1-inch headspace. Wipe the jar rims and threads. Place hot, metal lids on the jars and screw the bands firmly.

✴ Process in a pressure canner for the time and pressure shown in the PROCESSING TIMES AND POUNDS OF PRESSURE chart at the end of this recipe.

✴ Remove the jars from the canner and place them on a dry, wooden board that has been covered with a tea towel. Let the jars stand, *undisturbed*, 12 hours to cool completely.

NOTE: *A kitchen tool commonly known as a tomato "corer" (see illustration, page 96) is a handy, inexpensive kitchen tool to use for this task.*

**YIELDS ABOUT 5 PINTS**

| PROCESSING TIMES AND POUNDS OF PRESSURE | | | | | | |
|---|---|---|---|---|---|---|
| **Dial-Gauge Pressure Canner** | | | | | | |
| Style of Pack | Jar Size | Processing Time | Altitude of Canning Location | | | |
| | | | 0 to 2,000 ft | 2,001 to 4,000 ft | 4,001 to 6,000 ft | 6,001 to 8,000 ft |
| Hot | Pints | 20 min | 11 lbs | 12 lbs | 13 lbs | 14 lbs |
| | Quarts | 25 min | 11 lbs | 12 lbs | 13 lbs | 14 lbs |
| **Weighted-Gauge Pressure Canner** | | | | | | |
| Style of Pack | Jar Size | Processing Time | Altitude of Canning Location | | | |
| | | | 0 to 1,000 ft | Above 1,000 ft | | |
| Hot | Pints | 20 min | 10 lbs | 15 lbs | | |
| | Quarts | 25 min | 10 lbs | 15 lbs | | |

# CHERRY SAUCE

6½ cups pitted, tart, red cherries (see recipe
procedures, below)

1 1¾-ounce package powdered fruit pectin

5 cups sugar

＊ Place unpitted cherries in the sink
filled with cold water. Sort and stem the
cherries, discarding any cherries that
float. Drain the cherries in a colander.
Pit the cherries (see Note).

＊ Measure 6½ cups pitted cherries,
including the juice, and place in an
8-quart, heavy-bottomed, stainless steel
kettle; set aside. Place the sugar in a large
mixing bowl; set aside.

＊ Add the pectin to the cherries in the
kettle; stir to combine. Over high heat,
bring the cherry mixture to a rolling
boil, stirring constantly but carefully
to retain the wholeness of the cherries.
Immediately add the sugar and return
the cherry mixture to a rolling boil over
high heat, stirring continuously. Boil the
mixture at a rolling boil exactly 1 minute
(no longer; use a timer), stirring constantly. Immediately remove from the
heat and skim the foam off the cherry
mixture, using tableware tablespoons
and teaspoons. Stir and skim the cherry
mixture an additional 20 minutes, or
until the syrup thickens sufficiently that
the cherries will distribute evenly in the
sauce and not float to the top of the jars;
let stand.

＊ Drain hot, sterilized (page 19),
half-pint jars, upside down, on a clean
tea towel.

＊ Using a 1-cup measuring cup with a
pouring spout, pour the Cherry Sauce
into the drained jars, leaving ¼-inch
headspace. Wipe the jar rims and threads.
Place hot, metal lids on the jars and
screw the bands firmly.

＊ Process in a boiling-water canner for
the time shown in the PROCESSING TIMES
chart at the end of this recipe.

＊ Remove the jars from the canner and
place them on a dry, wooden board that
has been covered with a tea towel. Let
the jars stand, *undisturbed*, 12 hours to
cool completely.

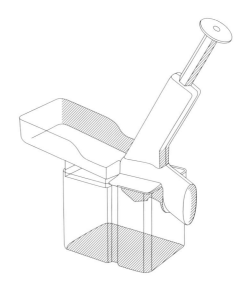

*Cherry Pitter*

**NOTE:** *The Westmark brand Kirschomat cherry pitter (see illustration, facing page) is an efficient tool to use for this task.*

**YIELDS ABOUT 6 HALF-PINTS**

*SERVING SUGGESTION*

• Serve as a topping over vanilla ice cream.

| PROCESSING TIMES | | | |
|---|---|---|---|
| *Jar Size* | *Altitude of Canning Location* | | |
| | 0 to 1,000 ft | 1,001 to 6,000 ft | Above 6,000 ft |
| Half-Pints | 5 min | 10 min | 15 min |

# CHERRY SAUCE WITH KIRSCHWASSER

1 half-pint canned Cherry Sauce (facing page)

3 tablespoons Kirschwasser (see Note)

✳ At serving time, place the Cherry Sauce in a small mixing bowl. Add the Kirschwasser; stir to blend.

**NOTE:** *Kirschwasser: Cherry brandy. A German word meaning "cherry water." It is pronounced "keersh-vahser."*

*SERVING SUGGESTION*

• Serve as a topping over vanilla ice cream.

# TUTTI-FRUTTI ICE CREAM TOPPING

✳ Follow the Tutti-Frutti Jam recipe, page 192, with the following exception: After adding the sugar and returning the fruit mixture to a rolling boil, boil the mixture for only 30 seconds, rather than 1 minute.

*SERVING SUGGESTION*

• Serve as a topping over vanilla ice cream.

**YIELDS ABOUT 6 HALF-PINTS**

*Blueberry Jam*

# Jams

Jam: A thick spread made with crushed or chopped fruit cooked with sugar. Jam has the same brilliance and color as jelly, but is softer in texture.

# APRICOT JAM

8 cups cold water

1 tablespoon white vinegar

1 tablespoon salt

3½ pounds apricots (5 cups chopped apricots; see recipe procedures, below)

7 cups sugar

¼ cup freshly squeezed, strained lemon juice

1 1¾-ounce package powdered fruit pectin

✳ In a 12-quart kettle, place the water, vinegar, and salt; stir until the salt dissolves; set aside.

✳ Wash ½ of the apricots. Blanch the apricots (page 36) 30 seconds and immediately immerse them in cold water; drain. Peel, cut in half, and pit the apricots. As the apricots are prepared, drop them into the vinegar solution to prevent discoloration. Repeat the procedure to prepare the remaining ½ of the apricots. Prepare only ½ of the apricots at a time because apricots darken quickly in their skins after being blanched. Let the apricots stand.

✳ Place the sugar in a large mixing bowl; set aside.

✳ Drain and rinse the apricots twice, using fresh, cold water. Drain the apricots well. In a food processor, chop ¼ of the apricots at a time, using about 3 quick on/off turns (see Note, page 177). Pieces of apricot should remain—be careful not to puree the fruit by overprocessing.

Place the chopped apricots, with the juice, in a mixing bowl.

✳ Measure 5 cups chopped apricots, including the juice, and place in an 8-quart, heavy-bottomed, stainless steel kettle. Add the lemon juice; stir to blend; set aside.

✳ Drain hot, sterilized (page 19), half-pint jars, upside down, on a clean tea towel; let stand.

✳ Add the pectin to the apricot mixture in the kettle; stir well to combine. Over high heat, bring the apricot mixture to a rolling boil, stirring constantly. Immediately add the sugar and return the apricot mixture to a rolling boil over high heat, stirring continuously. Boil the mixture at a rolling boil exactly 1 minute (use a timer), stirring constantly. Immediately remove from the heat and skim the foam off the jam, using tableware tablespoons and teaspoons.

✳ Using a 1-cup measuring cup with a pouring spout, quickly pour the hot jam into the drained jars, leaving ¼-inch headspace. Wipe the jar rims and threads. Place hot, metal lids on the jars and screw the bands firmly.

✳ Process in a boiling-water canner for the time shown in the PROCESSING TIMES chart at the end of this recipe.

✳ Remove the jars from the canner and place them on a dry, wooden board that

*continues*

has been covered with a tea towel. Let the jars stand, *undisturbed*, 12 hours to cool completely.

**NOTE:** *If a food processor is not available, hand-chop the apricots.*

YIELDS ABOUT 7 HALF-PINTS

| PROCESSING TIMES | | | |
| --- | --- | --- | --- |
| *Jar Size* | *Altitude of Canning Location* | | |
| | 0 to 1,000 ft | 1,001 to 6,000 ft | Above 6,000 ft |
| Half-pints | 5 min | 10 min | 15 min |

# BLUEBERRY JAM

6 cups blueberries (4 cups crushed blueberries; see recipe procedures, below)

2 tablespoons freshly squeezed, strained lemon juice

4 cups sugar

1 1¾-ounce package powdered fruit pectin

✳ Place the blueberries in a flat-bottomed pan. Sort and stem the blueberries. Transfer the berries to a colander. Run cold water over the blueberries to wash; set aside.

✳ Wash and dry the flat-bottomed pan. In the flat-bottomed pan, crush the blueberries, ¼ at a time, using a potato masher. Crush the blueberries until opened, but not pureed. Place the crushed blueberries, with the juice, in a mixing bowl.

✳ Measure 4 cups crushed blueberries, including the juice, and place in an 8-quart, heavy-bottomed, stainless steel kettle. Add the lemon juice, stir to blend; set aside. Place the sugar in a medium mixing bowl; set aside.

✳ Drain hot, sterilized (page 19), half-pint jars, upside down, on a clean tea towel; let stand.

✳ Add the pectin to the blueberry mixture in the kettle; stir well to combine. Over high heat, bring the blueberry mixture to a rolling boil, stirring constantly. Immediately add the sugar and return the blueberry mixture to a rolling boil over high heat, stirring continuously. Boil the mixture at a rolling boil exactly 1 minute (use a timer), stirring constantly. Immediately remove from the heat and skim the foam off the jam, using tableware tablespoons and teaspoons.

✳ Using a 1-cup measuring cup with a pouring spout, quickly pour the hot jam into the drained jars, leaving ¼-inch headspace. Wipe the jar rims and threads. Place hot, metal lids on the jars and screw the bands firmly.

*continues*

* Process in a boiling-water canner for the time shown in the PROCESSING TIMES chart at the end of this recipe.

* Remove the jars from the canner and place them on a dry, wooden board that has been covered with a tea towel. Let the jars stand, *undisturbed*, 12 hours to cool completely.

YIELDS ABOUT 6 HALF-PINTS

### PROCESSING TIMES

| *Jar Size* | Altitude of Canning Location | | |
|---|---|---|---|
| | 0 to 1,000 ft | 1,001 to 6,000 ft | Above 6,000 ft |
| Half-pints | 5 min | 10 min | 15 min |

# CHERRY JAM

*Awarded first place overall among all canned jams (twenty classes) at the 1992 Iowa State Fair.*

6 cups pitted, tart, red cherries (4 cups chopped cherries; see recipe procedures, below)

5 cups sugar

1 1¾-ounce package powdered fruit pectin

* Place unpitted cherries in the sink filled with cold water. Sort and stem the cherries, discarding any cherries that float. Drain the cherries in a colander. Pit the cherries (see Note 1).

* Measure 6 cups pitted cherries, including the juice. In a food processor, chop ¼ of the pitted cherries at a time, using 3 quick on/off turns (see Note 2). Place the chopped cherries, with the juice, in a mixing bowl.

* Measure 4 cups chopped cherries, including the accumulated juice, and place in an 8-quart, heavy-bottomed,

stainless steel kettle; set aside. Place the sugar in a large mixing bowl; set aside.

* Add the pectin to the chopped cherries in the kettle; stir well to combine. Over high heat, bring the cherry mixture to a rolling boil, stirring constantly. Immediately add the sugar and return the cherry mixture to a rolling boil over high heat, stirring continuously. Boil the mixture at a rolling boil exactly 2 minutes (use a timer), stirring constantly. Immediately remove from the heat and skim the foam off the jam, using tableware tablespoons and teaspoons. Stir and skim the jam 10 additional minutes, or until the mixture thickens sufficiently that the cherry pieces will distribute evenly in the jam and not float to the top of the jars (see Note 3); let stand.

* Drain hot, sterilized (page 19), half-pint jars, upside down, on a clean tea towel.

* Using a 1-cup measuring cup with a pouring spout, pour the hot jam into the drained jars, leaving ¼-inch headspace. Wipe the jar rims and threads. Place hot, metal lids on the jars and screw the bands firmly.

* Process in a boiling-water canner for the time shown in the PROCESSING TIMES chart at the end of this recipe.

* Remove the jars from the canner and place them on a dry, wooden board that has been covered with a tea towel. Let the jars stand, *undisturbed*, 12 hours to cool completely.

NOTE 1: *The Westmark brand Kirschomat cherry pitter (see illustration, page 170) is an efficient tool to use for this task.*

NOTE 2: *If a food processor is not available, cut the pitted cherries into eighths.*

NOTE 3: *Experience in jam making is the best teacher here, but the author finds that 10 minutes is, on average, about the correct amount of time for additional stirring and skimming of Cherry Jam after initially skimming the foam off the jam. (Many but not all fruit jams made with powdered fruit pectin are ready for pouring into the jars immediately after skimming.)*

YIELDS ABOUT 6 HALF-PINTS

| PROCESSING TIMES | | | |
|---|---|---|---|
| *Jar Size* | *Altitude of Canning Location* | | |
| | 0 to 1,000 ft | 1,001 to 6,000 ft | Above 6,000 ft |
| Half-pints | 5 min | 10 min | 15 min |

# GOOSEBERRY JAM

**NOTE**: *Gooseberries are naturally very high in pectin; therefore, Gooseberry Jam should not be made with added pectin, but should be made by boiling it to the jellying point (see the recipe procedures). Gooseberry Jam made with added pectin is nearly always too firm. (See the definition of Pectin on page 40, and the description of Sheeting in Jelly Making on page 196.)*

5⅓ cups sugar

8 cups (about 2½ pounds) gooseberries, divided

✳ Place the sugar in an 8-quart, heavy-bottomed, stainless kettle; cover and set aside.

✳ Wash 4 cups gooseberries and drain in a colander. Using a small, sharp paring knife, cut tiny portions off both ends of the gooseberries. Place the gooseberries in a medium mixing bowl; set aside. Wash, drain, and trim the remaining 4 cups gooseberries; place in a separate, medium mixing bowl.

✳ In a food processor, chop 4 cups of the gooseberries until medium-ground. Add the chopped gooseberries to the sugar in the kettle. Process the remaining 4 cups gooseberries in the food processor *just until the berries are crushed.* Add the crushed gooseberries to the sugar mixture in the kettle. Stir the mixture well to combine.

✳ Over medium-high heat, heat the gooseberry mixture until the sugar completely dissolves, stirring constantly. Attach a candy thermometer to the kettle. Increase the heat to high and bring the gooseberry mixture to a rolling boil, stirring constantly. Boil the mixture at a rolling boil until the temperature reaches 8°F above the boiling point of water at your canning location, stirring constantly. See "The Boiling Point of Water by Altitude," page 28, for information on how to find out the altitude of your canning location.

✳ Remove from the heat and detach the thermometer. Immediately skim the foam off the jam, using tableware tablespoons and teaspoons.

✳ Quickly drain hot, sterilized (page 19), half-pint jars, upside down, on a clean tea towel.

✳ Using a 1-cup measuring cup with a pouring spout, quickly pour the hot jam into the drained jars, leaving ¼-inch headspace. Wipe the jar rims and threads. Place hot, metal lids on the jars and screw the bands firmly.

✳ Process in a boiling-water canner for the time shown in the PROCESSING TIMES chart at the end of this recipe.

✳ Remove the jars from the canner and place them on a dry, wooden board that has been covered with a tea towel. Let the jars stand, *undisturbed*, 12 hours to cool completely.

**YIELDS ABOUT 5 HALF-PINTS**

PROCESSING TIMES

| Jar Size | Altitude of Canning Location | | |
|---|---|---|---|
| | 0 to 1,000 ft | 1,001 to 6,000 ft | Above 6,000 ft |
| Half-pints | 5 min | 10 min | 15 min |

# GRAPE JAM

9 cups stemmed Concord grapes (4 cups pressed grapes; see recipe procedures, below)

6 cups sugar

1 1¾-ounce package powdered fruit pectin

⁕ In small batches, place the grapes in a colander and wash them under cold, running water. Remove the grapes from the stems, selecting out only the fully ripe, unblemished fruit.

⁕ Measure 9 cups stemmed grapes. Place ½ of the grapes in a large, flat-bottomed pan. Using a potato masher, crush the grapes slightly. Place the crushed grapes, with the juice, in an 8-quart, heavy-bottomed, stainless steel kettle; set aside. Crush the remaining ½ of the grapes and with the juice, add to the kettle.

⁕ Over medium-high heat, bring the crushed grapes (and juice) to a simmer, stirring constantly. Reduce the heat. Cover the kettle and cook the grapes at a low simmer for 10 minutes, stirring frequently.

⁕ Remove from the heat. Press the cooked grapes and juice through a food mill to remove the seeds, pressing through as much of the skins as possible.

⁕ Measure 4 cups pressed grapes (including the juice) and place in a clean, 8-quart, heavy-bottomed, stainless steel kettle; set aside. Place the sugar in a large mixing bowl; set aside.

⁕ Drain hot, sterilized (page 19), half-pint jars, upside down, on a clean tea towel; let stand.

⁕ Add the pectin to the pressed grapes in the kettle; stir well to combine. Over high heat, bring the grape mixture to a rolling boil, stirring constantly. Immediately add the sugar and return the grape mixture to a rolling boil over high heat, stirring continuously. Boil the mixture at a rolling boil exactly 1 minute (use a timer), stirring constantly. Immediately remove from the heat and skim the foam off the jam, using tableware tablespoons and teaspoons.

⁕ Using a 1-cup measuring cup with a pouring spout, quickly pour the hot jam into the drained jars, leaving ¼-inch headspace. Wipe the jar rims and threads. Place hot, metal lids on the jars and screw the bands firmly.

⁕ Process in a boiling-water canner for the time shown in the PROCESSING TIMES chart at the end of this recipe.

* Remove the jars from the canner and place them on a dry, wooden board that has been covered with a tea towel. Let the jars stand, *undisturbed*, 12 hours to cool completely.

**YIELDS ABOUT 6 HALF-PINTS**

# PEACH JAM

8 cups cold water

1 tablespoon white vinegar

1 tablespoon salt

3 pounds peaches (4 cups chopped peaches; see recipe procedures, below)

5½ cups sugar

2 tablespoons freshly squeezed, strained lemon juice

1 1¾-ounce package powdered fruit pectin

* In a 12-quart kettle, place the water, vinegar, and salt; stir until the salt dissolves; set aside.

* Wash the peaches. Blanch the peaches (page 36) 45 seconds and immediately immerse them in cold water; drain. Peel, cut in half, and pit the peaches. If the peaches are large, cut each half in two. As the peaches are prepared, drop them into the vinegar solution to prevent discoloration. Let the peaches stand.

* Place the sugar in a large mixing bowl; set aside.

* Drain and rinse the peaches twice, using fresh, cold water. Drain the peaches well. In a food processor, chop ¼ of the peaches at a time, using 3 or 4 quick on/off turns (see Note, page 184). Pieces of peach should remain— be careful not to puree the fruit by over-processing. Place the chopped peaches, with the juice, in a mixing bowl.

* Measure 4 cups chopped peaches, including the juice, and place in an 8-quart, heavy-bottomed, stainless steel kettle. Add the lemon juice; stir to blend; set aside.

* Drain hot, sterilized (page 19), half-pint jars, upside down, on a clean tea towel; let stand.

*continues*

✳ Add the pectin to the peach mixture in the kettle; stir well to combine. Over high heat, bring the peach mixture to a rolling boil, stirring constantly. Immediately add the sugar and return the peach mixture to a rolling boil over high heat, stirring continuously. Boil the mixture at a rolling boil exactly 1 minute (use a timer), stirring constantly. Immediately remove from the heat and skim the foam off the jam, using tableware tablespoons and teaspoons. Stir and skim the jam 3 additional minutes, until the jam thickens slightly. This procedure will help achieve even distribution of the fruit pieces in the jam, preventing the fruit pieces from floating to the top of the jars.

✳ Using a 1-cup measuring cup with a pouring spout, pour the jam into the drained jars, leaving ¼-inch headspace. With the back of a teaspoon, push the fruit toward the bottom of each jar, making about 5 downward thrusts per jar, to further help distribute the pieces of fruit evenly.

✳ Wipe the jar rims and threads. Place hot, metal lids on the jars and screw the bands firmly.

✳ Process in a boiling-water canner for the time shown in the PROCESSING TIMES chart at the end of this recipe.

✳ Remove the jars from the canner and place them on a dry, wooden board that has been covered with a tea towel. Let the jars stand, *undisturbed*, 12 hours to cool completely.

N O T E : *If a food processor is not available, hand-chop the peaches.*

YIELDS ABOUT 6 HALF-PINTS

| PROCESSING TIMES | | | |
|---|---|---|---|
| *Jar Size* | *Altitude of Canning Location* | | |
| | 0 to 1,000 ft | 1,001 to 6,000 ft | Above 6,000 ft |
| Half-pints | 5 min | 10 min | 15 min |

# PINEAPPLE JAM

2 pineapples (4½ cups chopped pineapple;
  see recipe procedures, below)

5½ cups sugar

1 1¾-ounce package powdered fruit pectin

✳ Pare (page 40) the pineapples, carefully removing all the eyes and brown parts. Cut the pineapples into 1-inch slices and core (page 40). Then, cut the slices into 1-inch chunks.

✳ In a food processor, chop the pineapple chunks coarsely, in 1-cup batches, using about 3 quick on/off turns (see Note, page 186). Place the chopped pineapple, with the juice, in a mixing bowl.

✳ Measure 4½ cups chopped pineapple, including the juice, and place in an 8-quart, heavy-bottomed, stainless steel kettle; set aside. Place the sugar in a large mixing bowl; set aside.

✳ Add the pectin to the chopped pineapple in the kettle; stir well to combine. Over high heat, bring the pineapple mixture to a rolling boil, stirring constantly. Immediately add the sugar and return the pineapple mixture to a rolling boil over high heat, stirring continuously. Boil the mixture at a rolling boil exactly 1 minute (use a timer), stirring constantly. Immediately remove from the heat and skim the foam off the jam, using

tableware tablespoons and teaspoons. Stir and skim the jam about 8 additional minutes, until the jam thickens slightly. This procedure will help achieve even distribution of the fruit pieces in the jam, preventing the fruit pieces from floating to the top of the jars.

✳ Drain hot, sterilized (page 19), half-pint jars, upside down, on a clean tea towel.

✳ Using a 1-cup measuring cup with a pouring spout, pour the jam into the drained jars, leaving ¼-inch headspace. With the back of a teaspoon, push the fruit toward the bottom of each jar, making about 3 downward thrusts per jar, to further help distribute the pieces of fruit evenly.

✳ Wipe the jar rims and threads. Place hot, metal lids on the jars and screw the bands firmly.

✳ Process in a boiling-water canner for the time shown in the PROCESSING TIMES chart at the end of this recipe.

✳ Remove the jars from the canner and place them on a dry, wooden board that has been covered with a tea towel. Let the jars stand, *undisturbed*, 12 hours to cool completely.

*continues*

**YIELDS ABOUT 6 HALF-PINTS**

# RED PLUM JAM

4 pounds tart, ripe but firm, red plums (6 cups cooked plums; see recipe procedures, below)

8 cups sugar

1 1¾-ounce package powdered fruit pectin

✳ Wash, stem, quarter, and pit the plums. Do not pare (page 40) the plums. If the plums are especially large, cut each quarter in two.

✳ In a food processor, chop the plums fairly coarsely, in small batches, using about 5 quick on/off turns (see Note).

✳ Place the chopped plums, with the juice, in an 8-quart, heavy-bottomed, stainless steel kettle. Over medium-high heat, bring the plums to a boil, stirring constantly. Reduce the heat. Cover the kettle and simmer the plums 5 minutes, stirring frequently.

✳ Remove from the heat. Measure 6 cups cooked plums, including the juice, and place in a clean, 8-quart, heavy-bottomed stainless steel kettle; set aside.

Place the sugar in a large mixing bowl; set aside.

✳ Drain hot, sterilized (page 19), half-pint jars, upside down, on a clean tea towel; let stand.

✳ Add the pectin to the cooked plums in the kettle; stir well to combine. Over high heat, bring the plum mixture to a rolling boil, stirring constantly. Immediately add the sugar and return the plum mixture to a rolling boil over high heat, stirring continuously. Boil the mixture at a rolling boil exactly 1 minute (use a timer), stirring constantly. Immediately remove from the heat and skim the foam off the jam, using tableware tablespoons and teaspoons. Stir and skim the jam 3 additional minutes, until the jam thickens slightly. This procedure will help achieve even distribution of the fruit pieces in the jam, preventing the fruit pieces from floating to the top of the jars.

✳ Using a 1-cup measuring cup with a pouring spout, pour the jam into the drained jars, leaving ¼-inch headspace. With the back of a teaspoon, push the fruit toward the bottom of each jar, making about 3 downward thrusts per jar, to further help distribute the pieces of fruit evenly.

✳ Wipe the jar rims and threads. Place hot, metal lids on the jars and screw the bands firmly.

✳ Process in a boiling-water canner for the time shown in the PROCESSING TIMES chart at the end of this recipe.

✳ Remove the jars from the canner and place them on a dry, wooden board that has been covered with a tea towel. Let the jars stand, *undisturbed*, 12 hours to cool completely.

NOTE: *If a food processor is not available, hand-chop the plums.*

YIELDS ABOUT 10 HALF-PINTS

PROCESSING TIMES

| Jar Size | Altitude of Canning Location | | |
|---|---|---|---|
| | 0 to 1,000 ft | 1,001 to 6,000 ft | Above 6,000 ft |
| Half-pints | 5 min | 10 min | 15 min |

# RED RASPBERRY JAM

8 pints red raspberries (5 cups strained pulp; see recipe procedures, below)

7 cups sugar

1 1¾-ounce package powdered fruit pectin

✳ In a colander, wash and sort the raspberries, one pint at a time. Place ½ of the raspberries in a flat-bottomed pan. Using a potato masher, crush the raspberries. Place the crushed raspberries, with the juice, in a mixing bowl; set aside. Crush the remaining ½ of the raspberries. Press all the crushed raspberries and juice through a food mill to remove many of the seeds. Then, strain the raspberry pulp through a sieve to remove most of the remaining seeds.

✳ Measure 5 cups strained raspberry pulp and pour into an 8-quart, heavy-bottomed, stainless steel kettle; set aside. Place the sugar in a large mixing bowl; set aside.

✳ Drain hot, sterilized (page 19), half-pint jars, upside down, on a clean tea towel; let stand.

✳ Add the pectin to the raspberry pulp in the kettle; stir well to combine. Over high heat, bring the raspberry mixture to a rolling boil, stirring constantly. Immediately add the sugar and return the raspberry mixture to a rolling boil over high heat, stirring continuously. Boil the mixture at a rolling boil exactly 1 minute (use a timer), stirring constantly. Immediately remove from the heat and skim the foam off the jam, using tableware tablespoons and teaspoons.

✳ Using a 1-cup measuring cup with a pouring spout, quickly pour the hot jam into the drained jars, leaving ¼-inch headspace. Wipe the jar rims and threads. Place hot, metal lids on the jars and screw the bands firmly.

✳ Process in a boiling-water canner for the time shown in the PROCESSING TIMES chart at the end of this recipe.

✳ Remove the jars from the canner and place them on a dry, wooden board that has been covered with a tea towel. Let the jars stand, *undisturbed*, 12 hours to cool completely.

**YIELDS ABOUT 6 HALF-PINTS**

| PROCESSING TIMES | | | |
|---|---|---|---|
| *Jar Size* | *Altitude of Canning Location* | | |
| | 0 to 1,000 ft | 1,001 to 6,000 ft | Above 6,000 ft |
| Half-pints | 5 min | 10 min | 15 min |

# SEEDLESS WILD BLACK RASPBERRY JAM

9 cups crushed wild black raspberries* (see recipe procedures, below)

6 cups sugar

1 1¾-ounce package powdered fruit pectin

*If wild black raspberries are not available, commercial black raspberries may be substituted.*

❋ Gather fully ripe raspberries. In a colander, wash and sort the raspberries carefully. In batches, place the raspberries in a flat-bottomed pan and crush the raspberries, using a potato masher. Place the crushed raspberries, with the juice, in a mixing bowl.

❋ Measure 9 cups crushed raspberries, including the juice. Press the crushed raspberries and juice through a food mill to remove many of the seeds. Then, strain the raspberry pulp through a sieve to remove most of the remaining seeds.

❋ Pour the raspberry pulp into an 8-quart, heavy-bottomed, stainless steel kettle; set aside. Place the sugar in a large mixing bowl; set aside.

❋ Drain hot, sterilized (page 19), half-pint jars, upside down, on a clean tea towel; let stand.

❋ Add the pectin to the raspberry pulp in the kettle; stir well to combine. Over high heat, bring the raspberry mixture to a rolling boil, stirring constantly. Immediately add the sugar and return the raspberry mixture to a rolling boil over high heat, stirring continuously.

Boil the mixture at a rolling boil exactly 1 minute (use a timer), stirring constantly. Immediately remove from the heat and skim the foam off the jam, using tableware tablespoons and teaspoons.

❋ Using a 1-cup measuring cup with a pouring spout, quickly pour the hot jam into the drained jars, leaving ¼-inch headspace. Wipe the jar rims and threads. Place hot, metal lids on the jars and screw the bands firmly.

❋ Process in a boiling-water canner for the time shown in the PROCESSING TIMES chart at the end of this recipe.

❋ Remove the jars from the canner and place them on a dry, wooden board that has been covered with a tea towel. Let the jars stand, *undisturbed*, 12 hours to cool completely.

YIELDS 6 TO 7 HALF-PINTS

| PROCESSING TIMES | | | |
|---|---|---|---|
| Jar Size | Altitude of Canning Location | | |
| | 0 to 1,000 ft | 1,001 to 6,000 ft | Above 6,000 ft |
| Half-pints | 5 min | 10 min | 15 min |

# STRAWBERRY JAM

8 cups hulled (page 40) strawberries (5 cups crushed strawberries; see recipe procedures, below)

7 cups sugar

1 1¾-ounce package powdered fruit pectin

* Wash and sort the strawberries quickly in cold water; drain in a colander. Hull (see definition [1], page 40) the strawberries, using a strawberry huller (see illustration, page 72). Measure 8 cups hulled strawberries. In a flat-bottomed pan, crush the strawberries, ⅓ at a time, using a pastry blender (see illustration). Do not puree the strawberries; leave nice-sized pieces, which will be attractive in the jam. Place the crushed strawberries, with the juice, in a mixing bowl.

*Pastry Blender*

* Measure 5 cups crushed strawberries, including the juice, and place in an 8-quart, heavy-bottomed, stainless steel kettle; set aside. Place the sugar in a large mixing bowl; set aside.

* Drain hot, sterilized (page 19), half-pint jars, upside down, on a clean tea towel; let stand.

* Add the pectin to the crushed strawberries in the kettle; stir well to combine. Over high heat, bring the strawberry mixture to a rolling boil, stirring constantly. Immediately add the sugar and return the strawberry mixture to a rolling boil over high heat, stirring continuously. Boil the mixture at a rolling boil exactly 1 minute (use a timer), stirring constantly. Immediately remove from the heat and skim the foam off the jam, using tableware tablespoons and teaspoons.

* Using a 1-cup measuring cup with a pouring spout, quickly pour the hot jam into the drained jars, leaving ¼-inch headspace. Wipe the jar rims and threads. Place hot, metal lids on the jars and screw the bands firmly.

* Process in a boiling-water canner for the time shown in the PROCESSING TIMES chart at the end of this recipe.

* Remove the jars from the canner and place them on a dry, wooden board that has been covered with a tea towel. Let the jars stand, *undisturbed*, 12 hours to cool completely.

**YIELDS ABOUT 8 HALF-PINTS**

| PROCESSING TIMES | | | |
|---|---|---|---|
| *Jar Size* | *Altitude of Canning Location* | | |
| | 0 to 1,000 ft | 1,001 to 6,000 ft | Above 6,000 ft |
| Half-pints | 5 min | 10 min | 15 min |

# TUTTI-FRUTTI JAM

**NOTE:** *"Tutti-frutti" is an Italian term meaning "all fruits." Originally, tutti-frutti was the name for a mixture of fresh fruits, sugar, and brandy usually made in a crock and allowed to ferment. Fresh fruits were added as they came into season, along with additional sugar and brandy. The brandied fruits were used as accompaniments to meats, or the mixture was served as a dessert or a sauce over ice cream, puddings, or other desserts. Now, the term "tutti frutti" is sometimes applied to ice cream, confections, desserts, or other sweet foods containing mixed, chopped, candied, or fresh fruits.*

1 large orange, peeled, diced (page 40) ¼-inch square, and seeded (¾ cup diced orange pulp)

1 8-ounce can commercial crushed pineapple in 100 percent pineapple juice, well drained (⅔ cup drained pineapple)

¼ cup red maraschino cherries, diced (page 40) into eighths

¼ cup freshly squeezed, strained lemon juice

5 cups sugar

8 cups cold water

1 tablespoon white vinegar

1 tablespoon salt

3 cups (about 2 pounds) fresh Bartlett pears diced (page 40) ¼-inch square (see recipe procedures, below)

1 1¾-ounce package powdered fruit pectin

✳ Prepare the orange, pineapple, maraschino cherries, and lemon juice; cover each separately and set aside. Place the sugar in a large mixing bowl; set aside.

✳ In a 12-quart kettle, place the water, vinegar, and salt; stir until the salt dissolves; set aside.

✳ Wash, cut in half, core, and pare (page 40) the pears. As the pears are prepared, drop them into the vinegar solution to prevent discoloration.

✳ Drain and rinse the pears twice, using fresh, cold water. Drain the pears well. Dice the pears. Measure 3 cups diced pears.

✳ In an 8-quart, heavy-bottomed, stainless steel kettle, place the prepared pears, orange, pineapple, cherries, and lemon juice; set aside, *uncombined.*

✳ Drain hot, sterilized (page 19), half-pint jars, upside down, on a clean tea towel; let stand.

✳ Add the pectin to the fruit in the kettle; stir to combine. Over high heat, bring the fruit mixture to a rolling boil, stirring constantly. Immediately add the sugar and return the fruit mixture to a rolling boil over high heat, stirring continuously. Boil the mixture at a rolling boil exactly 1 minute (use a timer), stirring constantly. Immediately remove from the heat and skim the foam off the jam, using tableware tablespoons and teaspoons. Let the jam stand to cool *slightly* until sufficiently thick that the fruit will distribute evenly in the jars and not float to the top. Then, very briefly stir the jam to distribute the fruit evenly throughout the mixture.

＊ Using a 1-cup measuring cup with a pouring spout, pour the jam into the drained jars, leaving ¼-inch headspace. Wipe the jar rims and threads. Place hot, metal lids on the jars and screw the bands firmly.

＊ Process in a boiling-water canner for the time shown in the PROCESSING TIMES chart at the end of this recipe.

＊ Remove the jars from the canner and place them on a dry, wooden board that has been covered with a tea towel. Let the jars stand, *undisturbed*, 12 hours to cool completely.

**YIELDS ABOUT 6 HALF-PINTS**

| PROCESSING TIMES | | | |
|---|---|---|---|
| *Jar Size* | *Altitude of Canning Location* | | |
| | 0 to 1,000 ft | 1,001 to 6,000 ft | Above 6,000 ft |
| Half-pints | 5 min | 10 min | 15 min |

Blush Wine Jelly

# Jellies

Jelly: A semisolid mixture generally made with fruit juice and sugar. Flavored liquids other than fruit juice are sometimes used. Jelly is beautiful in color, translucent, and tender enough to cut easily with a spoon, yet firm enough to hold its shape when turned from the jar.

# APPLE JELLY

5 pounds tart apples (7 cups juice; see recipe procedures, below)

5 cups water

9 cups sugar

1 1¾-ounce package powdered fruit pectin

✳ Wash the apples; remove the stem and blossom ends. Do not pare (page 40) or core the apples. Cut the apples into small pieces and place them in an 8-quart, heavy-bottomed, stainless steel kettle. Add the water. Cover the kettle. Over high heat, bring the apples to a boil.

Reduce the heat and simmer the apples 10 minutes, stirring occasionally.

✳ Remove from the heat. Using a potato masher, crush the cooked apples in the kettle. Cover the kettle. Simmer the apples an additional 5 minutes, or until the apples are soft, stirring occasionally.

✳ Meanwhile, secure 4 layers of damp cheesecloth in a large sieve over a deep pan.

✳ Pour the cooked apples and juice over the cheesecloth in the sieve and let drain, *undisturbed*, at least 4 hours, until fully

---

## SHEETING IN JELLY MAKING

When making jellies *without added pectin*, a candy thermometer is the most reliable means of determining when the boiling jelly mixture reaches the jellying point and is done. The jellying point is reached when the jelly mixture reaches 8°F above the boiling point of water at sea level locations (page 28).

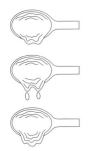

Another way to determine when the jellying point has been reached, is to test the jelly mixture for sheeting. To test for sheeting, dip a cool, metal tablespoon into the boiling jelly mixture and lift out a tablespoonful. Hold the spoon about 12 inches above the kettle (out of the steam) and pour the jelly mixture back into the kettle from the side of the spoon bowl. Before reaching the jellying point, the mixture first will drop off the spoon in syrupy drops. At the next stage before reaching the jellying point, two heavy drops of the jelly mixture will drop off the spoon. When the jellying point has been reached, the two drops of jelly mixture will flow together and break from the spoon in a single sheet. (See illustrations.)

drained. *Do not stir or squeeze the apple mixture in the cheesecloth*, as this may cause the jelly to be cloudy. Squeezed juice must be re-strained.

✳ Measure 7 cups strained apple juice and pour into a clean, 8-quart, heavy-bottomed, stainless steel kettle; set aside. Place the sugar in a large mixing bowl; set aside.

✳ Drain hot, sterilized (page 19), half-pint jars, upside down, on a clean tea towel; let stand.

✳ Add the pectin to the apple juice in the kettle; stir well to combine. Over high heat, bring the apple juice mixture to a rolling boil, stirring constantly. Immediately add the sugar and return the apple juice mixture to a rolling boil over high heat, stirring continuously. Boil the mixture at a rolling boil exactly 1 minute (use a timer), stirring constantly. Immediately remove from the heat and skim the foam off the jelly, using tableware tablespoons and teaspoons.

✳ Using a 1-cup measuring cup with a pouring spout, quickly pour the hot jelly into the drained jars, leaving ¼-inch headspace. Wipe the jar rims and threads. Place hot, metal lids on the jars and screw the bands firmly.

✳ Process in a boiling-water canner for the time shown in the PROCESSING TIMES chart at the end of this recipe.

✳ Remove the jars from the canner and place them on a dry, wooden board that has been covered with a tea towel. Let the jars stand, *undisturbed*, 12 hours to cool completely.

YIELDS ABOUT 10 HALF-PINTS

| PROCESSING TIMES | | | |
|---|---|---|---|
| *Jar Size* | *Altitude of Canning Location* | | |
| | 0 to 1,000 ft | 1,001 to 6,000 ft | Above 6,000 ft |
| Half-pints | 5 min | 10 min | 15 min |

# BLACKBERRY JELLY

14 cups blackberries (3½ cups juice; see
recipe procedures, below)

5 cups sugar

1 1¾-ounce package powdered fruit pectin

✳ Wash and sort the blackberries; drain
in a colander. In a flat-bottomed pan,
crush the blackberries, ⅓ at a time, using
a potato masher.

✳ Place the crushed blackberries, with
the juice, in an 8-quart, heavy-bottomed,
stainless steel kettle. Over medium-high
heat, bring the crushed blackberries to a
boil, stirring constantly. Reduce the heat.
Cover the kettle and simmer the blackberries 10 minutes, stirring occasionally.

✳ Meanwhile, secure 4 layers of damp
cheesecloth in a large sieve over a
deep pan.

✳ Pour the cooked blackberries and juice
over the cheesecloth in the sieve and
let drain, *undisturbed*, at least 5 hours,
until fully drained. *Do not stir or squeeze
the blackberry mixture in the cheesecloth*,
as this may cause the jelly to be cloudy.
Squeezed juice must be re-strained.

✳ Measure 3½ cups strained blackberry
juice (see Note) and pour into a clean,
8-quart, heavy-bottomed, stainless steel
kettle; set aside. Place the sugar in a large
mixing bowl; set aside.

✳ Drain hot, sterilized (page 19), half-
pint jars, upside down, on a clean tea
towel; let stand.

✳ Add the pectin to the blackberry juice
in the kettle; stir well to combine. Over
high heat, bring the blackberry juice
mixture to a rolling boil, stirring constantly. Immediately add the sugar and
return the blackberry juice mixture to
a rolling boil over high heat, stirring
continuously. Boil the mixture at a rolling boil exactly 1 minute (use a timer),
stirring constantly. Immediately remove
from the heat and skim the foam off the
jelly, using tableware tablespoons and
teaspoons.

✳ Using a 1-cup measuring cup with a
pouring spout, quickly pour the hot jelly
into the drained jars, leaving ¼-inch
headspace. Wipe the jar rims and threads.
Place hot, metal lids on the jars and
screw the bands firmly.

✳ Process in a boiling-water canner for
the time shown in the PROCESSING TIMES
chart at the end of this recipe.

✳ Remove the jars from the canner and
place them on a dry, wooden board that
has been covered with a tea towel. Let
the jars stand, *undisturbed*, 12 hours to
cool completely.

**NOTE:** *If there is less than 3 ½ cups strained blackberry juice, squeeze the cheesecloth containing the blackberry mixture over a separate pan or bowl to extract additional juice. Then, strain the newly extracted juice, undisturbed, through 4 layers of damp cheesecloth or a piece of damp cotton flannel, napped side up, and add to the already extracted juice.*

**YIELDS ABOUT 5½ HALF-PINTS**

| PROCESSING TIMES | | | |
|---|---|---|---|
| *Jar Size* | *Altitude of Canning Location* | | |
| | 0 to 1,000 ft | 1,001 to 6,000 ft | Above 6,000 ft |
| Half-pints | 5 min | 10 min | 15 min |

# CHERRY JELLY

12 cups pitted, tart, red cherries (3½ cups juice; see recipe procedures, below)

4½ cups sugar

1 1¾-ounce package powdered fruit pectin

* **THE FIRST DAY:** Place unpitted cherries in the sink filled with cold water. Sort and stem the cherries, discarding any cherries that float. Drain the cherries in a colander. Pit the cherries (see Note 1).

* Measure 12 cups pitted cherries, including the juice. In a food processor, chop approximately 2 cups of the pitted cherries at a time, using 3 quick on/off turns (see Note 2).

* Place the chopped cherries, with the accumulated juice, in an 8-quart, heavy-bottomed, stainless steel kettle. Over high heat, bring the cherries to a boil, stirring constantly. Reduce the heat to low. Cover the kettle and simmer the cherries 10 minutes, stirring intermittently. Keep the heat low to help prevent the cherries from boiling over.

* Meanwhile, secure 4 layers of damp cheesecloth in a large sieve over a deep pan.

* Pour the cooked cherries and juice over the cheesecloth in the sieve and let drain, *undisturbed*, at least 5 hours, until fully drained. *Do not stir or squeeze the cherry mixture in the cheesecloth.*

* Pour the strained cherry juice into a glass container; cover and refrigerate 24 hours.

**NOTE 1:** *The Westmark brand Kirschomat cherry pitter (see illustration, page 170) is an efficient tool to use for this task.*

**NOTE 2:** *If a food processor is not available, hand-chop the cherries.*

* **24 HOURS LATER:** Ladle the cherry juice from the glass container into a mixing bowl without disturbing any white, cloudy sediment that may have settled on the bottom of the container; discard the sediment. Re-strain the cherry juice through a piece of damp cotton flannel secured, napped side up, in a large sieve over a deep pan. *Do not stir or squeeze the juice in the cotton flannel,* as this may cause the jelly to be cloudy. Squeezed juice must be re-strained.

* Measure exactly 3½ cups re-strained juice and pour into a clean, 8-quart, heavy-bottomed, stainless steel kettle; set aside. Place the sugar in a medium mixing bowl; set aside.

* Drain hot, sterilized (page 19), half-pint jars, upside down, on a clean tea towel; let stand.

* Add the pectin to the cherry juice in the kettle; stir well to combine. Over high heat, bring the cherry juice mixture

*continues*

to a rolling boil, stirring constantly. Immediately add the sugar and return the cherry juice mixture to a rolling boil over high heat, stirring continuously. Boil the mixture at a rolling boil exactly 1 minute (use a timer), stirring constantly. Immediately remove from the heat and skim the foam off the jelly, using tableware tablespoons and teaspoons.

* Using a 1-cup measuring cup with a pouring spout, quickly pour the hot jelly into the drained jars, leaving ¼-inch headspace. Wipe the jar rims and threads. Place hot, metal lids on the jars and screw the bands firmly.

* Process in a boiling-water canner for the time shown in the PROCESSING TIMES chart at the end of this recipe.

* Remove the jars from the canner and place them on a dry, wooden board that has been covered with a tea towel. Let the jars stand, *undisturbed*, 12 hours to cool completely.

**YIELDS ABOUT 5 HALF-PINTS**

| PROCESSING TIMES | | | |
|---|---|---|---|
| *Jar Size* | *Altitude of Canning Location* | | |
| | 0 to 1,000 ft | 1,001 to 6,000 ft | Above 6,000 ft |
| Half-pints | 5 min | 10 min | 15 min |

# GRAPE JELLY

16 cups (about 5 pounds) Concord grapes (5 cups
  juice; see recipe procedures, below)

7 cups sugar

1 1¾-ounce package powdered fruit pectin

* THE FIRST DAY: Wash the grapes
well. Remove the grapes from the
stems, discarding underripe and overripe grapes. Measure 16 cups grapes. In a
flat-bottomed pan, crush the grapes, one
layer at a time, using a potato masher.

* Place the crushed grapes, with the
juice, in an 8-quart, heavy-bottomed,
stainless steel kettle. Over medium-high
heat, bring the crushed grapes to a boil,
stirring constantly. Reduce the heat.
Cover the kettle and simmer the grapes
10 minutes, stirring occasionally.

* Meanwhile, secure 4 layers of damp
cheesecloth in a large sieve over a
deep pan.

* Pour the cooked grapes and juice over
the cheesecloth in the sieve and let drain,
*undisturbed*, at least 6 hours, until fully
drained. *Do not stir or squeeze the grape
mixture in the cheesecloth.*

* Pour the strained juice into a glass
container; cover and refrigerate 48 hours
(see Note).

NOTE: *The tartaric acid in grapes, from which
cream of tartar is made, will frequently cause
tartrate crystals to form in grape jelly. The purpose
of refrigerating the grape juice for 48 hours is to
allow time for the formation of any tartrate crystals
in order that they can be removed before making
the jelly (instructions for removal of any tartrate
crystals from the grape juice are given later in the
recipe procedures).*

* 48 HOURS LATER: Ladle the grape
juice from the glass container into a
mixing bowl without disturbing any
sediment (tartrate crystals) that may
have settled on the bottom of the container; discard the sediment. Re-strain
the grape juice through a piece of damp
cotton flannel secured, napped side up, in
a large sieve over a deep pan. Do not stir
or squeeze the juice in the cotton flannel,
as this may cause the jelly to be cloudy.
Squeezed juice must be re-strained.

* Measure exactly 5 cups re-strained
juice and pour into a clean, 8-quart,
heavy-bottomed, stainless steel kettle; set
aside. Place the sugar in a large mixing
bowl; set aside.

* Drain hot, sterilized (page 19), half-
pint jars, upside down, on a clean tea
towel; let stand.

* Add the pectin to the grape juice in
the kettle; stir well to combine. Over
high heat, bring the grape juice mixture to a rolling boil, stirring constantly.

*continues*

Immediately add the sugar and return the grape juice mixture to a rolling boil, stirring continuously. Boil the mixture at a rolling boil exactly 1 minute (use a timer), stirring constantly. Immediately remove from the heat and skim the foam off the jelly, using tableware tablespoons and teaspoons.

✳ Using a 1-cup measuring cup with a pouring spout, quickly pour the hot jelly into the drained jars, leaving ¼-inch headspace. Wipe the jar rims and threads. Place hot metal lids on the jars and screw the bands firmly.

✳ Process in a boiling-water canner for the time shown in the PROCESSING TIMES chart at the end of this recipe.

✳ Remove the jars from the canner and place them on a dry, wooden board that has been covered with a tea towel. Let the jars stand, *undisturbed*, 12 hours to cool completely.

YIELDS ABOUT 8 HALF-PINTS

| PROCESSING TIMES | | | |
|---|---|---|---|
| *Jar Size* | *Altitude of Canning Location* | | |
| | 0 to 1,000 ft | 1,001 to 6,000 ft | Above 6,000 ft |
| Half-pints | 5 min | 10 min | 15 min |

# RED RASPBERRY JELLY

14 cups red raspberries (4 cups juice; see recipe procedures, below)

5½ cups sugar

1 1¾-ounce package powdered fruit pectin

✳ In a colander, wash and sort the raspberries, 2 cups at a time, and place in a mixing bowl. Place ½ of the raspberries in a flat-bottomed pan. Using a potato masher, crush the raspberries. Place the crushed raspberries, with the juice, in a mixing bowl; set aside. Crush the remaining ½ of the raspberries.

✳ Place all the crushed raspberries, with the juice, in an 8-quart, heavy-bottomed, stainless steel kettle. Do not add water unless necessary to prevent scorching. This will depend upon how much natural juice is in the raspberries. If water must be added, add as little as possible. Over medium-high heat, bring the crushed raspberries to a boil, stirring constantly. Reduce the heat. Cover the kettle and simmer the raspberries 10 minutes, stirring occasionally.

✳ Meanwhile, secure 4 layers of damp cotton flannel, napped side up, in a large sieve over a deep pan.

✳ Pour the cooked raspberries and juice over the cotton flannel in the sieve and let drain, *undisturbed*, at least 4 hours, until fully drained. *Do not stir or squeeze the raspberry mixture in the cotton flannel*, as this may cause the jelly to be cloudy. Squeezed juice must be re-strained.

✳ Measure 4 cups strained raspberry juice and pour into a clean, 8-quart, heavy-bottomed, stainless steel kettle; set aside. Place the sugar in a large mixing bowl; set aside.

✳ Drain hot, sterilized (page 19), half-pint jars, upside down, on a clean tea towel; let stand.

✳ Add the pectin to the raspberry juice in the kettle; stir well to combine. Over high heat, bring the raspberry juice mixture to a rolling boil, stirring constantly. Immediately add the sugar and return the raspberry juice mixture to a rolling boil over high heat, stirring continuously. Boil the mixture at a rolling boil exactly 1 minute (use a timer), stirring constantly. Immediately remove from the heat and skim the foam off the jelly, using tableware tablespoons and teaspoons.

✳ Using a 1-cup measuring cup with a pouring spout, quickly pour the hot jelly into the drained jars, leaving ¼-inch headspace. Wipe the jar rims and threads. Place hot, metal lids on the jars and screw the bands firmly.

✳ Process in a boiling-water canner for the time shown in the PROCESSING TIMES chart at the end of this recipe.

✳ Remove the jars from the canner and place them on a dry, wooden board that has been covered with a tea towel.

✳ Let the jars stand, *undisturbed*, 12 hours to cool completely.

**YIELDS ABOUT 6 HALF-PINTS**

| Processing Times | | | |
|---|---|---|---|
| *Jar Size* | *Altitude of Canning Location* | | |
| | 0 to 1,000 ft | 1,001 to 6,000 ft | Above 6,000 ft |
| Half-pints | 5 min | 10 min | 15 min |

# STRAWBERRY JELLY

14 cups strawberries (4 cups juice; see recipe procedures, below)

7½ cups sugar

2 3-ounce pouches liquid fruit pectin

* Wash and sort the strawberries in batches; drain in a colander. Hull (see definition [1], page 40) the strawberries, using a strawberry huller (see illustration, page 72). In a flat-bottomed pan, crush the strawberries, ⅓ at a time, using a potato masher.

* Place the crushed strawberries, with the juice, in an 8-quart, heavy-bottomed, stainless steel kettle. Do not add water unless necessary to prevent scorching. This will depend upon how much natural juice is in the strawberries. If water must be added, add as little as possible. Over medium-high heat, bring the crushed strawberries to a boil, stirring constantly. Reduce the heat. Cover the kettle and simmer the strawberries 10 minutes, stirring occasionally.

* Meanwhile, secure a piece of damp cotton flannel, napped side up, in a large sieve over a deep pan.

* Pour the cooked strawberries and juice over the cotton flannel in the sieve and let drain, *undisturbed*, at least 4 hours, until fully drained. *Do not stir or squeeze the strawberry mixture in the cotton flannel*, as this may cause the jelly to be cloudy. Squeezed juice must be re-strained.

* Measure 4 cups strained strawberry juice and pour into a clean, 8-quart, heavy-bottomed, stainless steel kettle. Add the sugar; stir to combine; set aside.

* Drain hot, sterilized (page 19), half-pint jars, upside down, on a clean tea towel; let stand.

* Over high heat, bring the strawberry juice mixture to a rolling boil, stirring constantly. Immediately add the pectin, stir to blend, and return the strawberry juice mixture to a rolling boil over high heat, stirring continuously. Boil the mixture at a rolling boil exactly 1 minute (use a timer), stirring constantly. Immediately remove from the heat and skim the foam off the jelly, using tableware tablespoons and teaspoons.

* Using a 1-cup measuring cup with a pouring spout, quickly pour the hot jelly into the drained jars, leaving ¼-inch headspace. Wipe the jar rims and threads. Place hot, metal lids on the jars and screw the bands firmly.

* Process in a boiling-water canner for the time shown in the PROCESSING TIMES chart at the end of this recipe.

* Remove the jars from the canner and place them on a dry, wooden board that has been covered with a tea towel. Let the jars stand, *undisturbed*, 12 hours to cool completely.

**YIELDS ABOUT 7 HALF-PINTS**

# WILD BLACK RASPBERRY JELLY

8 cups wild black raspberries* (2 cups juice; see recipe procedures, below)

5 cups sugar

1 3-ounce pouch liquid fruit pectin

*\* If wild black raspberries are not available, commercial black raspberries may be substituted.*

* Gather fully ripe raspberries. In a colander, wash and sort the raspberries carefully. Place the raspberries in a flat-bottomed pan. Using a potato masher, crush the raspberries.

* Place the crushed raspberries, with the juice, in an 8-quart, heavy-bottomed, stainless steel kettle. Do not add water unless necessary to prevent scorching. This will depend upon how much natural juice is in the raspberries. If water must be added, add as little as possible. Over medium-high heat, bring the crushed raspberries to a boil, stirring constantly. Reduce the heat. Cover the kettle and simmer the raspberries 10 minutes, stirring occasionally.

* Meanwhile, secure a piece of damp cotton flannel, napped side up, in a large sieve over a deep pan.

* Pour the cooked raspberries and juice over the cotton flannel in the sieve and let drain, *undisturbed*, at least 4 hours, until fully drained. *Do not stir or squeeze the raspberry mixture in the cotton flannel,* as this may cause the jelly to be cloudy. Squeezed juice must be re-strained.

* Measure 2 cups strained raspberry juice and pour into a clean, 8-quart, heavy-bottomed, stainless steel kettle. Add the sugar; stir to combine; set aside.

* Drain hot, sterilized (page 19), half-pint jars, upside down, on a clean tea towel; let stand.

* Over high heat, bring the raspberry juice mixture to a rolling boil, stirring constantly. Immediately add the pectin, stir to blend, and return the raspberry

*continues*

juice mixture to a rolling boil over high heat, stirring continuously. Boil the mixture at a rolling boil exactly 1 minute (use a timer), stirring constantly. Immediately remove from the heat and skim the foam off the jelly, using tableware tablespoons and teaspoons.

✳ Using a 1-cup measuring cup with a pouring spout, quickly pour the hot jelly into the drained jars, leaving ¼-inch headspace. Wipe the jar rims and threads. Place hot, metal lids on the jars and screw the bands firmly.

✳ Process in a boiling-water canner for the time shown in the PROCESSING TIMES chart at the end of this recipe.

✳ Remove the jars from the canner and place them on a dry, wooden board that has been covered with a tea towel. Let the jars stand, *undisturbed*, 12 hours to cool completely.

| PROCESSING TIMES | | | |
|---|---|---|---|
| *Jar Size* | *Altitude of Canning Location* | | |
| | 0 to 1,000 ft | 1,001 to 6,000 ft | Above 6,000 ft |
| Half-pints | 5 min | 10 min | 15 min |

YIELDS ABOUT 4 HALF-PINTS

# BASIL JELLY

**NOTE:** *The flavor of an herb usually is imparted in jelly by means of an infusion, as in this recipe. An infusion is a liquid, such as water, flavored by steeping in it a product, such as an herb or tea. Infusions are easily made. When making an infusion for use in an herb jelly, it is highly important to use very fresh herbs—preferably straight from the garden—to achieve superior flavor.*

1½ cups finely chopped, fresh basil leaves

3¼ cups water

A few drops green liquid food coloring

4 cups sugar

1 1¾-ounce package powdered fruit pectin

✳ In a medium, stainless steel saucepan, place the basil and water; stir to combine. Over high heat, bring the mixture to a boil. Remove from the heat; cover and let stand 1 hour.

✳ Then, secure a piece of damp cotton flannel, napped side up, in a sieve over a deep pan. Pour the basil and liquid (infusion) over the cotton flannel in the sieve and let fully drain, *undisturbed. Do not stir or squeeze the infusion in the cotton flannel.* Squeezed infusion must be re-strained.

✳ Measure 3 cups basil infusion and pour into an 8-quart, heavy-bottomed, stainless steel kettle. Add the food coloring; stir to blend; set aside. Place the sugar in a medium mixing bowl; set aside.

✳ Drain hot, sterilized (page 19), half-pint jars, upside down, on a clean tea towel; let stand.

✳ Add the pectin to the basil infusion in the kettle; stir well to combine. Over high heat, bring the infusion mixture to a rolling boil, stirring constantly. Immediately add the sugar and return the basil infusion mixture to a rolling boil over high heat, stirring continuously. Boil the mixture at a rolling boil exactly 1 minute (use a timer), stirring constantly. Immediately remove from the heat and skim the foam off the jelly, using tableware tablespoons and teaspoons.

✳ Using a 1-cup measuring cup with a pouring spout, quickly pour the hot jelly into the drained jars, leaving ¼-inch headspace. Wipe the jar rims and threads. Place hot, metal lids on the jars and screw the bands firmly.

✳ Process in a boiling-water canner for the time shown in the PROCESSING TIMES chart at the end of this recipe.

✳ Remove the jars from the canner and place them on a dry, wooden board that has been covered with a tea towel. Let the jars stand, *undisturbed*, 12 hours to cool completely.

*continues*

*SERVING SUGGESTIONS*

- Serve either as a garnish or as a sweet spread (with butter) for dinner rolls with pork, veal, lamb, and wild game dinners.

- Serve with toasted English muffins or toasted minibagels at an omelet or scrambled egg brunch.

| PROCESSING TIMES | | | |
|---|---|---|---|
| *Jar Size* | *Altitude of Canning Location* | | |
| | 0 to 1,000 ft | 1,001 to 6,000 ft | Above 6,000 ft |
| Half-pints | 5 min | 10 min | 15 min |

# MINT JELLY

**NOTE:** *Mint Jelly is often made using an apple jelly base, as in this recipe. The mint flavor is achieved by making an infusion (see the headnote for Basil Jelly, page 209) and then pressing the mint leaves in the infusion, together with the liquid, in a ricer to produce a more pronounced mint flavor. Because the mint leaves are pressed, the infusion becomes an extract, which is strained through a paper coffee filter before it is added to the apple juice. Green liquid food coloring is traditionally used in this jelly to give it that pretty, minty appearance.*

1½ cups firmly packed, fresh mint leaves

1½ cups boiling water

5 pounds tart apples (6 cups plus 2 tablespoons juice; see recipe procedures, below)

5 cups water

½ teaspoon plus 3 drops green liquid food coloring

9 cups sugar

1 1¾-ounce package powdered fruit pectin

✳ Place the mint leaves in a heatproof glass bowl. Pour 1½ cups boiling water over the leaves; cover and let stand 1 hour.

✳ Then, press the leaves and liquid firmly in a potato ricer. Strain the mint liquid (extract) through a paper coffee filter. Measure ¾ cup plus 2 tablespoons mint extract; pour it into a clean glass bowl; cover and refrigerate.

✳ Wash the apples; remove the stem and blossom ends. Do not pare (page 40) or core the apples. Cut the apples into small pieces and place them in an 8-quart, heavy-bottomed, stainless steel kettle. Add 5 cups water. Cover the kettle. Over high heat, bring the apples to a boil. Reduce the heat and simmer the apples 10 minutes, stirring occasionally.

✳ Remove from the heat. Using a potato masher, crush the cooked apples in the kettle. Cover the kettle. Simmer the apples an additional 5 minutes, or until the apples are soft, stirring occasionally.

✳ Meanwhile, secure 4 layers of damp cheesecloth in a large sieve over a deep pan.

✳ Pour the cooked apples and juice over the cheesecloth in the sieve and let drain, *undisturbed*, at least 4 hours, until fully drained. *Do not stir or squeeze the apple mixture in the cheesecloth*, as this may cause the jelly to be cloudy. Squeezed juice must be re-strained.

✳ Measure 6 cups plus 2 tablespoons strained apple juice and pour into a clean, 8-quart, heavy-bottomed, stainless steel kettle. Add the refrigerated mint extract and food coloring; stir until evenly blended; set aside. Place the sugar in a large mixing bowl; set aside.

✳ Drain hot, sterilized (page 19), half-pint jars, upside down, on a clean tea towel; let stand.

✳ Add the pectin to the mint mixture in the kettle; stir well to combine. Over high heat, bring the mint mixture to a rolling boil, stirring constantly. Immediately add the sugar and return the mint mixture to a rolling boil over high heat, stirring continuously. Boil the mixture at a rolling boil exactly 1 minute (use a timer), stirring constantly. Immediately remove from the heat and skim the foam off the jelly, using tableware tablespoons and teaspoons.

✳ Using a 1-cup measuring cup with a pouring spout, quickly pour the hot jelly into the drained jars, leaving ¼-inch headspace. Wipe the jar rims and threads. Place hot, metal lids on the jars and screw the bands firmly.

✳ Process in a boiling-water canner for the time shown in the PROCESSING TIMES chart at the end of this recipe.

✳ Remove the jars from the canner and place them on a dry, wooden board that has been covered with a tea towel. Let the jars stand, *undisturbed*, 12 hours to cool completely.

**YIELDS ABOUT 10 HALF-PINTS**

| Jar Size | Altitude of Canning Location | | |
|---|---|---|---|
| | 0 to 1,000 ft | 1,001 to 6,000 ft | Above 6,000 ft |
| Half-pints | 5 min | 10 min | 15 min |

PROCESSING TIMES

# BLUSH WINE JELLY

**NOTE:** *Wine jelly is quick and easy to make because wine is a ready-to-go ingredient, in contrast to the special processing of fruit required for fruit jelly.*

½ cup plus 2 tablespoons freshly squeezed lemon juice (½ cup strained juice; see recipe procedures, below)

1 750-milliliter bottle white zinfandel (blush) wine (about 3¼ cups)

4½ cups sugar

1 1¾-ounce package powdered fruit pectin

* Secure a small piece of damp cotton flannel, napped side up, in a small sieve over a bowl. Pour the lemon juice over the cotton flannel in the sieve and let drain, *undisturbed*, until fully drained. *Do not stir or squeeze the lemon juice in the cotton flannel*, as this may cause the jelly to be cloudy. Squeezed juice must be re-strained.

* Measure ½ cup strained lemon juice and pour into an 8-quart, heavy-bottomed, stainless steel kettle. Add the wine; stir to blend with the lemon juice; set aside. Place the sugar in a medium mixing bowl; set aside.

* Drain hot, sterilized (page 19), half-pint jars, upside down, on a clean tea towel; let stand.

* Add the pectin to the wine mixture in the kettle; stir well to combine. Over high heat, bring the wine mixture to a rolling boil, stirring constantly. Immediately add the sugar and return the wine mixture to a rolling boil over high heat, stirring continuously. Boil the mixture at a rolling boil exactly 1 minute (use a timer), stirring constantly. Immediately remove from the heat and skim the foam off the jelly, using tableware tablespoons and teaspoons.

* Using a 1-cup measuring cup with a pouring spout, quickly pour the hot jelly into the drained jars, leaving ¼-inch headspace. Wipe the jar rims and threads. Place hot, metal lids on the jars and screw the bands firmly.

* Process in a boiling-water canner for the time shown in the PROCESSING TIMES chart at the end of this recipe.

* Remove the jars from the canner and place them on a dry, wooden board that has been covered with a tea towel. Let the jars stand, *undisturbed*, 12 hours to cool completely.

**YIELDS ABOUT 5 HALF-PINTS**

**SERVING SUGGESTION**

- This beautiful, delicate, pale-pink colored jelly is sublimely appropriate to pass in a crystal dish at a dinner party for guests to spread thinly on their hot, buttered dinner rolls.

| PROCESSING TIMES | | | |
|---|---|---|---|
| Jar Size | Altitude of Canning Location | | |
| | 0 to 1,000 ft | 1,001 to 6,000 ft | Above 6,000 ft |
| Half-pints | 5 min | 10 min | 15 min |

# Preserves

Preserve: Small, whole fruit or uniformly sized, medium-large pieces of fruit in a clear, heavy, slightly jelled syrup. A preserve contains plump, tender fruit with natural color and flavor.

# CHERRY PRESERVES

6 cups pitted, tart, red cherries (see recipe
   procedures, below)

5 cups sugar

⅓ cup light corn syrup

* **THE FIRST DAY:** Place unpitted cherries in the sink filled with cold water. Sort and stem the cherries, discarding any cherries that float. Drain the cherries in a colander. Pit the cherries, reserving the juice (see Note).

* Measure 6 cups pitted cherries, including the juice, and place in an 8-quart, heavy-bottomed, stainless steel kettle. Add the sugar and corn syrup; using a wooden mixing spoon, stir to combine, being careful not to break up the whole cherries. Over medium-high heat, bring the cherry mixture to a boil, stirring constantly and carefully with the wooden mixing spoon. Boil the cherry mixture rapidly for 15 minutes, stirring constantly and carefully with the wooden mixing spoon.

* Remove from the heat and skim the foam off the cherry mixture, using tableware tablespoons and teaspoons.

* Pour the hot cherry mixture into a 12-x-18-x-1-inch cookie pan. Let the cherry mixture stand, uncovered, in a cool place, 24 hours.

**NOTE:** *The Westmark brand Kirschomat cherry pitter (see illustration, page 170) is an efficient tool to use for this task.*

* **24 HOURS LATER:** Place the cherry mixture in a clean, 8-quart, heavy-bottomed, stainless steel kettle. Over high heat, bring the cherry mixture to a rapid boil, stirring constantly and carefully with a wooden mixing spoon. Boil the mixture rapidly for 1 minute, stirring constantly and carefully with the wooden mixing spoon. Immediately remove from the heat and skim the foam off the preserves, using tableware tablespoons and teaspoons. Then, using the wooden mixing spoon and the tableware tablespoons and teaspoons, continue to stir and skim (if necessary) the preserves 10 additional minutes, or until the mixture thickens sufficiently that the cherries will distribute evenly in the preserves and not float to the top of the jars; let stand.

* Drain hot, sterilized (page 19), half-pint jars, upside down, on a clean tea towel.

* Using a 1-cup measuring cup with a pouring spout, pour the preserves into the drained jars, leaving ¼-inch headspace. Wipe the jar rims and threads. Place hot, metal lids on the jars and screw the bands firmly.

* Process in a boiling-water canner for the time shown in the PROCESSING TIMES chart at the end of this recipe.

* Remove the jars from the canner and place them on a dry, wooden board that has been covered with a tea towel. Let the jars stand, *undisturbed*, 12 hours to cool completely.

**YIELDS ABOUT 5 HALF-PINTS**

| PROCESSING TIMES | | | |
|---|---|---|---|
| *Jar Size* | *Altitude of Canning Location* | | |
| | 0 to 1,000 ft | 1,001 to 6,000 ft | Above 6,000 ft |
| Half-pints | 5 min | 10 min | 15 min |

# STRAWBERRY PRESERVES

**NOTE:** *The most elegant strawberry preserves are made with very small, whole strawberries, which can be difficult to find nowadays unless you have your own strawberry patch. Commercial strawberries purchased at supermarkets and produce markets keep getting bigger and bigger (and, may I say, less and less endowed with that wonderful, old-fashioned strawberry flavor). For making these preserves, I used to pick tiny, deep red, fabulously flavored strawberries in a U-Pick strawberry field in Dallas County (Iowa). The proprietor kept about three long rows of those special strawberries principally for use in preserves. Unfortunately, the strawberry field is no longer there, and I erred in not previously finding out what variety the little strawberries were, but I think they may have been a variety called "sparkle."*

8 cups small, firm, uniformly sized strawberries

4 cups sugar

2 cups sugar

2 tablespoons freshly squeezed, strained lemon juice

✳ **THE FIRST DAY:** Wash and sort the strawberries quickly in cold water; drain in a colander. Using a strawberry huller (see illustration, page 72), remove only the green, leafy sepals at the stem of the strawberries. Do not remove the center pith of the strawberries. Place the strawberries in a mixing bowl; let stand.

✳ Pour enough hot water into an 8-quart, heavy-bottomed, stainless steel kettle to cover the strawberries when added later. Cover the kettle. Over high heat, bring the water to a boil. Uncover the kettle. Add the strawberries and leave the strawberries in the kettle, uncovered, over high heat exactly 2 minutes (use a timer). Immediately remove from the heat and drain the strawberries well. (Leave the strawberries in the kettle.)

✳ Add 4 cups sugar to the strawberries in the kettle; using a wooden mixing spoon, carefully stir very briefly to partially combine. Try to prevent crushing the strawberries. Over medium-high heat, heat the strawberry mixture until the sugar dissolves, stirring carefully with the wooden spoon. When the sugar dissolves, increase the heat to high. Bring the mixture to a rolling boil; boil exactly two minutes (use a timer), using the wooden spoon to stir only sufficiently to prevent scorching. Immediately remove from the heat.

✳ After the bubbling stops, add 2 cups sugar and the lemon juice; using the wooden mixing spoon, stir carefully to combine. Over high heat, bring the mixture to a rolling boil, using the wooden mixing spoon to stir only minimally (to help avoid breaking up the whole strawberries). Boil the mixture exactly 5 minutes (use a timer), using the wooden mixing spoon to stir only minimally.

* Immediately remove from the heat and skim the foam off the strawberry mixture, using tableware tablespoons and teaspoons.

* Pour the hot strawberry mixture into a 10½-x-15½-x-1-inch cookie pan. Let the strawberry mixture stand, uncovered, in a cool place, overnight or about 12 hours.

* THE NEXT DAY: Using a wooden mixing spoon, carefully transfer the strawberry mixture in the cookie pan to a clean, 8-quart, heavy-bottomed, stainless steel kettle. Over medium heat, heat the strawberry mixture to under boiling, using the wooden mixing spoon to gently stir the mixture and prevent scorching. Avoid breaking up the strawberries. Immediately remove from the heat and, if necessary, skim any foam off the preserves, using tableware tablespoons and teaspoons. Then, if necessary, stir the preserves, using the wooden mixing spoon, until the mixture thickens sufficiently that the strawberries will distribute evenly in the preserves and not float to the top of the jars; let stand.

* Drain hot, sterilized (page 19), half-pint jars, upside down, on a clean tea towel.

* Using a 1-cup measuring cup with a pouring spout, pour the preserves into the drained jars, leaving ¼-inch headspace. Wipe the jar rims and threads. Place hot, metal lids on the jars and screw the bands firmly.

* Process in a boiling-water canner for the time shown in the PROCESSING TIMES chart at the end of this recipe.

* Remove the jars from the canner and place them on a dry, wooden board that has been covered with a tea towel. Let the jars stand, *undisturbed*, 12 hours to cool completely.

YIELDS ABOUT 5 HALF-PINTS

| PROCESSING TIMES | | | |
|---|---|---|---|
| *Jar Size* | *Altitude of Canning Location* | | |
| | 0 to 1,000 ft | 1,001 to 6,000 ft | Above 6,000 ft |
| Half-pints | 5 min | 10 min | 15 min |

Grape Conserve

# Conserves

Conserve: Similar to jam, with the same consistency. A conserve generally—but not always—contains two or more fruits, one of which is usually a citrus fruit. It contains nuts and/or raisins and/or coconut. In its purest form, a conserve contains both nuts and raisins. Conserves are favored for meat and poultry accompaniments; however, they also may be used as spreads on bread products.

# APRICOT-ALMOND CONSERVE

3 medium oranges

1 cup slivered, blanched almonds

16 cups cold water

2 tablespoons white vinegar

2 tablespoons salt

5 pounds apricots

10 cups sugar

¼ cup Amaretto (see page 65)

✳ Wash the oranges. Cut off the ends and quarter the oranges lengthwise. Using a grapefruit knife, remove the pulp from each orange quarter by cutting next to the peel using a sawing motion. Set the peels aside.

✳ Trim away any white peel membrane remaining on the orange pulp. Cut the pulp into ½-inch cubes (see *Cube*, page 40), removing and discarding any seeds. Place the orange cubes in a bowl; cover and set aside.

✳ Cut the quarters of orange peel in half lengthwise. Using the grapefruit knife, cut away and discard as much of the white membrane from the orange peels as possible. Using a meat grinder (page 37), finely grind the orange peels. Place the ground orange peel in a mixing bowl; cover and set aside.

✳ Using the meat grinder, coarsely grind the almonds. Place the ground almonds in a mixing bowl; cover and set aside.

✳ In a 12-quart kettle, place the water, vinegar, and salt; stir until the salt dissolves; set aside.

✳ Wash ½ of the apricots. Blanch the apricots (page 36) 30 seconds and immediately immerse them in cold water; drain. Peel, cut in half, and pit the apricots. As the apricots are prepared, drop them into the vinegar solution to prevent discoloration. Repeat the procedure to prepare the remaining ½ of the apricots. Prepare only ½ of the apricots at a time because apricots darken quickly in their skins after being blanched.

✳ Drain and rinse all the apricots twice, using fresh, cold water. Drain the apricots well. Cut each apricot half into ninths.

✳ In an 8-quart, heavy-bottomed, stainless steel kettle, place the apricots, orange cubes, orange peel, almonds, sugar, and Amaretto; stir to combine. Over low heat, heat the apricot mixture until the sugar completely dissolves, stirring constantly. Attach a candy thermometer to the kettle. Increase the heat to medium-high and bring the mixture to a rapid

*continues*

boil, stirring constantly. Rapidly boil the mixture until the temperature reaches 8°F above the boiling point of water at your canning location, stirring constantly. **Important: See "The Boiling Point of Water by Altitude," page 28, for information on how to find out the altitude of your canning location.**

✳ Remove from the heat and detach the thermometer. If any foam remains on the surface of the conserve, immediately skim it off, using tableware tablespoons and teaspoons; let stand.

✳ Quickly drain hot, sterilized (page 19), half-pint jars, upside down, on a clean tea towel.

✳ Using a 1-cup measuring cup with a pouring spout, pour the hot conserve into the drained jars, leaving ¼-inch headspace. Wipe the jar rims and threads. Place hot, metal lids on the jars and screw the bands firmly.

✳ Process in a boiling-water canner for the time shown in the PROCESSING TIMES chart at the end of this recipe.

✳ Remove the jars from the canner and place them on a dry, wooden board that has been covered with a tea towel. Let the jars stand, *undisturbed*, 12 hours to cool completely.

YIELDS ABOUT 12 HALF-PINTS

| PROCESSING TIMES | | | |
|---|---|---|---|
| *Jar Size* | *Altitude of Canning Location* | | |
| | 0 to 1,000 ft | 1,001 to 6,000 ft | Above 6,000 ft |
| Half-pints | 5 min | 10 min | 15 min |

# GOOSEBERRY CONSERVE

6 cups gooseberries, stem and blossom ends
    removed*

¾ cup finely diced (page 40) unpeeled orange
    (about 1 medium orange)

4 cups sugar

1 cup golden raisins

*Use a small, sharp paring knife to cut tiny portions
off both ends of the gooseberries.*

✳ In an 8-quart, heavy-bottomed, stain-less steel kettle, place the gooseberries, orange, sugar, and raisins; stir to combine. Over low heat, heat the gooseberry mixture until the sugar completely dissolves, stirring constantly. Attach a candy thermometer to the kettle. Increase the heat to medium-high and bring the mixture to a rapid boil, stirring constantly. Rapidly boil the mixture until the temperature reaches 8°F above the boiling point of water at your canning location, stirring constantly. **Important: See "The Boiling Point of Water by Altitude," page 28, for information on how to find out the altitude of your canning location.**

✳ Remove from the heat and detach the thermometer. If any foam remains on the surface of the conserve, immediately skim it off, using tableware tablespoons and teaspoons; let stand.

✳ Quickly drain hot, sterilized (page 19), half-pint jars, upside down, on a clean tea towel.

✳ Using a 1-cup measuring cup with a pouring spout, pour the hot conserve into the drained jars, leaving ¼-inch headspace. Wipe the jar rims and threads. Place hot, metal lids on the jars and screw the bands firmly.

✳ Process in a boiling-water canner for the time shown in the PROCESSING TIMES chart at the end of this recipe.

✳ Remove the jars from the canner and place them on a dry, wooden board that has been covered with a tea towel. Let the jars stand, *undisturbed*, 12 hours to cool completely.

YIELDS ABOUT 5 HALF-PINTS

| PROCESSING TIMES | | | |
|---|---|---|---|
| *Jar Size* | *Altitude of Canning Location* | | |
| | 0 to 1,000 ft | 1,001 to 6,000 ft | Above 6,000 ft |
| Half-pints | 5 min | 10 min | 15 min |

# GRAPE CONSERVE

5 pounds Concord grapes

8 cups sugar

1½ cups raisins

⅔ cup freshly squeezed, strained orange juice

1 cup chopped (page 36) English walnuts

✳ Wash the grapes and drain them. Remove the grapes from the stems, discarding any green or underripe fruit. Over a large, flat-bottomed pan, separate the grape pulp from the skins by squeezing each grape between your fingers, letting the pulp drop into the pan and placing the skins in an 8-quart, heavy-bottomed, stainless steel kettle. Set aside the kettle containing the skins.

✳ Pour off ½ cup of the grape juice accumulated in the flat-bottomed pan and add it to the skins in the kettle. If necessary, crush the grape pulp, using a potato masher, to extract additional juice to make ½ cup grape juice. Cover the pan containing the pulp; set aside.

✳ Over medium to medium-high heat, bring the skins and juice to a simmer, stirring constantly. Simmer the mixture 15 minutes, stirring nearly constantly. Remove from the heat and set aside.

✳ Place the grape pulp, with the remaining accumulated juice, in a clean, heavy-bottomed, stainless kettle. Do not add water. Over medium to medium-high heat, bring the grape pulp to a boil,

stirring constantly. Boil the grape pulp 3 minutes, stirring constantly. Remove from the heat.

✳ Press the cooked pulp (including the juice) through a food mill to remove the seeds.

✳ Measure 6 cups pressed grape pulp and place in the kettle containing the cooked skins. Add the sugar, raisins, and orange juice; stir to combine. Over low heat, heat the grape mixture until the sugar completely dissolves, stirring constantly. Attach a candy thermometer to the kettle. Increase the heat to medium-high and bring the mixture to a rapid boil, stirring constantly. Rapidly boil the mixture until the temperature reaches 8°F above the boiling point of water at your canning location, stirring constantly. **Important: See "The Boiling Point of Water by Altitude," page 28, for information on how to find out the altitude of your canning location.** Add the walnuts halfway through the boiling process (or when the mixture temperature reaches 4°F above the boiling point of water at your canning location), continuing to stir constantly.

✳ Remove from the heat and detach the thermometer. If any foam remains on the surface of the conserve, immediately skim it off, using tableware tablespoons and teaspoons; let stand.

✳ Quickly drain hot, sterilized (page 19), half-pint jars, upside down, on a clean tea towel.

✳ Using a 1-cup measuring cup with a pouring spout, pour the hot conserve into the drained jars, leaving ¼-inch headspace. Wipe the jar rims and threads. Place hot, metal lids on the jars and screw the bands firmly.

✳ Process in a boiling-water canner for the time shown in the PROCESSING TIMES chart at the end of this recipe.

✳ Remove the jars from the canner and place them on a dry, wooden board that has been covered with a tea towel. Let the jars stand, *undisturbed*, 12 hours to cool completely.

YIELDS ABOUT 7 HALF-PINTS

PROCESSING TIMES

| Jar Size | Altitude of Canning Location | | |
|---|---|---|---|
| | 0 to 1,000 ft | 1,001 to 6,000 ft | Above 6,000 ft |
| Half-pints | 5 min | 10 min | 15 min |

# RHUBARB-STRAWBERRY CONSERVE

1 large orange

1 cup water

1 cup golden raisins

3 cups fresh rhubarb sliced ¼-inch thick (see recipe procedures, below)

3 cups crushed strawberries (about 6 cups fresh strawberries) (see recipe procedures, below)

5 cups sugar

✻ Using a sharp knife, dice (page 40) the entire orange (both the peel and pulp) very finely.

✻ Place the diced orange in a small, stainless steel saucepan. Add 1 cup water. Cover the saucepan. Over medium heat, bring the orange mixture to a simmer. Uncover the saucepan and reduce the heat to medium-low. Simmer the orange mixture until the peel is softened (about 30 minutes).

✻ Remove the orange mixture from the heat. Add the raisins; stir to combine; set aside.

✻ If possible, select rhubarb stalks not exceeding ½ inch in width. If the stalks are wider, cut them in half lengthwise before slicing. Slice the rhubarb ¼ inch thick. Measure 3 cups sliced rhubarb and place in a medium mixing bowl; set aside.

✻ Hull (see definition [1], page 40) the strawberries, using a strawberry huller (see illustration, page 72). Cut the hulled strawberries into quarters or halves, depending upon their size, and place in a medium, stainless steel mixing bowl. Using a pastry blender (see illustration page 190), crush the strawberries until the mixture is part juice and part strawberry flesh. (Do not puree.)

✻ Measure 3 cups crushed strawberries, including the juice, and place in an 8-quart, heavy-bottomed, stainless steel kettle. Add the orange-raisin mixture (including the liquid), rhubarb, and sugar; stir well to combine. Over low heat, heat the mixture until the sugar completely dissolves, stirring constantly. Attach a candy thermometer to the kettle. Increase the heat to medium-high and bring the mixture to a rapid boil, stirring constantly. Rapidly boil the mixture until the temperature reaches 8°F above the boiling point of water at your canning location, stirring constantly. **Important: See "The Boiling Point of Water by Altitude," page 28, for information on how to find out the altitude of your canning location.**

✻ Remove from the heat and detach the thermometer. If any foam remains on the surface of the conserve, immediately skim it off, using tableware tablespoons and teaspoons; let stand.

✳ Quickly drain hot, sterilized (page 19), half-pint jars, upside down, on a clean tea towel.

✳ Using a 1-cup measuring cup with a pouring spout, pour the hot conserve into the drained jars, leaving ¼-inch headspace. Wipe the jar rims and threads. Place hot, metal lids on the jars and screw the bands firmly.

✳ Process in a boiling-water canner for the time shown in the PROCESSING TIMES chart at the end of this recipe.

✳ Remove the jars from the canner and place them on a dry, wooden board that has been covered with a tea towel. Let the jars stand, *undisturbed*, 12 hours to cool completely.

**YIELDS ABOUT 7 HALF-PINTS**

| PROCESSING TIMES | | | |
|---|---|---|---|
| *Jar Size* | *Altitude of Canning Location* | | |
| | 0 to 1,000 ft | 1,001 to 6,000 ft | Above 6,000 ft |
| Half-pints | 5 min | 10 min | 15 min |

# Marmalades

Marmalade: A soft fruit jelly containing small pieces of fruit or fruit peel evenly suspended in the translucent jelly. Marmalade often contains citrus fruit.

# KUMQUAT MARMALADE

1 pound kumquats (about 30 large kumquats)

About 2 large oranges (see recipe procedures, below)

½ large lemon (cut a whole lemon in half lengthwise)

6½ cups water

About 6 cups sugar (see recipe procedures, below)

✳ **THE FIRST DAY:** Wash the kumquats. Using a small, sharp, thin-bladed knife, thinly cut off the ends of the kumquats. Then, cut each kumquat widthwise into 1/16-inch slices, removing and discarding the seeds. Measure 3 cups sliced kumquats and place in an 8-quart, heavy-bottomed, stainless steel kettle; cover and set aside.

✳ Wash the oranges. Using a sharp, thin-bladed knife, cut off the ends of the oranges. Then, quarter the oranges lengthwise. Using a grapefruit knife, remove the pulp from each orange quarter by cutting next to the peel using a sawing motion. Place the orange pulp in a bowl; set aside.

✳ Using the small, sharp, thin-bladed knife, cut each quarter of orange peel widthwise into 1/16-inch slices. Measure 2 cups sliced orange peel and place in the kettle containing the sliced kumquats; cover and set aside.

✳ Cut each quarter of the orange pulp in half lengthwise. Then, cut each of the halves widthwise into ¼-inch slices, removing and discarding any seeds. Use all of the pulp, including the fruit meat and the membrane. Measure 1¼ cups sliced orange pulp and place in the kettle containing the sliced kumquats; cover and set aside.

✳ Cut the ½ lemon in half lengthwise. Using the small, sharp, thin-bladed knife, cut each piece of lemon widthwise into 1/16-inch slices, removing and discarding the seeds. (Slice the peel and pulp together.) Measure ½ cup lemon slices and place in the kettle containing the sliced kumquats.

✳ Add the water to the fruit in the kettle; stir to combine. Over high heat, bring the fruit mixture to a boil, uncovered, stirring intermittently. Reduce the heat and simmer the mixture (uncovered) 5 minutes, stirring occasionally.

✳ Remove from the heat and cover the kettle. Let the fruit mixture stand 18 to 24 hours in a cool place.

✳ **18 TO 24 HOURS LATER:** Over medium-high to high heat, bring the covered fruit mixture to a rapid boil, stirring intermittently. Rapidly boil the fruit mixture, covered, 45 minutes, stirring often to prevent the mixture from sticking to the bottom of the kettle.

* Remove from the heat and measure the fruit mixture. Place the fruit mixture back in the kettle. Add to the kettle the exact amount of sugar as the measured fruit mixture. (For 1 cup of fruit mixture, add 1 cup of sugar.) Stir the mixture to combine. Over low heat, heat the mixture until the sugar completely dissolves, stirring constantly. Attach a candy thermometer to the kettle. Increase the heat to medium-high and bring the mixture to a rapid boil, stirring constantly to prevent the mixture from sticking to the bottom of the kettle. The mixture will be foaming, but do not reduce the heat. Rapidly boil the mixture until the temperature reaches 8°F above the boiling point of water at your canning location, stirring constantly. **Important: See "The Boiling Point of Water by Altitude," page 28, for information on how to find out the altitude of your canning location.**

* Remove from the heat and detach the thermometer. If any foam remains on the surface of the marmalade, immediately skim it off, using tableware tablespoons and teaspoons; let stand.

* Quickly drain hot, sterilized (page 19), half-pint jars, upside down, on a clean tea towel.

* Using a 1-cup measuring cup with a pouring spout, pour the hot marmalade into the drained jars, leaving ¼-inch headspace. Wipe the jar rims and threads. Place hot, metal lids on the jars and screw the bands firmly.

* Process in a boiling-water canner for the time shown in the PROCESSING TIMES chart at the end of this recipe.

* Remove the jars from the canner and place them on a dry, wooden board that has been covered with a tea towel. Let the jars stand, *undisturbed*, 12 hours to cool completely.

YIELDS ABOUT 6 HALF-PINTS

| PROCESSING TIMES | | | |
|---|---|---|---|
| *Jar Size* | *Altitude of Canning Location* | | |
| | 0 to 1,000 ft | 1,001 to 6,000 ft | Above 6,000 ft |
| Half-pints | 5 min | 10 min | 15 min |

# ORANGE MARMALADE

5 or 6 large oranges

1 large lemon

6 cups water

About 5¾ to 6 cups sugar (see recipe procedures, below)

✳ THE FIRST DAY: Wash the oranges. Using a small, sharp, thin-bladed knife, cut off the ends of the oranges. Then, quarter the oranges lengthwise. Using a grapefruit knife, remove the pulp from each orange quarter by cutting next to the peel using a sawing motion. Place the orange pulp in a bowl; set aside.

✳ Using the small, sharp, thin-bladed knife, cut each quarter of orange peel widthwise into ¹⁄₁₆-inch slices. Measure 4 cups sliced orange peel and place in an 8-quart, heavy-bottomed, stainless steel kettle; set aside.

✳ Cut each quarter of orange pulp in half lengthwise. Cut each of the halves widthwise into ¼-inch slices, removing and discarding any seeds. Use all of the pulp, including the fruit meat and the membrane. Measure 3½ cups sliced orange pulp and add to the orange peel in the kettle; set aside.

✳ Using the small, sharp, thin-bladed knife, quarter the lemon lengthwise. Cut each quarter widthwise into ¹⁄₁₆-inch slices (slice the peel and pulp together), removing and discarding any seeds.

Measure 1 cup lemon slices and add to the kettle containing the orange peel and pulp.

✳ Add the water to the fruit in the kettle; stir to combine. Over high heat, bring the fruit mixture to a boil, uncovered, stirring intermittently. Reduce the heat and simmer the mixture (uncovered) 5 minutes, stirring occasionally.

✳ Remove from the heat and cover the kettle. Let the fruit mixture stand 18 to 24 hours in a cool place.

✳ 18 TO 24 HOURS LATER: Over medium-high to high heat, bring the covered fruit mixture to a rapid boil, stirring intermittently. Rapidly boil the fruit mixture, covered, 1 hour, stirring often to prevent the mixture from sticking to the bottom of the kettle.

✳ Remove from the heat and measure the fruit mixture. Place the fruit mixture back in the kettle. Add to the kettle the exact amount of sugar as the measured fruit mixture. (For 1 cup of fruit mixture, add 1 cup of sugar.) Stir the mixture to combine. Over low heat, heat the mixture until the sugar completely dissolves, stirring constantly. Attach a candy thermometer to the kettle. Increase the heat to medium-high and bring the mixture to a rapid boil, stirring constantly to prevent the mixture from sticking to the bottom of the kettle. The mixture will be foaming, but do not reduce the heat. Rapidly boil the mixture until the temperature reaches 8°F above the boiling point of water at your canning location, stirring constantly. **Important: See "The Boiling Point of Water by Altitude," page 28, for information on how to find out the altitude of your canning location.**

＊ Remove from the heat and detach the thermometer. If any foam remains on the surface of the marmalade, immediately skim it off, using tableware tablespoons and teaspoons; let stand.

＊ Quickly drain hot, sterilized (page 19), half-pint jars, upside down, on a clean tea towel.

＊ Using a 1-cup measuring cup with a pouring spout, pour the hot marmalade into the drained jars, leaving ¼-inch headspace. Wipe the jar rims and threads. Place hot, metal lids on the jars and screw the bands firmly.

＊ Process in a boiling-water canner for the time shown in the PROCESSING TIMES chart at the end of this recipe.

＊ Remove the jars from the canner and place them on a dry, wooden board that has been covered with a tea towel. Let the jars stand, *undisturbed*, 12 hours to cool completely.

YIELDS ABOUT 6 HALF-PINTS

| Processing Times | | | |
|---|---|---|---|
| *Jar Size* | *Altitude of Canning Location* | | |
| | 0 to 1,000 ft | 1,001 to 6,000 ft | Above 6,000 ft |
| Half-pints | 5 min | 10 min | 15 min |

*Apple Butter*

# Butters

Butter: Fruit pulp and sugar cooked to a rather thick
consistency, but not jellied. A butter often contains spices.

# APPLE BUTTER

12 cups apple pulp (about 9 pounds apples) (see recipe procedures, below)

1½ cups water

6 cups sugar

2 teaspoons ground cinnamon

¾ teaspoon ground cloves

¾ teaspoon ground allspice

* Wash, pare (page 40) (see Note), quarter, and core the apples.

* Place the apples in a 12-quart, heavy-bottomed, stainless steel kettle. Add the water. Over medium-high heat, bring the apples to a simmer, uncovered. Reduce the heat and simmer the apples, uncovered, until very tender (about 30 minutes, depending upon the apples), stirring frequently to prevent the apples from burning on the bottom of the kettle.

* Remove from the heat. Press the cooked apples and liquid through a food mill (see illustration, page 72).

* Measure 12 cups apple pulp and place it in a clean, 12-quart, heavy-bottomed, stainless steel kettle. Add the sugar, cinnamon, cloves, and allspice; stir to combine. Over medium heat, bring the mixture to a simmer, stirring constantly. Reduce the heat and simmer the mixture gently for 10 to 15 minutes, or until it is reduced to the proper consistency (see To Test for Doneness of Butters, facing

page), stirring constantly to prevent scorching. Remove from the heat; let stand.

* Drain hot, sterilized (page 19), half-pint or pint jars, upside down, on a clean tea towel.

* Using a 1-cup measuring cup with a pouring spout, pour the hot Apple Butter into the drained jars, leaving ¼-inch headspace. Wipe the jar rims and threads. Place hot, metal lids on the jars and screw the bands firmly.

* Process in a boiling-water canner for the time shown in the PROCESSING TIMES chart at the end of this recipe.

* Remove the jars from the canner and place them on a dry, wooden board that has been covered with a tea towel. Let the jars stand, *undisturbed*, 12 hours to cool completely.

NOTE: *A Back to Basics® brand apple "peeler" (parer) (see illustration, page 47) helps accomplish this task expeditiously and efficiently.*

YIELDS ABOUT 14 HALF-PINTS (OR 7 PINTS)

| PROCESSING TIMES | | | |
|---|---|---|---|
| *Jar Size* | Altitude of Canning Location | | |
| | 0 to 1,000 ft | 1,001 to 6,000 ft | Above 6,000 ft |
| Half-pints | 10 min | 15 min | 20 min |
| Pints | 15 min | 20 min | 25 min |

# APRICOT BUTTER

16 cups cold water

2 tablespoons white vinegar

2 tablespoons salt

6 cups apricot pulp (about 5½ pounds apricots) (see recipe procedures, below)

¼ cup water

3 cups sugar

2 tablespoons freshly squeezed, strained lemon juice

¼ teaspoon almond extract


✳ In a 12-quart kettle, place 16 cups water, vinegar, and salt; stir until the salt dissolves; set aside.

✳ Wash ½ of the apricots. Blanch the apricots (page 36) 30 seconds and immediately immerse them in cold water; drain. Peel, cut in half, and pit the apricots. As the apricots are prepared, drop them into the vinegar solution to prevent their discoloration. Repeat the procedure to prepare the remaining ½ of the apricots. Prepare only ½ of the apricots at a time because apricots darken quickly in their skins after being blanched.

✳ Drain and rinse the apricots twice, using fresh, cold water. Drain the apricots well. Place the apricots in an 8-quart, heavy-bottomed, stainless steel kettle. Add ¼ cup water. Over medium heat, bring the apricots to a simmer, stirring constantly. Simmer the apricots until soft, stirring constantly.

✳ Remove from the heat. Press the cooked apricots and liquid through a food mill (see illustration page 72).

✳ Measure 6 cups apricot pulp and place it in a clean, 8-quart, heavy-bottomed, stainless steel kettle. Add the sugar; stir to combine. Over medium heat, bring the mixture to a simmer, stirring constantly. Simmer the mixture, uncovered, 30 minutes, or until it reaches the proper consistency (see to Test for Doneness of

*continues*

---

## TO TEST FOR DONENESS OF BUTTERS

To determine when a butter has cooked down adequately and is thick enough to can, scoop a teaspoonful from the kettle and hold it away from the steam for 2 minutes. If properly done, the butter should remain mounded on the spoon.

Another test for doneness is to place a teaspoonful of the hot butter on a room-temperature plate. If liquid does not run off around the edge of the butter, it is ready to be canned.

Butters, page 239), stirring frequently to prevent sticking.

✳ Remove from the heat. Add the lemon and almond extract; stir well to blend; let stand.

✳ Drain hot, sterilized (page 19), half-pint jars, upside down, on a clean tea towel.

✳ Using a 1-cup measuring cup with a pouring sprout, pour the hot Apricot Butter into the drained jars, leaving ¼-inch headspace. Wipe the jar rims and threads. Place hot, metal lids on the jars and screw the bands firmly.

✳ Process in a boiling-water canner for the time shown in the PROCESSING TIMES chart at the end of this recipe.

✳ Remove the jars from the canner and place them on a dry, wooden board that has been covered with a tea towel. Let the jars stand, *undisturbed*, 12 hours to cool completely.

YIELDS ABOUT 6 HALF-PINTS

| PROCESSING TIMES | | | |
|---|---|---|---|
| *Jar Size* | *Altitude of Canning Location* | | |
| | 0 to 1,000 ft | 1,001 to 6,000 ft | Above 6,000 ft |
| Half-pints | 5 min | 10 min | 15 min |

# PEAR BUTTER

16 cups cold water

2 tablespoons white vinegar

2 tablespoons salt

8 cups Bartlett pear pulp (about 7 pounds Bartlett pears) (see recipe procedures, below)

¼ cup water

4 cups sugar

⅓ cup freshly squeezed, strained orange juice

1¼ teaspoons finely grated orange rind (page 37)

1 teaspoon ground nutmeg

✳ In a 12-quart kettle, place 16 cups water, vinegar, and salt; stir until the salt dissolves; set aside.

✳ Wash, quarter, and core (page 40) the pears. (Do not pare [page 40] the pears.) As the pears are prepared, drop them into the vinegar solution to prevent their discoloration.

✳ Drain and rinse the pears twice, using fresh, cold water. Drain the pears well. Place the pears in an 8-quart,

*continues*

heavy-bottomed, stainless steel kettle. Add ¼ cup water. Over medium heat, bring the pears to a simmer, stirring constantly. Simmer the pears 10 minutes, or until soft, stirring constantly.

✳ Remove from the heat. Press the cooked pears and liquid through a food mill (see illustration, page 72).

✳ Measure 8 cups pear pulp and place it in a clean, 8-quart, heavy-bottomed, stainless steel kettle. Add the sugar, orange juice, orange rind, and nutmeg; stir to combine. Over medium heat, bring the mixture to a simmer, stirring constantly. Simmer the mixture, uncovered, 30 minutes, or until it reaches the desired consistency (see To Test for Doneness of Butters, page 239), stirring frequently to prevent sticking. Remove from the heat; let stand.

✳ Drain hot, sterilized (page 19), half-pint jars, upside down, on a clean tea towel.

✳ Using a 1-cup measuring cup with a pouring spout, pour the hot Pear Butter into the drained jars, leaving ¼-inch headspace. Wipe the jar rims and threads. Place hot, metal lids on the jars and screw the bands firmly.

✳ Process in a boiling-water canner for the time shown in the PROCESSING TIMES chart at the end of this recipe.

✳ Remove the jars from the canner and place them on a dry, wooden board that has been covered with a tea towel. Let the jars stand, *undisturbed*, 12 hours to cool completely.

YIELDS ABOUT 8 HALF-PINTS

| PROCESSING TIMES | | | |
|---|---|---|---|
| *Jar Size* | *Altitude of Canning Location* | | |
| | 0 to 1,000 ft | 1,001 to 6,000 ft | Above 6,000 ft |
| Half-pints | 5 min | 10 min | 15 min |

# WILD PLUM BUTTER

4 cups wild plum pulp (see recipe procedures, below)

Water

3 cups sugar

* Wash and sort the plums. Cut them in half and pit them.

* Place the plums in an 8-quart, heavy-bottomed, stainless steel kettle. Add a very small amount of water—only enough to prevent sticking. Over medium heat, bring the plums to a simmer, stirring constantly.

* Remove from the heat. Press the cooked plums and liquid through a food mill (see illustration, page 72).

* Measure 4 cups plum pulp and place it in a clean, 8-quart, heavy-bottomed, stainless steel kettle. Add the sugar (¾ cup sugar for each cup of pulp); stir to combine. Over medium heat, bring the mixture to a simmer, stirring constantly. Simmer the mixture until it reaches the proper consistency (see To Test for Doneness of Butters, page 239), stirring constantly to prevent sticking. Remove from the heat; let stand.

* Drain hot, sterilized, half-pint jars, upside down, on a clean tea towel.

* Using a 1-cup measuring cup with a pouring spout, pour the hot Plum Butter into the drained jars, leaving ¼-inch headspace. Wipe the jar rims and threads. Place hot, metal lids on the jars and screw the bands firmly.

* Process in a boiling-water canner for the time shown in the PROCESSING TIMES chart at the end of this recipe.

* Remove the jars from the canner and place them on a dry, wooden board that has been covered with a tea towel. Let the jars stand, *undisturbed*, 12 hours to cool completely.

YIELDS ABOUT 4 HALF-PINTS

| PROCESSING TIMES | | | |
|---|---|---|---|
| *Jar Size* | *Altitude of Canning Location* | | |
| | 0 to 1,000 ft | 1,001 to 6,000 ft | Above 6,000 ft |
| Half-pints | 5 min | 10 min | 15 min |

# SOURCES CONSULTED

Cooperative Extension Service. The University of Georgia. College of Family and Consumer Sciences. College of Agricultural and Environmental Sciences. *Bulletin 989: So Easy to Preserve*, 5th ed., by Susan Reynolds and Paulette Williams. Revised by Elizabeth L. Andress and Judy A. Harrison. Athens, 2006.

Cooperative Extension Service. The University of Georgia. National Center for Home Food Preservation. *Preserving Food: Using Pressure Canners*. Rev. ed., by Elizabeth L. Andress. Athens, 2011.

Cooperative Extension Service. The University of Georgia. National Center for Home Food Preservation. *Using Boiling Water Canners*. Rev. ed., by Elizabeth L. Andress. Athens, 2011.

United States Department of Agriculture. National Institute of Food and Agriculture. *Agriculture Information Bulletin No. 539: Complete Guide to Home Canning*. Washington, D.C.: Government Printing Office, August 2009.

Corn Relish

# ACKNOWLEDGMENTS

First and foremost, I want to thank my sister-in-law and brother, Dee and Gary Staples, to whom this cookbook is dedicated. Their abiding encouragement and support have been, and are central to my cookbook and food endeavors.

Coleen O'Shea, my agent, is the best that a writer could have. Her experience, knowledge, and loyalty are so very much appreciated, and I thank her.

A technical cookbook, like *Blue Ribbon Country Canning,* is uniquely challenging to publish, especially with the critical issue of safe home canning at the heart of the copy. Publisher of the book is Egg & Dart®, a division of Dynamic Housewares, Inc., of which Pamela Falk is President. Pam put her "all" into the book's production and personally oversaw the project from beginning through publication. She framed the detailed, scientific, general canning information and recipes with beautiful and, at the same time, instructional photographs as well as an appealing book design. Many thanks to you, Pam, for your undying involvement with the book and for working with me and my penchant for detail. Designing and putting together a book like *Blue Ribbon Country Canning* is no small task. Leslie Jonath, Creative Director; Gretchen Scoble, Designer; and Lisa McGuinness, Managing Editor, deserve the highest accolades for their incredible dedication and tireless work in designing *Blue Ribbon Country Canning.*

Erin Scott's photographs are gorgeous and, at the same time, instructive. Thank you for your patience with the demands of this unique photographic project, Erin. And Prop Stylist, Ethel Brennan, deserves accolades for her creative artistry.

The instructive illustrations in the book, all to scale, were rendered by Sharon Soder. Sharon is a masterful artist, and we have worked together for many years. Thanks, Sharon.

Linda Heiken, Louise Piper, and Pat Berry, three of Iowa's finest canners as well as major blue ribbon winners at the Iowa State Fair, augmented my inventory of canned foods by supplying some of their perfect and most beautiful jars for the photographs. The book wouldn't be the book without these exemplary jars of the very finest in home canning. My deepest admiration and thanks!

In addition to one's own garden, canners are greatly assisted by knowledgeable produce people and food experts at supermarkets and elsewhere. Many thanks to Barry Brauch, Aaron Grant, Ron DeYoung, and Kevin Helm who have helped me immeasurably in securing special foods for canning.

I want to acknowledge and thank Arlette Hollister, Superintendent of Foods at the Iowa State Fair, for her phenomenal expertise in directing the Food Department at the Iowa State Fair, the largest food department of all state fairs in the country; and particularly in this book, to extend recognition for her great support and promotion of safe home canning.

# INDEX

— A —

Acidity, 23, 24
Almonds
    Apricot-Almond Conserve,
        223–24
    chopping, 36
    Pears Amaretto, 65–66
Altitude, boiling point of
    water by, 28
Amaretto
    Apricot-Almond Conserve,
        223–24
    Pears Amaretto, 65–66
Apples, 46–47
    Apple Butter, 238
    Apple Jelly, 196–97
    Applesauce, 47–48
    Brandied Mincemeat,
        105–6
    Mint Jelly, 210–11
    Mixed Fruit, 62–63
    Peach-Apple Salsa, 159–61
    Spiced Apple Rings, 75–76
Apricots, 50–51
    Apricot-Almond Conserve,
        223–24
    Apricot Butter, 239–40
    Apricot Jam, 175–77
    Mixed Fruit, 62–63
Asparagus
    Asparagus Spears, 82–84
    Cut Asparagus, 84

— B —

Basil Jelly, 209–10
Beans
    Dilly Beans, 112–14

Green and Wax Beans,
    84–86
Beets, Pickled, 115–16
Bell peppers
    Bell Pepper Relish, 142–43
    Chili Sauce, 143–45
    Corn Relish, 146–47
    Corn with Red Peppers and
        Basil, 90–91
    Jicama Relish, 148–49
    Peach-Apple Salsa, 159–61
    Piccalilli, 152–53
    Pickled Mixed Vegetables,
        119–20
    Zucchini Relish, 154–55
Blackberry Jelly, 198–99
Blanching, 36, 40
Blueberries, 53–54
    Blueberry Jam, 177–78
Blush Wine Jelly, 212–13
Boiling-water bath canning,
    28–31
Botulism, 14, 23–24, 34
Bread and Butter Pickles,
    110–11
Brines, definition of, 40
Butters
    Apple Butter, 238
    Apricot Butter, 239–40
    definition of, 237
    Pear Butter, 240–42
    testing, for doneness, 239
    Wild Plum Butter, 243

— C —

Cabbage
    Piccalilli, 152–53
    Sauerkraut, 136–39
Canned foods
    opening jars of, 34
    storing, 34
    suspect jars of, 34–35
Canning
    acidity and, 23, 24
    boiling-water bath, 28–31
    equipment for, 15–17, 19
    measuring ingredients for,
        17
    pressure, 31–33
    procedures for, 19–33
    rewards of, 12–13
    safety information for, 14,
        17, 23–24, 26–27
    selection of foods for, 15
    time allocation for, 18
Canning powders, 27
Carrots, 87
Catsup
    definition of, 166
    Tomato Catsup, 166–67
Cheesecloth bags, 38
Cherries
    Cherry Jam, 178–79
    Cherry Jelly, 200–202
    Cherry Preserves, 216–17
    Cherry Sauce, 170–71
    Cherry Sauce with
        Kirschwasser, 171
    Fruit Cocktail, 55–57
    Tutti-Frutti Ice Cream
        Topping, 171

Tutti-Frutti Jam, 192–93
White Cherries, 54–55
Chile peppers
    Tomato-Chile Salsa, 161–63
    varieties of, 156
Chili Sauce, 143–45
Chutney, Peach, 150–51
Condiments, definition of,
    40. *See also* Relishes; Salsas;
    Sauces
Conserves
    Apricot-Almond Conserve,
        223–24
    definition of, 221
    Gooseberry Conserve, 225
    Grape Conserve, 226–27
    Rhubarb-Strawberry
        Conserve, 228–29
    tips for, 17–18
Coring, 40
Corn
    Corn Relish, 146–47
    Corn with Red Peppers and
        Basil, 90–91
    Cream-Style Corn, 92–93
    Whole-Kernel Corn, 89
Crock Pots, 27
Cubing, 40
Cucumbers
    Bread and Butter Pickles,
        110–11
    Easy Refrigerator Sweet
        Dill Pickles, 111–12
    Fermented Dill Pickles,
        134–35
    Fermented Kosher Dill
        Pickles, 136
    Pickled Mixed Vegetables,
        119–20

— D —
Dicing, 40
Dishwashers, canning with,
    27

— E —
Equipment, 15–17

— F —
Fermented foods
    Fermented Dill Pickles,
        134–35
    Fermented Kosher Dill
        Pickles, 136
    Sauerkraut, 136–39
    tips for, 133
Figs, acidity of, 24
Fish, 106–7
Fruits. *See also individual*
    *fruits*
    Fruit Cocktail, 55–57
    grating rind of citrus, 37
    Mixed Fruit, 62–63
    spiced, without vinegar, 45

— G —
Ginger
    Peach Chutney, 150–51
    using fresh, 39
Gooseberries, 58–59
    Gooseberry Conserve, 225
    Gooseberry Jam, 180–81
Grapes, 60
    Fruit Cocktail, 55–57
    Grape Conserve, 226–27
    Grape Jam, 182–83
    Grape Jelly, 203–4
    Mixed Fruit, 62–63
Grating, 37, 40
Grinding, 37–38, 40

— H —
Herbs, cheesecloth bags for, 38
Hot packing, 21
Hulling, 40

— I —
Ice Cream Topping, Tutti-
    Frutti, 171
Inversion method, 27

— J —
Jams
    Apricot Jam, 175–77
    Blueberry Jam, 177–78
    Cherry Jam, 178–79
    definition of, 173
    Gooseberry Jam, 180–81
    Grape Jam, 182–83
    lower-sugar, 18
    Peach Jam, 183–84
    Pineapple Jam, 185–86
    Red Plum Jam, 186–87
    Red Raspberry Jam, 188
    Seedless Wild Black
        Raspberry Jam, 189
    Strawberry Jam, 190
    tips for, 17–18
    Tutti-Frutti Jam, 192–93
Jars
    checking, for sealing,
        30–31, 33
    filling and capping, 21
    preparing and sterilizing,
        19–20
    processing filled, 29–30, 32
    sealing, with paraffin, 27
    types of, 19
    unsealed, reprocessing or
        refrigerating, 31, 33
Jellies
    Apple Jelly, 196–97
    Basil Jelly, 209–10
    Blackberry Jelly, 198–99
    Blush Wine Jelly, 212–13
    Cherry Jelly, 200–202
    definition of, 195
    Grape Jelly, 203–4
    jellying point for, 196
    lower-sugar, 18
    Mint Jelly, 210–11

Red Raspberry Jelly, 204–5
Strawberry Jelly, 206–7
testing, for sheeting, 196
tips for, 17–18
Wild Black Raspberry Jelly,
207–8
Jicama Relish, 148–49

— K —
Kiwis, 61
Kumquat Marmalade, 232–33

— L —
Lids
preparing, 20–21
types of, 19
Low-temperature
pasteurization, 24–25

— M —
Mangos
Mango Salsa, 156–57
preparing, 38–39
Marmalades
definition of, 231
Kumquat Marmalade,
232–33
Orange Marmalade, 234–35
Meat
Brandied Mincemeat,
105–6
Cubes, Strips, or Chunks of
Boneless Meat, 102–4
Meat grinders, 37–38
Melons
Melon Ball Pickles, 123–24
Watermelon Rind Pickles,
129–30
Microwave ovens, 27
Mincemeat, Brandied, 105–6
Mint Jelly, 210–11
Mushrooms, Marinated,
120–21

— N —
Nuts, chopping, 36. See also
individual nuts

— O —
Okra, Pickled, 122–23
Onions, peeling pearl, 38
Open-kettle canning, 26
Oranges
Apricot-Almond Conserve,
223–24
Gooseberry Conserve, 225
Grape Conserve, 226–27
grating rind of, 37
Kumquat Marmalade,
232–33
Orange Marmalade, 234–35
Rhubarb-Strawberry
Conserve, 228–29
Tutti-Frutti Ice Cream
Topping, 171
Tutti-Frutti Jam, 192–93
Ovens
conventional, 27
microwave, 27

— P —
Paraffin, sealing jars with, 27
Paring, 40
Peaches, 64–65
Fruit Cocktail, 55–57
Mixed Fruit, 62–63
Peach-Apple Salsa, 159–61
Peach Chutney, 150–51
Peach Jam, 183–84
Spiced Peaches, 125–26
Pears
Fruit Cocktail, 55–57
Mixed Fruit, 62–63
Pear Butter, 240–42
Pears Amaretto, 65–66
Peppermint Pears, 78–79
Plain Pears, 66
Spiced Seckel Pears, 127–28

Tutti-Frutti Ice Cream
Topping, 171
Tutti-Frutti Jam, 192–93
Pecans
chopping, 36
Rhubarb-Strawberry
Conserve, 228–29
Pectin, 40
Peppermint Pears, 78–79
Piccalilli, 152–53
Pickles
Bread and Butter Pickles,
110–11
definition of, 109
Dilly Beans, 112–14
Easy Refrigerator Sweet
Dill Pickles, 111–12
Fermented Dill Pickles,
134–35
Fermented Kosher Dill
Pickles, 136
low-temperature
pasteurization for, 24–25
Marinated Mushrooms,
120–21
Melon Ball Pickles, 123–24
Pickled Beets, 115–16
Pickled Mixed Vegetables,
119–20
Pickled Okra, 122–23
salt for, 18
Spiced Peaches, 125–26
Spiced Seckel Pears, 127–28
vinegar for, 18
Watermelon Rind Pickles,
129–30
Pineapple
Fruit Cocktail, 55–57
Pineapple Jam, 185–86
Tutti-Frutti Ice Cream
Topping, 171
Tutti-Frutti Jam, 192–93
Plums
Mixed Fruit, 62–63

Plain Plums, 68
Plums in Port Wine, 67–68
Red Plum Jam, 186–87
Wild Plum Butter, 243
Preserves
    Cherry Preserves, 216–17
    definition of, 215
    Strawberry Preserves,
        218–19
    tips for, 17–18
Pressure canning, 31–33
Pressure cookers, 26–27
Pureeing, 40

— R —
Raisins
    Brandied Mincemeat,
        105–6
    Gooseberry Conserve, 225
    Grape Conserve, 226–27
    Rhubarb-Strawberry
        Conserve, 228–29
Raspberries, 68–69
    Red Raspberry Jam, 188
    Red Raspberry Jelly, 204–5
    Seedless Wild Black
        Raspberry Jam, 189
    Wild Black Raspberry Jelly,
        207–8
Raw packing, 21
Relishes
    Bell Pepper Relish, 142–43
    Chili Sauce, 143–45
    Corn Relish, 146–47
    definition of, 141
    Jicama Relish, 148–49
    Peach Chutney, 150–51
    Piccalilli, 152–53
    salt for, 18
    vinegar for, 18
    Zucchini Relish, 154–55
Rhubarb, 70
    Rhubarb-Strawberry
        Conserve, 228–29

Rind
    definition of, 40
    grating, 37
    Watermelon Rind Pickles,
        129–30
Rolling boil, definition of, 40

— S —
Safety information, 14, 17,
    23–24, 26–27
Salmon in Pint Jars, 106–7
Salsas
    definition of, 141
    Mango Salsa, 156–57
    Peach-Apple Salsa, 159–61
    Tomato-Chile Salsa, 161–63
Salt, 18
Sauces. See also Salsas
    Applesauce, 47–48
    Cherry Sauce, 170–71
    Cherry Sauce with
        Kirschwasser, 171
    Chili Sauce, 143–45
    Spaghetti Sauce, 168–69
    Tomato Catsup, 166–67
    Tutti-Frutti Ice Cream
        Topping, 171
Sauerkraut, 136–39
Sautéing, 41
Scalding, 41
Shredding, 41
Shucking, 41
Slow cookers, 27
Spaghetti Sauce, 168–69
Spices, cheesecloth bags for, 38
Steam canners, 26
Storage tips, 34
Strawberries, 72–73
    Rhubarb-Strawberry
        Conserve, 228–29
    Strawberry Jam, 190
    Strawberry Jelly, 206–7

Strawberry Preserves,
    218–19
Sun, canning with, 27

— T —
Tomatoes, 95–97
    acidity of, 24
    blanching, 36
    Chili Sauce, 143–45
    Peach-Apple Salsa, 159–61
    Piccalilli, 152–53
    seeding and coring, 39
    Spaghetti Sauce, 168–69
    Tomato Catsup, 166–67
    Tomato-Chile Salsa, 161–63
    Tomato Juice, 97–98
Tutti-Frutti Ice Cream
    Topping, 171
Tutti-Frutti Jam, 192–93

— V —
Vegetables. See also individual
    vegetables
    Piccalilli, 152–53
    Pickled Mixed Vegetables,
        119–20
Vinegar, 18
Vitamins, 15

— W —
Walnuts
    chopping, 36
    Grape Conserve, 226–27
Water, boiling point of, 28
Watermelon Rind Pickles,
    129–30
Wine
    Blush Wine Jelly, 212–13
    Plums in Port Wine, 67–68

— Z —
Zucchini Relish, 154–55

# METRIC CONVERSION TABLES

| To Convert (U.S.) | To (Metric) | Multiply By[1] |
|---|---|---|
| Teaspoons | Milliliters | 4.9289 |
| Tablespoons | Milliliters | 14.787 |
| Fluid Ounces | Milliliters | 29.5735 |
| Cups (Liquid) | Milliliters | 236.5882 |
| Fluid Ounces | Liters | 0.0296 |
| Pints (Dry) | Liters | 0.5506 |
| Pints (Liquid) | Liters | 0.4732 |
| Quarts (Dry) | Liters | 1.1012 |
| Quarts (Liquid) | Liters | 0.9464 |
| Gallons (Dry) | Liters | 4.4048 |
| Gallons (Liquid) | Liters | 3.7854 |
| Pecks (Dry) | Liters | 8.8098 |
| Bushels (Dry) (Struck[2]) | Liters | 35.2391 |
| Ounces (Avoirdupois) | Grams | 28.3495 |
| Pounds (Avoirdupois) | Grams | 453.5924 |
| Ounces (Avoirdupois) | Kilograms | 0.0283 |
| Pounds (Avoirdupois) | Kilograms | 0.4536 |

| To Convert (Metric) | To (U.S.) | Multiply By[1] |
|---|---|---|
| Milliliters | Teaspoons | 0.2029 |
| Milliliters | Tablespoons | 0.0676 |
| Milliliters | Fluid Ounces | 0.0338 |
| Milliliters | Cups (Liquid) | 0.0042 |
| Liters | Fluid Ounces | 33.8140 |
| Liters | Pints (Dry) | 1.8162 |
| Liters | Pints (Liquid) | 2.1134 |
| Liters | Quarts (Dry) | 0.9081 |
| Liters | Quarts (Liquid) | 1.0567 |
| Liters | Gallons (Dry) | 0.2270 |
| Liters | Gallons (Liquid) | 0.2642 |
| Liters | Pecks (Dry) | 0.1135 |
| Liters | Bushels (Dry) (Struck[2]) | 0.0284 |
| Grams | Ounces (Avoirdupois) | 0.0353 |
| Grams | Pounds (Avoirdupois) | 0.0022 |
| Kilograms | Ounces (Avoirdupois) | 35.274 |
| Kilograms | Pounds (Avoirdupois) | 2.2046 |

| To Convert (Metric) | To (Metric) | Multiply By[1] |
|---|---|---|
| Milliliters | Liters | 0.001 |
| Liters | Milliliters | 1000.0 |
| Grams | Kilograms | 0.001 |
| Kilograms | Grams | 1000.0 |

[1]Approximate factors.
[2]Struck measure. A heaped bushel is equal to 1¼ struck bushels.

# VOLUME AND WEIGHT MEASURES

## VOLUME MEASURES

| U.S. Customary Measures | | | | Metric Measures[1] | |
|---|---|---|---|---|---|
| Dash[2] | = | Less than ⅛ tsp | | | |
| ¼ tsp | = | 15 drops | .04 fl oz | 1.23 | mL |
| ½ tsp | = | 30 drops | .08 fl oz | 2.46 | mL |
| ¾ tsp | = | 45 drops | .13 fl oz | 3.70 | mL |
| 1 tsp | = | 60 drops | ⅙ fl oz | 4.929 | mL |
| ¼ Tbsp | = | ¾ tsp | .13 fl oz | 3.70 | mL |
| ⅓ Tbsp | = | 1 tsp | | | |
| ⅜ Tbsp | = | 1⅛ tsp | .19 fl oz | 5.55 | mL |
| ½ Tbsp | = | 1½ tsp | ¼ fl oz | 7.39 | mL |
| ⅝ Tbsp | = | 1⅞ tsp (1¾ tsp + ⅛ tsp) | .31 fl oz | 9.24 | mL |
| ⅔ Tbsp | = | 2 tsp | ⅓ fl oz | 9.86 | mL |
| ¾ Tbsp | = | 2¼ tsp | .37 fl oz | 11.09 | mL |
| ⅞ Tbsp | = | 2½ tsp | .44 fl oz | 12.94 | mL |
| 1 Tbsp | = | 3 tsp | ½ fl oz | 14.787 | mL |
| ⅛ cup | = | 2 Tbsp | 1 fl oz | 29.574 | mL |
| ¼ cup | = | 4 Tbsp | 2 fl oz | 59.15 | mL |
| ⅓ cup | = | 5⅓ Tbsp (5 Tbsp + 1 tsp) | 2⅔ fl oz | 78.85 | mL |
| ⅜ cup | = | 6 Tbsp | 3 fl oz | 88.72 | mL |
| ½ cup | = | 8 Tbsp | 4 fl oz | 118.29 | mL |
| ⅝ cup | = | 10 Tbsp | 5 fl oz | 147.87 | mL |
| ⅔ cup | = | 10⅔ Tbsp (10 Tbsp + 2 tsp) | 5⅓ fl oz | 157.71 | mL |
| ¾ cup | = | 12 Tbsp | 6 fl oz | 177.44 | mL |
| ⅞ cup | = | 14 Tbsp | 7 fl oz | 207.01 | mL |
| 1 cup (liq) | = | 16 Tbsp | 8 fl oz | 236.582 | mL |
| ½ pt (dry) | = | 1 cup | | 275.31 | mL |
| ½ pt (liq) | = | 1 cup (liq) | 8 fl oz | 236.589 | mL |
| 1 pt (dry) | = | 2 cups | | 550.610 | mL |
| 1 pt (liq) | = | 2 cups (liq) | 16 fl oz | 473.177 | mL |
| 1 qt (dry) | = | 2 pt (dry) or 4 cups (dry) | | 1.101 | L |
| 1 qt (liq) | = | 2 pt (liq) or 4 cups (liq) | 32 fl oz | 0.946 | L |
| 1 gal (dry) | = | 4 qt or 8 pt | | 4.405 | L |
| 1 gal (liq) | = | 4 qt (liq) or 8 pt (liq) | 128 fl oz | 3.785 | L |
| 1 peck (dry) | = | 2 gal (dry) or 8 qt (dry) | | 8.810 | L |
| 1 bu (dry) (struck[3]) | = | 4 pecks (dry) or 8 gal (dry) | | 35.239 | L |

[1]Approximate measures.
[2]Not a standard volume measure.
[3]Struck measure. A heaped bushel is equal to 1¼ struck bushels.

## WEIGHT MEASURES

| U.S. Ounces and Pounds (Avoirdupois Weight) | | | Metric Measures[1] |
|---|---|---|---|
| ¼ oz | = | | 7.087 g |
| ½ oz | = | | 14.175 g |
| ¾ oz | = | | 21.262 g |
| 1 oz | = | | 28.350 g |
| 16 oz | = | 1 lb | 453.592 g |
| 1 lb | = | | 0.4536 kg |
| 2 lbs | = | | 0.9072 kg |

[1]Approximate measures.

## METRIC CONVERSIONS

| Metric Measures | | U.S. Measures[1] |
|---|---|---|
| 1 milliliter | = | 0.203 tsp |
| | | 0.0676 Tbsp |
| | | 0.0338 fl oz |
| | | 0.0042 cups |
| | | 0.0021 pt (liq) |
| | | 0.0011 qt (liq) |
| | | 0.00026 gal (liq) |
| 1 liter | = | 33.8140 fl oz |
| | | 4.2268 cups |
| | | 1.8162 pt (dry) |
| | | 2.1134 pt (liq) |
| | | 0.9081 qt (dry) |
| | | 1.0567 qt (liq) |
| | | 0.2270 gal (dry) |
| | | 0.2642 gal (liq) |
| | | 0.1135 peck (dry) |
| | | 0.0284 bu (dry) |
| 1 gram | = | 0.0353 oz (avdp) |
| 1 kilogram | = | 2.2046 lb (avdp) |

[1]Approximate measures.

## ABBREVIATIONS[1]

| | | | |
|---|---|---|---|
| Avoirdupois | avdp | Milliliter | mL |
| Bushel | bu | Ounce | oz |
| Fluid Ounce | fl oz | Peck | pk |
| Gallon | gal | Pint | pt |
| Gram | g | Pound | lb |
| Kilogram | kg | Quart | qt |
| Liquid | liq | Tablespoon | Tbsp |
| Liter | L | Teaspoon | tsp |

[1]Used for both singular and plural items.

# DIANE ROUPE

An ardent and accomplished canner, Diane Roupe is a notable winner of numerous blue ribbons for her canning entries at the eminent Iowa State Fair, where she now serves as a primary canning judge. She is author of the American cookbook classic, *The Blue Ribbon Country Cookbook*.

Prior to devoting full time to her interest in food, she served as Executive Director of the National Rehabilitation Association in Washington, D.C., and Vice President for Public Affairs of Blue Cross and Blue Shield of Greater New York. She taught at New York University in the Food and Hotel Management program. A graduate of Northwestern University, she now lives in West Des Moines, Iowa.

Christopher Maharry